YouTube® Channels

2nd Edition

by Rob Ciampa, Theresa Go, Matt Ciampa, and Rich Murphy

for dummies®

A Wiley Brand

YouTube® Channels For Dummies®, 2nd Edition

Published by: **John Wiley & Sons, Inc.**, 111 River Street, Hoboken, NJ 07030-5774, www.wiley.com

Copyright © 2020 by John Wiley & Sons, Inc., Hoboken, New Jersey

Published simultaneously in Canada

For general information on our other products and services, please contact our Customer Care Department within the U.S. at 877-762-2974, outside the U.S. at 317-572-3993, or fax 317-572-4002. For technical support, please visit https://hub.wiley.com/community/support/dummies.

Wiley publishes in a variety of print and electronic formats and by print-on-demand. Some material included with standard print versions of this book may not be included in e-books or in print-on-demand. If this book refers to media such as a CD or DVD that is not included in the version you purchased, you may download this material at http://booksupport.wiley.com. For more information about Wiley products, visit www.wiley.com.

Library of Congress Control Number: 2020941187

ISBN: 978-1-119-68805-1 (pbk); 978-1-119-68810-5 (ebk); 978-1-119-68798-6 (ebk)

10 9 8 7 6 5 4 3 2 1

MIX
Paper from responsible sources
FSC
www.fsc.org   FSC® C013604

Contents at a Glance

Table of Contents

Introduction

Maybe you're looking to become a YouTube sensation with your next video or you simply want to share your insights or your particular expertise with the world. Perhaps you'd even like to use YouTube and video to help your business, which could be a local coffee shop or a Fortune 500 company. No matter how you plan to make use of your video-making skills, YouTube has made sharing the results of those skills easy. And with the tips and techniques included within the pages of this second edition of *YouTube Channels For Dummies*, you'll be ready to take full advantage of YouTube's user-friendly platform when creating your very own YouTube channel.

To get a better sense of how YouTube has changed the entertainment playing field, cast your mind back to ten or so years before the turn of the millennium — if you can remember back that far. Despite an explosion of ever better and ever cheaper video equipment for consumers, sharing a video still meant gathering family and friends around your giant 70-inch, LED television screen so that every-one could watch your latest video masterpiece. Back in those days, someone who wasn't in the room watching along was clean out of luck.

YouTube changed all that. It globalized the viewing experience, reinventing how people show videos by making it possible to share with audiences considerably larger than that bunch of friends and family gathered around the TV set eating popcorn. Any viewer who wanted to see any video anywhere in the world only had to type www.youtube.com into their favorite browser, search for the video they wanted to see, and click the Play button — and there it was.

As easy as it is for a viewer to take full advantage of YouTube, it's almost as easy for a contributor to become part of the YouTube mix. After setting up an account, it's a snap to start uploading video. And, if the video you're uploading takes off, you could become famous and even earn a good chunk of change from your YouTube exploits.

Notice that we said "if the video you're uploading takes off." That can be a very big *if*. Not just any video will do. The truth of the matter is that the low-quality, badly shot videos that were still popular a few years ago no longer cut the mustard. Viewers expect higher quality these days, which is why you need to step up your game and produce the best possible content. This book can help show you the way.

About This Book

In some ways, reading a book to find out all about YouTube channels seems a bit odd. Isn't YouTube the place that specializes in videos designed to teach you about any topic on earth? Why not just stick with the YouTube videos that are all about YouTube?

First off, it's a bit self-referential and incestuous to get all your information about YouTube channels from YouTube videos. Second, that video purporting to tell you how to strike it rich on YouTube may have been shot and edited by the neighbor kid down the street who has never made a dime from YouTube and who may never move out of Mom and Dad's basement. In other words, just as you shouldn't believe everything you read on the Internet, you shouldn't believe everything you see on YouTube. Sometimes it pays to listen to the true experts (like us) who have a track record in advising folks how to put their best foot forward on YouTube.

We also know that there are only so many hours in a day and that everyone's schedules seem to be getting more and more hectic each day. That's why we've written a book that doesn't beat around the bush — in other words, it gets straight to the point so that you can get in and get out with the information you need. In that sense, *YouTube Channels For Dummies* is the exact opposite of all those wordy instructional manuals that spell out a hundred ways to do something but never get around to telling you the best way. No matter if you're looking to set up a channel, create an effective header, or figure out ways to maximize your monetization potential, we show you the quickest, most effective way to get the job done.

Preparing the 2nd Edition of *YouTube Channels For Dummies* was quite involved. Since the 1st Edition, the YouTube community has grown by leaps and bounds. There are many more creators putting out great videos. And when it comes to major brands and agencies, being on YouTube is no longer an option; it's a necessity. We can go on for pages. Regardless, YouTube has continued to evolve as much as its community. For this edition, we made sure to make our way through all parts of the platform, checking out the new things, such as YouTube Studio, but also noting which stuff has been removed. The YouTube advertising world has also changed considerably, including full integration into the Google Ads suite. Want to make money? You'll find that Google AdSense has improved too.

Foolish Assumptions

Whether you're an experienced videographer or you just bought your first camcorder, you should treat YouTube with an open mind. Just because it's easy to make a video and upload it to YouTube doesn't mean that you won't hit the occasional bump in the road, so don't fool yourself into thinking you don't need help from time to time.

That goes for pretty much everyone, from pros who make a living producing video to ambitious students looking to showcase edgy movie shorts to absolute beginners looking to upload their first video. Regardless of whether you identify with one of these situations or you have a truly unique one, you'll find content in these pages just for you. See whether you can see yourself in one of these categories:

>> **Newbies:** You shoot lots of videos but have never uploaded one to YouTube. But then the feeling overtook you to upload your best ones and share them with the world. No problem: This book can answer some of your most basic questions.

You want your movies to look really cool so that you can post them on YouTube and all your other favorite social media haunts, and if you use this book to answer your most basic questions, trust us — your movies will be awesome.

This book doesn't require your fluency in technospeak. Instead, it's written using a down-to-earth tone. Through clearly written explanations, lists, illustrations, and tips, you'll find out how to best use your equipment, set up video shoots, and navigate the YouTube upload process.

>> **Creators:** There's never been a better place for independent creators to build their brands. It doesn't matter if you're a budding fashion and beauty expert or a seasoned small-engine repair technician; YouTube is where you can showcase your expertise and connect with people who care about what you do, no matter if they're next door or in another part of the world. Even if you've been doing this for some time, you'll find that there are now more capabilities that will make you even better.

>> **Students:** If making movies is what you do and you're interested in sharing your work, this book can get you started by helping you set up your own YouTube channel as your stage. Since you already understand the fundamentals of making a movie, you can concentrate on creating and maintaining your channel. Before long, you'll be uploading videos, building a following, and transforming yourself into the next Steven Spielberg.

- >> **Videographers:** You're already comfortable making movies, you know all about effective editing practices, and you're ready to share your professional work with the world. You'll find tons of info in this book to help set up your channel and grow your audience so that you can transform your video page into a moneymaking endeavor. Ripe with tips, this guide puts you in the easy chair, filling in the blanks with the best ways to showcase your videos and effectively monetize your content.

- >> **Business professionals:** YouTube is great for business because it can help drive awareness and increase sales. These days, consumers turn to YouTube to learn more about the products or services they're considering. YouTube creators have become trusted advisors for viewers and more frequently collaborate with many of the world's most famous brands to give buyers (or potential buyers) all the information they need to enhance their product choices.

- >> **Entrepreneurs:** You may already have a moderate following on YouTube, whereas others are new to the game. Regardless of your level of success, you share the same goal, and that's to use YouTube as a business tool. Whether you're looking for the best ways to earn money with your channel or looking at the bigger picture to promote your business or service, this book has much to offer to find the most effective strategy.

How This Book Is Organized

This new edition of *YouTube Channels For Dummies* is divided into five sections, with each section detailing the various phases of setting up and mastering your channel. Each reader will no doubt prefer a particular area. Some may relish the section that pertains to making a home on YouTube, for example, whereas others may skip ahead to the section on growing and knowing your audience or the cool ways you can build a following. Think of it as a smorgasbord of information.

Part 1: Getting Started with YouTube Channels

This section provides a swift overview of YouTube and how to set up your channel. Whether you're a beginner looking to share videos with a global audience, a working video professional looking to take advantage of monetization, a business owner looking to close the distance, or anyone in between, this group of chapters covers all you need to know to get started.

Part 2: Making Good Videos and Not Making Bad Videos

Regardless of the device or camera used, the language of cinema remains the most important aspect of making good videos — and not making bad ones. The chapters in this part cover fundamental moviemaking for YouTube channels, from using the right tools to putting all the pieces together in postproduction.

Part 3: Growing and Knowing Your Audience

After understanding how to build your channel and fill it with great content, it's time to concentrate on building your audience. The chapters in this part can help you find your way to building a healthy following.

Part 4: YouTube Channels Are Serious Business

This part covers what you need to get started with the business side of YouTube. Whether you're looking to raise brand awareness or considering collaboration with your fellow YouTubers, the chapters in this part can help you get the job done.

Part 5: The Part of Tens

The *For Dummies* version of a top ten list found in this part of the book provides insight into the common and not-so-common aspects of mastering your YouTube channel. More specifically, you'll find out all about the steps you can take to improve your YouTube search results so that viewers are better able to track down your masterpiece. You'll also find out ten things everyone should know about copyright so that you can keep the lawyers off your back.

Icons Used in This Book

What's a *For Dummies* book without icons pointing you in the direction of truly helpful information that's sure to help you along your way? In this section, we briefly describe each icon used in this book.

This icon points out helpful suggestions and useful nuggets of information.

This icon marks a generally interesting and useful fact — something you might want to remember for later use.

When you see this icon, you know that there's techie stuff nearby. If you're not feeling techie, feel free to skip it.

The Warning icon highlights lurking danger. With this icon, we're telling you to pay attention and proceed with caution.

Beyond the Book

In addition to the pages you're reading right now, this book comes with a free access-anywhere cheat sheet that offers a number of YouTube-related pearls of wisdom. To get this cheat sheet, visit www.dummies.com and type **youtube for dummies cheat sheet** in the Search box.

Where to Go from Here

You can either read this book straight through or skip from chapter to chapter. If you need to brush up on some of the YouTube basics, turn the page. If tips on producing that great YouTube video is what you're looking for, go straight to Part 2. Use this book to find out how you, too, can create and manage great content on the YouTube platform.

1

Getting Started with YouTube

Find out how to set up a home on YouTube.

Master all the YouTube basics.

See what's involved in building your own YouTube channel.

Chapter **1**

Making a Home on YouTube

YouTube is the new business-and-entertainment frontier, which means there's as much excitement and creativity associated with creating and managing a YouTube channel these days as was the case during the early days of television, when the sky seemed the limit. YouTube — like television before it — is caught up in the same adventure that comes from defining its target audience as well as finding out what audiences are willing to watch.

For television, the adventurous nature of its early endeavors could be traced to the fact that TV was so new that audiences really didn't know what they wanted. For YouTube, working in today's market, it's much more about meeting the diverse interests and needs of an audience that attracts more than a billion people from all over the planet.

Anyone who wants to show off their video prowess or share their vision with the world can hang a virtual shingle on YouTube by starting their own channel. Of course, when television began, we humans had more toes than the TV had channels. These days, YouTube has billions of users. That makes running a successful YouTube channel seem a bit more daunting.

Having more than 2 billion monthly active users can make getting noticed on your channel feel like searching for a virtual needle in an online haystack. Yet regardless of the steep increase in competition, the intention has always been the same — get people to watch your channel. But it's not all bad news: You also have an advantage over your counterpart in the 1940s. Back then, it took a great deal of capital to get started on television. Today? Not so much. In fact, if you just want a platform for presenting some of your video work, YouTube can make that possible without your having to fork over one thin dime.

Knowing that YouTube is free to use should reduce some of your worries — at least from a financial perspective. Couple that with the size and diversity of the YouTube audience — and the endless number of topics that interest them — and it's easy to believe that you have a fair chance of success for your channel. That's true, up to a point — if the point is you want your channel to thrive, you need to provide your viewers with compelling content.

Saying that your channel needs to host solid content that people actually want to see seems as glaringly obvious as saying a hamburger joint must make a good burger in order to survive. But content merely makes up the first part of the equation. The rest depends on how you bring viewers to that content: While YouTube is free, video production certainly is not. Unless you want to shell out money from your own pocket, you need to generate some funds to produce high quality content for your channel. In the world of YouTube, one major way to generate such funds is with advertising revenue — and it should come as no surprise that the more viewers you can attract, the greater your potential to generate advertising revenue. How much depends on your needs and ambitions, but increased revenue can lead to better production values, which brings it all back to more revenue.

But before you start worrying about all that money you're going to make, let's take a look at what it takes to get started on a YouTube channel for you or your business.

The YouTube Phenomenon: Why You Need to Be on YouTube

Like snowflakes on a winter day, or episodes of *The Simpsons,* YouTube has more topics that viewers can appreciate than any human can count. And because you already love making videos and most likely exhibit some expertise or viewpoint to share with the world, YouTube may be your best creative outlet.

On the downside, you're not the only one hoping to get noticed on YouTube. Many others with the very same intention are looking to build an audience for their YouTube channels, too. ("How many?" you may ask. The number exceeds the number of those preapproved credit card applications that plague your mailbox, so we're talking *lots.*)

Your journey on YouTube begins with knowing your strengths. Some users relish documenting the quirks of their existence to the gentle amusement of others. Others have some type of expertise to share. Then you have performers who regard the video hosting site as their personal stage — the list goes on and on. Even businesses realize it's a great place to inform consumers about their products or provide a great level of customer service. Regardless of your passion, a potential audience is waiting for you.

Audience, audience, audience

Have you ever noticed the repetitive way people describe the most important aspect of a piece of real estate? Yes, we know it's all about location, so much so that real estate agents, among others, feel compelled to say it three times, as though saying it once doesn't get the point across.

Maybe that need for the special emphasis that comes with repetition is justified because, when it comes to success on your YouTube channel, we're of the opinion that saying the word *audience* just once doesn't do justice to its importance. In paying homage to our real estate buddies, we can agree that success for your YouTube channel depends on [drum roll, please] audience, audience, audience!

What's a YouTube audience actually like? You'll find people from all walks of life, and you'll soon discover that they can spend a great deal of time meandering through YouTube's seemingly endless virtual walls, sometimes just entertaining themselves, sometimes educating themselves, sometimes engaging quite passionately with what they see, sometimes letting it all just wash over them. Given the amount of time folks spend on the site, there's a good chance that someone ends up seeing your video. Not a great chance, of course, given that the site has so much content and only so many viewers to watch that content — but still a good chance.

So, how do you move from "good chance" to "great chance"? First and foremost, your success depends on the strength of your content. Right behind strong content, though, you'll find that you need to be a virtual wrangler, capable of bringing to your channel people who may not know anything about you. To do that, you need to know what excites your viewers, what they're looking for in video content, and how they consume what they like. With that information in hand, you can fine-tune your content to better serve your (current or potential) audience.

REMEMBER

Gathering information on the viewing habits of your audience is a crucial first step in determining what they want to see and how long they're willing to watch your videos. YouTube makes it easy to gather lots of information about your viewers — YouTube Analytics, covered in Chapter 11, is a big help here — but consulting friends and family about their viewing preferences is sometimes a good place to start.

Incorporating YouTube into your business and marketing plans

Just like cool sheets on a summer evening, YouTube goes perfectly with social media when it comes to your business and marketing needs. Why not? You already know that your presence on Facebook, LinkedIn, or Twitter keeps you connected with all the right people. Guess what? YouTube can help raise your social media profile as well. (See Figure 1-1.)

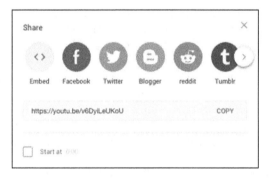

FIGURE 1-1:
Using social media can let people not on YouTube know there's something for them to check out.

By integrating your video content with social media, you can drive interested parties to your channel; your channel, in turn, can point them back to your social media platforms and your contact information. This synergy helps build a strong following, because you can inform potential customers about your business via multiple avenues.

REMEMBER

Video is the perfect partner when it comes to showing products, giving demonstrations, providing tutorials, or showcasing other features designed to increase awareness of your brand. And YouTube is the perfect partner to host your videos.

When coming up with a plan to incorporate your YouTube-based video content into your business and marketing plans, here are some areas to consider:

>> **Give your videos effective titles:** Your video should have clear and succinct titles. The titles should get to the point about your product or service so that people can easily find your video.

>> **Create eye-catching thumbnails:** Make your videos stand out from the crowd. Thumbnails are a great way to catch viewers' attention and compel them to click through.

>> **Add more metadata:** On YouTube, metadata is comprised of the title, video tags, and description of your videos. Coming up with a strong title is a good place to start, but it doesn't end there. You should also add a detailed description of the video, as shown in Figure 1-2, and use as many *keywords* — specific words that are representative of your video's subject matter — as are appropriate for the content. The more information that's included with each video, the easier it is for viewers to find exactly what you have to offer in a Google search.

>> **Include your contact info on the video:** Always add your business or personal information to the video and its description fields, such as email address and social media sites.

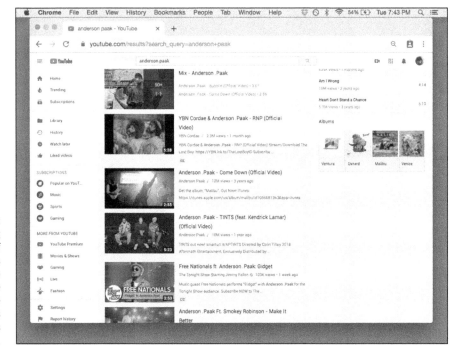

FIGURE 1-2:
The strong metadata of these videos allow them to show up on the first page of the search results for this popular artist.

Becoming a star!

Are you ready for your close-up? Or maybe framing one is your thing. It doesn't matter, because YouTube gives you a platform right up there with radio, film, and television as yet another means of achieving stardom. By doing so, YouTube has created a dedicated community that offers one more way for the world to notice you.

The thought of stardom often leans toward actors and musicians — and the creators behind them. Many have found great success after being discovered on YouTube. (Can you say "Shawn Mendes"?) The rock band Journey found its current lead singer on YouTube. Aerosmith guitarist Joe Perry also found a singer for his other band, The Joe Perry Project.

Actors have also found work by showcasing their clip reels, performances, and auditions. YouTube has made many stars of its own — personalities offering everything from rap parodies to lip-syncing to video game analysis and commentary have made a name for themselves on YouTube. MrBeast, to take one example, has been watched by hundreds of millions of viewers. (See Figure 1-3.)

So, proof positive that YouTube can provide a stage big enough to start, and perhaps sustain, a career.

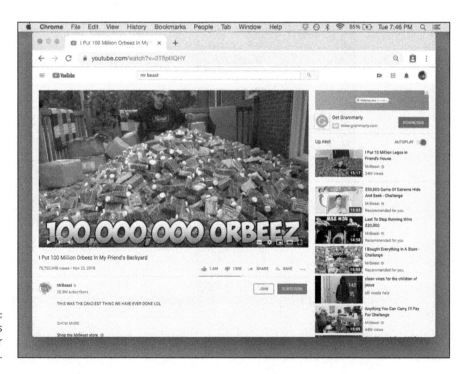

FIGURE 1-3:
One of MrBeast's more popular videos.

Going viral

If you're a millennial or someone who remembers the world before the turn of the century, the phrase "going viral" could have two different meanings. So, in addition to meaning the spread of a virus, which is a bad thing, the term refers to the rapid spread of a video, and that's a great thing.

When an uploaded video goes viral in the good sense, it becomes a sensation that users share and share and share — in the process gathering more numbers of viewers than there are grains of sand in an hourglass. Having your video go viral is like releasing a hit record or having your book make the *New York Times* best seller list, except that you're unlikely to get anywhere near as rich from going viral even if you get a couple of million hits.

TIP

Planning on a video going viral is like planning on winning the lottery. It *could* happen, but you shouldn't bet on it. If you are seriously interested in earning some ad revenue from your video content, work on creating a range of compelling content for your channel, rather than hoping on that one-shot, grand slam home run.

There's no way of telling whether a video will go viral, but there are some traits that successful ones share. Though we discuss ways throughout this book to improve the odds of your video going viral, here are some factors that can make a video a runaway success:

>> **Spontaneity:** There's a real in-the-moment feel to a viral video that captures a random and decisive moment that you could never repeat. The popular video "Charlie bit my finger — again!" and its more than 800 million clicks comes to mind.

>> **Be light-hearted:** People love stuff that's silly and that makes them laugh and think — or that even make them consider trying something, much like the Coke-and-Mentos video collection that has drawn hundreds of millions of views.

>> **Get it out on social media:** Yeah, you can rely on chance that someone stumbles across your video, but that's sort of passive, like waiting by the phone for someone to "find you" for the job. A better tack is for you to let social media know about your latest masterpiece. Just a few tweets here, a Facebook post there, and then maybe an announcement on Reddit can instantly start turning the wheels of virality.

Wasting lots and lots of time

One person's waste of time is another's quest for information, or someone's need to laugh or learn about something, so YouTube viewers simply spend a lot of time watching videos.

That's a good thing, and a win-win situation all around. The audience gets its dose of entertainment, education, and exploration. And your channel benefits because, as viewership increases, so does the potential for someone to find you. And, when that someone finds your channel and you happen to have set it up for receiving advertising revenue (the YouTube term here is *monetization*), you can earn some money.

Here are some numbers, provided by YouTube, that indicate how much (potential) time-wasting is really going on:

>> More than 2 billion unique users visit YouTube each month.

>> Over 1 billion hours of video are watched daily on YouTube

>> According to Nielsen, YouTube reaches more U.S. adults ages 18 to 34 than any cable network.

Seeing What Makes a YouTube Channel Unique

Four walls do not make a home — but it does provide a good start. How you adorn those walls and furnish those halls is what makes it uniquely yours — uniquely your home, in other words. Well, your YouTube channel isn't much different.

When you first create a YouTube channel, it's nothing more than an empty template on a page. Over time, you add videos, organize videos into playlists, and create channel art with your own logo, designs, and branding. Obviously, your video content plays a big part in what makes your channel special, but so does the channel's look and feel. Everything from the layout and font color to the type of content and its subscribers helps set one channel apart from the others.

Though this book takes pride in describing effective ways to create and maintain your YouTube channel for the next couple of hundred pages, let's look at some basics first:

>> **Have people find your channel.** If a tree falls in the forest and nobody hears it fall, does it make a sound? Who knows? More appropriately, if you create a YouTube channel and nobody visits it, it's a safe bet to say that all your good work has come to nothing.

Viewers have to know that your channel exists before they can visit. The main way you have of letting people know you exist is by making sure your content shows up high in the search results of both Google and YouTube itself. (Don't forget that YouTube is the second-most-popular search engine, just behind Google.) To get those high rankings, you have titles, tags, and descriptive text to associate tons of search-engine-friendly keywords with each of your videos — doing that will bring viewers searching for content in contact with *your* content rather than with someone else's content. It's also important that viewers watch, like, comment on, and share your video — yet more indications to the search engines and YouTube's algorithms that your content and channel are important. For good measure, use social media to prep your audience for content that's coming down the pike — just like a movie studio creates a buzz for a big summer blockbuster by teasing you with previews and trailers weeks before release.

REMEMBER

Users often take advantage of YouTube's personalized video recommendations, such as the home screen Recommended feed (see Figure 1-4) and the Up Next feature. If a user clicks on your video and enjoys the content, there's a good chance they'll visit your channel to see what else you have to offer. The more appealing your channel looks at first glance, the more likely a viewer will be to stop and spend some time exploring your channel and your other videos.

>> **Connect with your viewers.** You definitely want to build a community of followers, and for that to happen, you need to actively communicate with them. That means everything from having them subscribe to your channel, engaging with them in your channel's Comments section and on the Community tab, and exposing them to your other social media accounts. You can do all this directly on your channel page.

>> **Provide them with a clear description of your channel.** When viewers know what your channel has to offer, and if it appeals to their interests, they're more likely to visit often, and maybe even subscribe to it. But you need to get the word out.

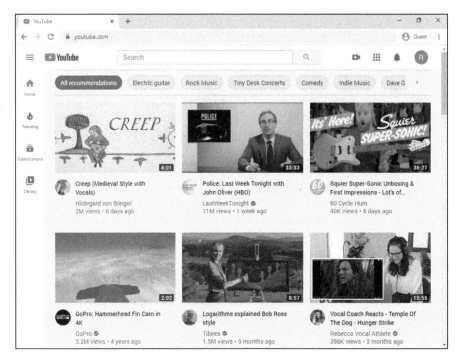

FIGURE 1-4:
The YouTube
Recommended
feed.

Angling for subscriptions

Viewers who like your content will come back and watch more, but viewers who love your content will want to subscribe. Why not? When you keep reaching for the same print magazine whenever you see it, eventually you just subscribe to it so that it regularly comes to the mailbox at your front door. YouTube offers repeat viewers of your channel the same option. Basically, all they have to do is click the Subscribe button, as shown in Figure 1-5, on your channel's home page.

After viewers subscribe to your channel, you have to make it worth their while to view it or else they'll unsubscribe faster than you can say "Jack Nicholson." Here's what "making it worth their while" entails:

>> **Stay in touch with subscribers.** According to YouTube, viewers subscribe to millions of channels every day, so it's important to stay in touch if you want to stay uppermost in their minds.

TIP

Suggest to your viewers that they follow you on social media so that you can let them know when new content is available. This strategy helps your audience grow as you amass a devoted fan base.

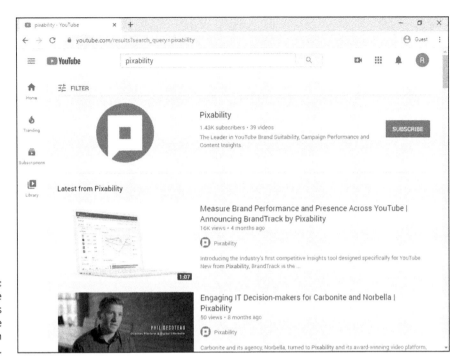

>> **Actively upload videos.** It's difficult to imagine a television station maintaining viewers if it doesn't add new programs. Even if it were all *Seinfeld* all the time, chances are good that viewers would eventually drift off to something else. Well, the same concept applies for your YouTube channel. If you don't upload new video content, you'll lose the interest of your subscriber base. The takeaway here? Always provide new content.

>> **Pay close attention to tagging.** When you *tag* a video, you categorize it after uploading it to YouTube. When a video is properly identified, it increases the possibility of someone else finding it, and that extends to future subscribers.

Establishing your brand

Whether it's a consumer or a viewer, a brand makes your product or service immediately identifiable. Imagine that the Coca-Cola logo looked different every time you saw it, or maybe the apple on your PowerBook wasn't the same apple you saw embossed on your iPhone. This lack of consistency could shatter your confidence in the product; you may start wondering whether what you had was a cheap knock-off of the real thing rather than the genuine article.

Branding is designed to restore confidence in the product — that familiar logo makes you relax, knowing that you're sure to get the real thing. When it comes to your YouTube channel, branding becomes the identifiable element that lets viewers know who you are and what you're all about, thus creating a similar feeling of confidence. Just like consumers flock to brands they identify with, your audience will do the same with your brand.

Branding takes on many forms on YouTube:

>> **Intro clip:** Before each video runs on your channel, you can insert a 3-second clip that acts as a label for your content. The torch-carrying lady wrapped in a flag for Columbia Pictures and the roaring MGM lion are good examples of a branding element. Your job, if you choose to accept it, is to come up with an intro of your own that is equally compelling.

>> **Channel header:** This element is the banner on top of your main page, and at first it's as empty as a blank page. (See Figure 1-6.) You'll definitely want to click that Add Channel Art button to add a compelling picture or another graphic along with the name of your channel. The channel header can also include your contact info and specify how often you intend to upload new videos.

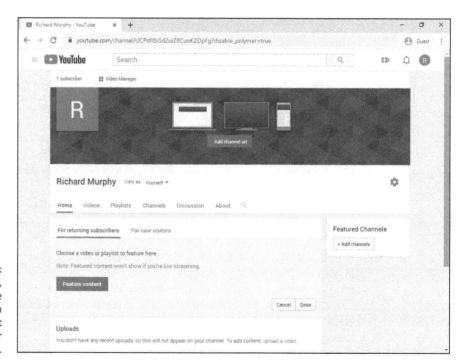

FIGURE 1-6:
An empty header, waiting to be filled with an image that represents your content.

>> **Logo:** Companies spend millions on branding when they have to come up with a new logo, because they have to track down and replace every single instance of the old logo. We're guessing that's not your problem — you just have to come up with your own logo, perhaps using a simple image and your name. If you feel graphically challenged, you can find places on the web that can create one for you inexpensively. Or just have an artistic friend design a logo for you.

>> **Playlists:** If you have enough videos on your channel, you can create a running order of them. This playlist can provide an overview of your content or a specific subtopic of your videos. You can name every playlist, and even rearrange them.

>> **Trailer:** In a YouTube context, a *trailer* is a video that can automatically play whenever visitors come to your channel. You can use the video most representative of your content as a kind of advertisement for your offerings, or you can make a short video that shows viewers what your channel is all about and how they can benefit from watching your videos.

Managing Channels for Fun and/or Profit

Everybody has a reason for making a video, and YouTube doesn't discriminate on why you do it. Whether you were influenced a little too much by the silly, everyday situations depicted on television a series like *America's Funniest Home Videos* or you want to show off your post-film-school prowess or you're looking to educate the masses with a series of how-to videos, there's a place for you on YouTube — and (you hope!) an audience that's willing to follow your exploits.

In addition to the pleasure that comes from a job well done, there's (potentially) a business side to running a YouTube channel. If you post videos that draw a lot of views, it's worth your time to *monetize* your channel — generate some income from ad revenue, in other words. But that's not the only business purpose YouTube channels can help with: They can serve as a great showcase for your particular skills or services or act as a delivery system for product descriptions, tutorials, and testimonials associated with whatever your business is selling.

Creating content

Whether you grab a 10-second video of a gathering of friends, have something meaningful to say on your video blog, or plan a highly structured production with sets and actors, you're creating content.

Almost every topic under the sun is represented on YouTube. That diversity in topics is matched by an equally broad range of production levels. Some videos are quite sophisticated, displaying amazing production values, but many are fairly average. And a great deal are just poorly done and end up getting shown in film classes as examples of what not to do.

Better production values increase your ability to grab viewers' attention — maybe enough for them to watch the entire video and maybe enough for them to even consider watching whatever else you have to offer. The holy grail, of course, is having them feel so enthusiastic about what they see that they then share it with others.

But great video quality doesn't happen accidentally; rather, it's done consciously, from conception to upload. Though the topic is more thoroughly represented throughout this book, here are some key suggestions to always keep in mind:

REMEMBER

>> **Plan before you film.** Great videos begin in preproduction. That means having an idea of the shooting location and working with some sort of script (or at least a storyboard of the kind of shots you want for the video).

Great planning leads to great production.

>> **Know your audience.** When you're just getting started, you try to make solid videos with good descriptions and hope that your audience finds you. After you have attracted a following, it's still important to understand who they are and whether your content is right for them. For example, if you start a channel that talks about SAT and college prep, you should use language that's consistent with a high-school-age demographic. Don't overlook the importance of being highly aware of your potential audience.

>> **Keep viewers entertained.** Regardless of the subject matter, it's important for viewers to enjoy the experience so that you hold their attention. Remember that hooking a viewer's attention starts with the first five seconds of the video. (Why? Because viewers may leave before the good stuff starts!)

>> **Let them learn something.** People generally click on a video description link in search of information. If they find it quickly and they were entertained, chances are good that they will love you and click through to products or services mentioned in the video.

Building an audience

After you create great content, you have to find people to watch it. After all, isn't that the entire purpose of sharing your video with the world? Whether it starts with the ten people who just happen to run across your student film or a million people viewing your talking puppy video, building your audience is essential.

YouTube is no different from other media when it comes to emphasizing the importance of building an audience. For example, you may have the catchiest song of all time, but if no one has ever heard it or even knows it exists, then that song cannot by any stretch of the imagination be called a success. The same is true for your videos — you need to work at getting as many people as possible to watch them.

Successfully building your audience depends on understanding their needs and making sure you can deliver on what your channel promises. Catering to your audience — whether it consists of one person or ten million — centers on understanding them and satisfying their appetite. (For more on building your audience, check out Chapter 10.)

Building a business

In addition to letting you upload your videos to satisfy the fun side of your personality, YouTube can work wonders for your business side. You can easily set your account to monetize video content, as mentioned in the next section; as long as you meet the minimum requirements for monetization and enough viewers watch your videos, you can earn some extra money. If you have something to sell or a service to offer, you can also leverage YouTube for some pretty cool and powerful advertising. As you can see in Chapter 13, it's simple enough for anyone to do it.

Monetizing

You can earn money with your YouTube channel every time someone views a YouTube ad before watching one of your videos. The more people who view your content, the more money you can potentially make. The minimum eligibility requirements to turn on monetization features for your channel have dramatically changed over the past couple of years, primarily because of what are referred to as brand safety issues with advertisers.

So, what's all this about "brand safety"? Actually, it's not that complicated. An advertiser wants to place its ads on videos that are suitable for its brand image, culture, and vision. An advertiser doesn't want its brands associated with bad press or negative content. What is suitable for one brand advertiser might not be suitable for another brand. For example, a video game manufacturer might be okay with advertising on first-person-shooter videos, but a beauty brand may find that kind of content inappropriate for its video's ads or just not relevant for its target audience.

Your first hurdle for making money on YouTube is to get accepted into the YouTube Partner Program. To apply for the program, you need to have 1,000 subscribers and 4,000 public video watch-hours over the past year.

Now that users have found the potential to make money on YouTube, it's become like the California gold rush of 1849. Motivated entrepreneurs are setting up shop in the hope of striking it big with their YouTube channels.

As you might expect, not everybody will strike it rich. In fact, very few will strike it rich. Nevertheless, it's possible to earn a side hustle, especially if you take advantage of the multiple ways you can make money by way of your YouTube channel, including advertising revenue, channel membership, your merchandise shelf, Super Chat and Super Stickers, and YouTube Premium Revenue. Just keep in mind that slow-and-steady wins the race — making money takes time, or at least it will take time until you build a massive following. (For more on monetization, check out Chapter 14.)

IN THIS CHAPTER

» **Navigating the basics of the YouTube interface**

» **Watching YouTube videos**

» **Creating a YouTube account**

» **Setting up a unique channel URL**

» **Checking out the YouTube Partner Program**

Chapter **2**

The Basics of YouTube

n the simplest sense, *YouTube* is a website designed for sharing video. Before YouTube's founding in 2005, posting and sharing a video online was difficult: The bandwidth and storage needed to stream video were expensive, and many copyright risks were involved in letting people upload whatever they wanted. Because YouTube was willing to absorb the costs and ignore the risks, it provided, for free, the infrastructure for users to upload and view as much video as they want. This proposition turned out to be a popular one.

Google acquired YouTube in 2006, and YouTube's growth continued. As of 2019, viewers watch more than a billion hours of video per day, and more than 500 hours of video are uploaded every minute.

Let us say that last part again: 500 hours of video are uploaded to YouTube *every minute.*

Given that amount of content, you, as an individual, could never watch everything that's available on YouTube. For every minute of video you watch, you're 500 hours behind. For every work of genius, such as "Cat in a shark costume chases a duck while riding a Roomba," YouTube has literally tens of thousands of poorly shot, poorly edited videos of family vacations, dance recitals, and bad jokes that could possibly be of interest only to the uploader. This chapter serves as your (essential) guide to finding the good parts while skipping the bad. (Hey, it's a tough job, but somebody had to do it, and that somebody was us.) We help you navigate the YouTube interface, establish an account, and start looking ahead to planning a channel. If you're new to YouTube or you need to dig a bit deeper as a user, this is the chapter for you.

What You'll Find on YouTube

You'll find, in a word, videos on YouTube. You'll find, in several words, just about anything on YouTube. We would say that you'll find anything you can imagine, but even we never would have imagined that anyone would make a compilation of animal clips from the defunct app Vine, and we definitely would never have imagined that the compilation would have been viewed over 214 million times. The best way to describe what's on YouTube may be to start with the categories that YouTube lists on its home page.

Managing your identity

Your entire YouTube experience is driven by whether YouTube knows who you are. It doesn't use any magic to figure it out. Instead, YouTube simply determines whether you're logged in or logged out. When you log in, YouTube can make video recommendations based on your viewing behavior. In other words, after YouTube knows what you like, it does its best to bring more of that great video content to you.

REMEMBER

YouTube and its parent, Google, are in the advertising business and are not promoting online video for the betterment of mankind (though some channels on YouTube actually help achieve that goal). By understanding your viewing behavior when you're logged in, YouTube and Google are able to serve better and more relevant ads to you. That's good for them, for the advertiser, and for the viewer. Sure, most people don't like ads, but YouTube is truly trying to do a better job of targeting ads. (Chapter 13 covers this topic in more detail.)

As you can see in this chapter and throughout the book, you need to be logged in to do most of the important things on YouTube. Sure, you can watch videos without being logged in, but you'll miss a good part of the experience. You need a Google account to log in, and we show you how to set up one of those a little later in this chapter, in the section "Working with a YouTube Account." You also have the option to create a YouTube channel for an existing Google account.

REMEMBER

You don't need a YouTube channel to log in to YouTube — you just need a Google account. Having a channel though, as you'll soon find out, helps you organize your YouTube viewing without having to create any videos.

Nav[igating]

The ho[me] ... [p]ast. It was once the fount o[f] ... [f]or new content, the home [page] ... YouTube changed the hom[e] ... [th]e company's desire to know ... [wan]ts and who have a history ... [th]em based on past usage. N[ow] ... are currently most popular ...

The lo[gged-in home page]

As long a[s] ... , the site is busily keeping t[rack] ... [a]bout what kind of videos yo[u] ... page you see, and YouTube ... [you]r home page will come to b[e] ... [y]ou've watched in the past.

Here's a q[uick look] ... [wh]en you log on to www.youtube.com after you create an account. (Again, we tell you more about creating an account later in this chapter, in the section "Working with a YouTube Account.") Take a look at Figure 2-1 to see how a YouTube home page looks when you log in.

Sometimes a picture is worth a thousand words, and sometimes you need a thousand words to explain what that picture is actually trying to show you. When it comes to the YouTube home page, you definitely need the thousand words. The list in the following section offers descriptions of what's on the home page.

Along the top

These are essentially YouTube's main controls, and with them, you can access most of the site's essential functions.

>> **The Guide icon:** This button, consisting of three horizontal bars, sits next to the YouTube button. Clicking it brings up a guide of channels and topics that may be of interest to the viewer.

>> **The YouTube button:** Though it looks exactly like the YouTube logo, this button actually does something in addition to looking pretty; clicking it always brings you back to the YouTube home page.

>> **The Search box:** Whenever you need to search for a video, this is where you go. Enter keywords to find videos that may match what you're looking for.

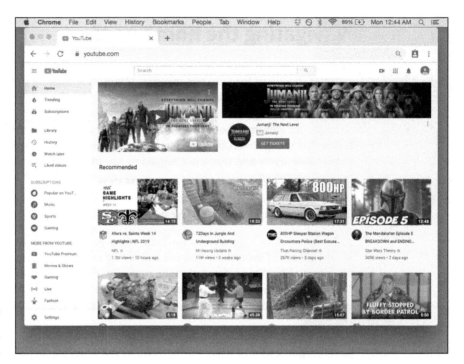

FIGURE 2-1:
The logged-in
YouTube
home page.

» **The Upload icon:** When you're ready to upload a video, you get started by using this camera-shaped button. Clicking it opens a dropdown menu, giving you the option to post a video or do a livestream. (Read more about the Upload icon in Chapter 9.)

» **The YouTube Apps icon:** This button, consisting of nine tiny squares, allows you to access a suite of other YouTube applications, including its own television service, YouTube TV; music streaming, via YouTube Music; and a safer, child-oriented site, YouTube Kids. It also has helpful tools for creators. The Creator Academy provides instructional guides for users hoping to maximize their channel's effectiveness. YouTube for Artists offers musicians a means of promoting and growing their content.

» **The Notifications bell:** Notifications of any activity relevant to your user experience appear here. As a YouTube creator, you're alerted whenever activity happens on your channel, including comments, video sharing, and more. As a viewer who has notifications turned on, you're notified whenever channels upload videos or make posts.

» **Channel icon:** A round image button shows either the Channel icon you come up with or an image associated with your Google ID when you're logged in. Use this button to get to YouTube Studio, which is your YouTube Mission Control, or to configure your YouTube account settings.

TIP

You can log on to YouTube through your Google account, but we recommend having an associated YouTube channel, to get all the benefits of your YouTube experience, such as creating playlists. (For more on playlists, see Chapter 3.)

Down the left side

TIP

The menu functions running down the left side of the screen complement the functionality of the ones that run across the top and focus more on content. You can toggle what's shown on the left side by clicking the Guide icon:

>> **Home:** This option is selected by default when you arrive at the YouTube home page. When this section is selected, the main window of the site shows you lists of channels and videos that YouTube assumes you'll like.

>> **Trending:** Videos that are now popular on YouTube can be found here. A video can make it to the trending list for many reasons, but it appears the same for all viewers, regardless of personal preference. The list is updated frequently as videos dip in and out of relevance.

>> **Subscriptions:** See the most recent uploads for all the channels you've subscribed to, from most recent to oldest. If your channel is new and you haven't subscribed to anyone yet, this listing displays suggested genres and creators to get you started. Subscriptions are a good way to keep track of the channels you like on YouTube. You can control how your subscriptions are organized on your home page by using the following tools:

Manage: Clicking this link takes you to a separate page listing all your subscriptions, as shown in Figure 2-2. Here you're given the option to unsubscribe from any channels as well as alter their notification settings. (Notifications are denoted by the Bell icon in the top right of the screen.) You have the choice of All, Personalized, or None. All notifies you of any and all upload activity. Personalized notifies you of only certain uploads, based on a variety of variables, including your watch history. Finally, None turns off all notifications, if you really just don't want to be bothered (or if you just like surprises).

Arrangement: To the right of Manage are two icons. The leftmost icon, featuring a cluster of six boxes, reconfigures the page to display as a grid, showing only thumbnails, titles, and views. The icon to the right, with three squares and three rectangles, lists all uploads instead, allowing you to view the first part of the video description without having to click the actual video.

FIGURE 2-2:
A list of your
subscriptions.

>> **Library:** This gives you quick, abridged views inside all the other menu functions on the left.

- *History:* By default, you can easily access the eight most recent videos you've watched. You can view a more extensive record of your watch history by clicking See All, which we delve into a bit more below."

- *Watch Later:* Videos you've flagged for viewing at a later time can be found using the clock-shaped icon. We go over how to manage this playlist later in this chapter, also in the section "Down the left side."

- *Playlists:* Playlists are a great way to organize videos you've discovered on YouTube. This section highlights some of your playlists, if and when you've made them. We go into more detail about playlists and their importance in Chapter 3.

- *Liked Videos:* Any videos you *like* (covered later in the chapter, in the section Watching a Video) will populate on this automatically generated playlist.

- *Purchases:* Any movies or content you buy on YouTube appear here, to view at your convenience.

>> **History:** Clicking History — or See All on the Library — takes you to a new page cataloging all your account activity, including your watch history, search history, comments, community, and live chat, as shown in Figure 2-3. This page can be deeply embarrassing to visit, because it can reveal to you just how many unboxing videos and TikTok compilations you've watched in the past week. But whereas this section can lead to feelings of shame and regret for time wasted, it can also be an interesting insight into your viewing.

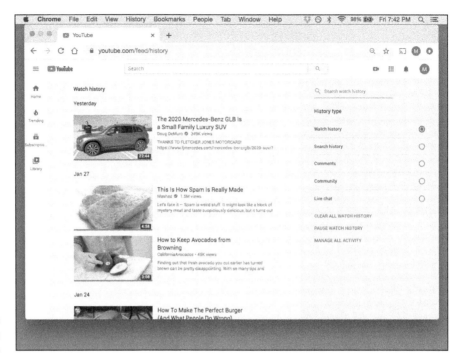

FIGURE 2-3:
The Watch History page.

TIP

REMEMBER

You'll end up seeing a lot of videos on YouTube, and at some point you'll want to go back to see what you've viewed or to watch a particular video again. The History section is a great way to keep track of what you've watched and to analyze your viewing.

Your watch history is what YouTube's algorithms pay attention to when populating the suggested videos on the front page of your account.

Unlike with real-world history — the stuff recorded in encyclopedias and history books — you do have some control over this list. A few controls here let you "rewrite history," as described in this list:

- *Clear All Watch History:* This is the nuclear option. If you're ready to undo everything you've ever watched and start over with a clean slate, this does just what it says and deletes all the information from your watch history. If you don't want to clear your whole watch history, you can also delete individual videos on a case-by-case basis by hovering the mouse cursor over them and clicking the X that appears.

- *Pause Watch History:* This puts your memory on hold and allows you to watch videos without their being added to either your history or your video recommendations from YouTube. If you know that you're about to binge-watch a bunch of funny animal videos and don't want to be recommended videos like these, this is the option to select. Of course, this strategy works only if you pause before you watch the videos. Otherwise, you'll be in there clearing your watch history before you know it.

- *Manage All Activity:* This takes you to a separate page that allows you to access more info about your account's activity, including reviewing YouTube searches you've conducted. This is helpful when you forget to save a video, and you want to reconstruct the search history. Clickable links allow you to instantly return to the YouTube search results for that query. You can also access various other activity settings associated with your Google account.

» **Watch Later:** The Watch Later link opens a new page that shows you a private playlist of all the videos you've chosen to watch at a later time. Your channel subscribers can't see this playlist unless you make it public. After you've watched the content, you can quickly remove it from the playlist. If you use a streaming device attached to your TV, this can be your TV line-up for the evening. You can easily add videos to the Watch Later playlist — or any playlist, for that matter — as described in the following list:

- *Add Videos:* If you hover the mouse cursor over a video thumbnail, a clock-shaped icon appears. Clicking this icon automatically adds a video to your Watch Later playlist. Or if you're watching a video but don't have time to finish it, you can save it to your Watch Later playlist (as discussed later in this chapter, in the section "Watching a video"). A playlist is useful for organizing the videos you like or want to watch later. For example, you can collect all the Taylor Swift videos you've watched into one country power-house playlist. A playlist is also a great way to engage viewers with your content. (For more on how content engages viewers, see Chapter 3.)

Hovering the mouse cursor over a video thumbnail also reveals a secondary button, named Add to Queue. If you want to watch a series of videos back-to-back in one session without adding them to a playlist, use this button to queue them up so that they play, one after the other, without interruption.

- *Removing Videos:* When you hover over a video, you see a small icon on the right, composed of a row of three small dots. Clicking this icon opens a dropdown menu that gives you the option to remove the video from your Watch Later playlist. (This function applies to other playlists as well.) This is a great way to clean out your Watch Later playlist if it's getting tedious. You can also move a video to the top or bottom of the list, add it to the queue, or add it to a more unique playlist. You can also rearrange the play order of the videos on your list by hovering over the two lines on the left of each video, clicking, and then dragging.

If an uploader deletes a video, it's automatically removed from any and all of your playlists.

- *Play All:* This option allows you to play all videos on the Watch Later playlist as they appear. However, if you want to spice things up, you can set it to Shuffle.

» **Liked Videos:** This is the final section that appears by default on your home page when you first start your YouTube account. It functions in exactly the same capacity as your Watch Later playlist, except that videos are added whenever you click to like them, a function we explore later in this chapter, in the section "Watching a video."

» **Purchases:** If you happen to purchase any content on YouTube, an additional option appears. You use this option to view all purchases you have made on YouTube or Google Play. You can watch again any movies you have purchased — and at any time.

» **Playlists:** The playlist section is where you can see all the recent playlists you have created or saved. You can click on any one of your playlists here to easily access and modify a playlist.

» **Subscriptions:** Not to be confused with the previous Subscriptions button, this section alphabetically lists the channels you're subscribed to and denotes, with a small blue dot, whether you've seen their most recent activity. Clicking any of the subscriptions takes you straight to that channel. (Keep in mind that subscriptions are a good way to keep track of the channels you like on YouTube.)

REMEMBER

You may have now seen in the Guide more than a few references to subscriptions. Subscriptions and subscription management are a big deal on YouTube because they serve to support a strong connection between a viewer and a channel.

» **More from YouTube:** This list gives you quick access to some popular features and video categories:

- *YouTube Premium:* This paid-subscription service lets you view YouTube without ads, play videos in the background of your phone or mobile device, access exclusive original content, and download content, including on YouTube Music's app.

- *Movies/Shows:* These items are available for purchase here. YouTube also offers some movies and television programs for free.

- *Gaming:* This one showcases popular gaming content and live streams across all of YouTube. You can subscribe to the category as a whole or browse individually.

- *Live:* Live displays popular live content streaming on YouTube. You can also subscribe to the category as a whole.

- *Fashion:* You can find popular content here. As with the previous two categories, you can subscribe or view at your pleasure.

>> **Masthead:** Last but not least, the largest element on the YouTube landing page is an advertisement called a masthead — sometimes with and sometimes without its own, embedded video. The ad probably isn't what you came to YouTube to see, but ad revenue keeps the lights on and the video flowing.

TIP

If you'd rather not look at the big banner ad, you can usually close it by clicking the Close Ad button in one of the banner's corners.

The logged-out experience

When you arrive at YouTube before you've taken the trouble to create an account, you see the pure, innocent YouTube of the viewer with no viewing history. Treasure this moment, this innocence, this pure instant of seeing the site in its purest form. You'll soon become a jaded viewer, with a viewing history filled with reminders of the hours spent watching Billie Eilish videos. Have a look at Figure 2-4 to see what YouTube looks like to the user who is logged out.

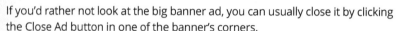

WHY DOES YouTube HAVE ADS?

It's always flattering when people listen to you and seem to be interested in knowing exactly who you are. You might think that YouTube is an avid listener, just because it takes a great interest in the kinds of videos you're watching, but that's not because YouTube has suddenly decided that you two should be Best Friends Forever. The truth is that YouTube's *product* — the way it makes money — is *not* streaming video. In fact, the streaming video part costs the company quite a bit of money because it's expensive for it to host the GoPro videos you made of your dog's bath.

So, if YouTube isn't making money hosting and serving videos, how is it making money? Here's the dirty secret: *It's making money selling advertisements!* That means *you* are YouTube's product. It's selling your attention to advertisers, and that's why YouTube wants so badly to know you. It wants to be able to tell its ad-buying customers exactly who is watching their ads.

Though all this information may seem to be much like part of a dystopian police state, it turns out that it's something that can work in your favor when you launch a channel with an eye toward making money from your content. We get to the details of grabbing your share of YouTube ad revenue in Chapter 13.

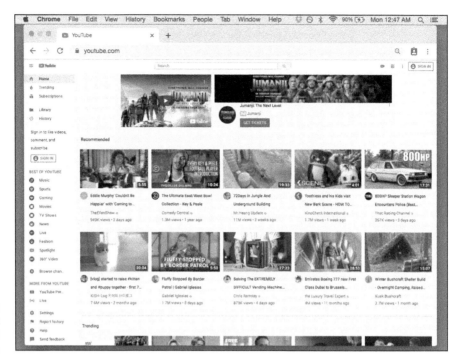

On the left side of the screen, scroll down and you'll see a list of links to the Best of YouTube channels. These verticals, as they're called, are the primary content divisions on YouTube. *Verticals* resemble the sections of a newspaper. Like a newspaper, YouTube is organized into sections so that you can find the type of content you want to watch. You can subscribe to any of these verticals like it's a normal user channel.

TECHNICAL STUFF

The programming on YouTube is divided into verticals. (Anywhere else, these content divisions would be called *genres.*) Verticals are all a combination of YouTube *native* content (content produced by regular YouTube users) and content produced by traditional media companies, like CNN and The Onion. One amazing aspect of YouTube is that individuals can still manage to have a voice just as loud as the major media players (which is one fundamental point of this book).

It's time to see what the verticals have to offer:

» **Music:** Music is a big deal on YouTube. Thirty-nine of the 100 most-subscribed channels are music channels. Though MTV was once the go-to place for showing music videos, that niche is now filled by YouTube, and much of that traffic is dominated by VEVO, which offers music videos from big-name entertainment conglomerates, such as Universal Music Group and Sony Music Entertainment.

>> **Sports:** Sports videos are also extremely popular on YouTube. The Sports vertical is an interesting blend of mainstream sports video — from sources like ESPN, the NFL, and other major sports leagues to Parkour and extreme sports videos shot with the extremely popular GoPro camera line.

>> **Gaming:** This vertical is one of the most exciting. It includes not only live streaming but also non-live videos, trending gamers, and autogenerated content from Minecraft, Fortnite, Grand Theft Auto, World of Tanks, and more.

>> **Movies & Shows:** This one is home to YouTube's movie-and-television-show purchase or rental business. You can even watch many things here for free, though there will be ads.

>> **News:** The News vertical consists of channels that cover a wide range of beats, including national news, world news, science, sports, and entertainment.

>> **Live:** You can catch live events from gaming to music to sports and much more.

>> **Fashion:** This subject is one of the most popular on YouTube. Consisting of everything from clothing to makeup, this is one of the site's most popular and influential categories.

>> **Spotlight:** This one is somewhat different from the one named Popular on YouTube in that it itemizes what's new-and-emerging. Because it covers a collection of topics, you may find yourself spending more time in this section than you originally planned.

>> **360° Video:** These omnidirectional videos allow viewers to see what happens from any angle. Once considered somewhat gimmicky, 360° is becoming increasingly popular because of its virtual reality applications.

>> **Browse Channels:** This vertical consists of a summary look at channels across different categories and interest groups.

TIP

You can get a look at the home page at any time without all the baggage of your past video views. That way, you'll be sure to see (unfiltered) what's trending on the site. Just put your browser in a private browsing mode, such as Chrome's Incognito option, and you'll see the YouTube home page with new eyes. You'll see which videos are hot on the site with none of the context of your past browsing.

REMEMBER

In Apple's Safari browser and Mozilla Firefox, incognito browsing is called *private browsing*. In Internet Explorer, it's called *InPrivate browsing*.

Watching a video

The reason that most people visit YouTube is to watch videos. That should probably be one of the first things you do when you arrive. After familiarizing yourself with the home page, try clicking on a video. You're taken to a Watch page, which should look a lot like the one shown in Figure 2-5.

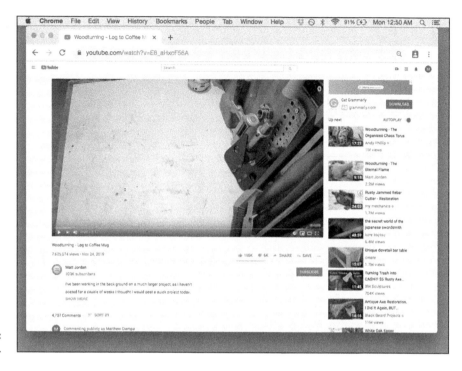

FIGURE 2-5:
The Watch page.

The Watch page is, first and foremost, for viewing videos, but it has a number of other functions as well. You'll want to become familiar with a number of elements on this page:

>> **Video Player:** Front and center is the video player, which you use to watch the video.

>> **Video Info:** Tucked beneath the video player you'll see the video info, including its title, view count, and description field.

>> **Comments:** Everybody has an opinion, right? What's true about the world outside is equally true in the world of YouTube. Here's where viewers can comment on and discuss the video, and where the uploader occasionally joins in the discussion.

>> **Suggestions:** Along the right side of the screen are the suggested videos, which are YouTube's best guesses about what you might want to watch next, based on the video you're watching and your overall watch history.

That's the bird's-eye view. The next few sections take a closer look at some of these features in a bit more detail.

TECHNICAL STUFF

The YouTube *algorithm*, the mysterious piece of code responsible for guessing what you want to watch next, is uncannily effective a lot of the time. The suggested videos can suck you into what is known as the YouTube spiral, in which you can potentially lose hours of your life clicking on video after video and eventually end up watching infomercials from the mid-1980s with no clear idea how you got there.

The player

The most noticeable item on the Watch page is the video player. As with most video players, the YouTube version has a number of controls ranging along the bottom. Here's an overview of what each control does:

>> **The scrubber:** This bar, which runs the length of the video player, allows the viewer to jump around in the video. Hover the mouse cursor over the bar, and then click on the red circle and drag it to the right to "scrub" forward in the video.

>> **The Play/Pause button:** This button stops and starts the video stream.

>> **The Next button:** This button allows the viewer to skip to the next video. Next can mean a recommended video from YouTube or the subsequent video if watching a playlist.

>> **The mute/volume control:** When you roll over the Speaker symbol, the volume bar appears. Click the speaker to mute the audio. Use the volume slider to adjust the volume.

>> **The counter:** This is the timer for the video. It shows you how much viewing time has elapsed as well as the total length of the video.

>> **Closed Captions:** This button, marked CC, toggles the captions (on-screen text of the dialogue and sounds) on and off. Not every video has good captions. (For more on captions — good, bad, and indifferent — check out Chapter 9.)

>> **Settings:** You have to click the little Gear icon to access the Settings menu, but that's not too hard to do. For most videos, the available settings include toggling autoplay, turning annotations on and off (graphics superimposed on the video), changing the video speed, switching subtitles and captioning, and setting the resolution of the video. We're big fans of watching the videos at normal speed and at the highest available resolution.

>> **Display Controls:** You can change the size of the default player to become smaller so that you can continue to browse the site (miniplayer), show across the width of the browser (theater mode), cast to a compatible television or device (play on TV), or take over the entire display (full screen).

TIP

When it comes to resolution, most videos don't default to 1080p or 720p HD. The default playback is often 480p or lower, which doesn't look that great. If you want to watch videos in high definition, you have to become familiar with the Settings menu. Keep in mind that your Internet connection needs to be fast enough to stream HD video to avoid interruption.

The video info section

Directly below the video player, you'll find a bunch of information about the video that we usually call the *video info.* You can see a lot of data about each video there, as you can see in Figure 2-6.

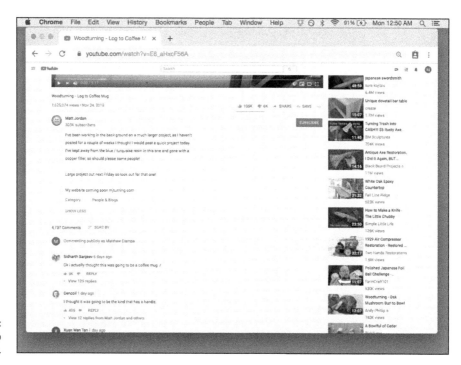

FIGURE 2-6:
The video info section.

Here's a list of the most important information to pay attention to in the video info:

>> **Title:** In large type just below the video player is the title of the video. If the video is trending, a small message denoting so appears above the title. (We talk more about titles — more effective titles, to be specific — in Chapter 9. For now, think "catchy and relevant.")

>> **Like or Dislike:** The Thumbs Up and Thumbs Down buttons give you a quick, simple way to let your feelings about a video be known. Just to be clear, punch the Thumbs Up button if you like the video; punch the Thumbs Down if you don't.

>> **Share:** Next up is the Share link. When you click the Share link, you're shown a few different ways that you can share the video and entice the world to look at it. (You can see the various Share settings in Figure 2-7.) Don't forget that YouTube is also a social media platform that's quite capable of letting you easily share to Facebook, LinkedIn, reddit, and other sites. YouTube also lets you share video on a website with simple HTML embed code, and if that's not your style, you can simply email a video link to your friends.

FIGURE 2-7:
Sharing videos.

>> **Save:** Over time, you'll want to keep track and organize the video you're viewing. If you're using YouTube videos to help you with a kitchen renovation, you may want to keep all the videos about cabinet installation in one place. That place is the playlist, and you learn about it in Chapter 3. You can save a list of all the videos you want to watch later or videos that are your favorites.

>> **More:** This catch-all button — the one with the three dots (. . .) — lets you see more information about the video. This includes reading the transcript of the video or adding translations. You can also report this video to YouTube if you see inappropriate content. This last piece should be used only sparingly.

>> **Channel information:** Just below the title, you'll find the channel name and a logo known as the Channel icon. A small check mark appears next to the channel name if it's *verified,* meaning a person or brand behind the account is the real deal.

>> **Subscription status and control:** In Chapter 10, you discover that subscriptions are important to creators and viewers because subscriptions provide a better level of engagement among the two. The Subscribe button, which is to the right of the Channel icon, appears in red with a subscriber count number if the viewer is *not* subscribed. Simply clicking the button enables the subscription, and the button turns gray while adding a secondary subscription setting button that looks like a gear. Click this secondary button to control how you want to receive updates from the channel. To unsubscribe from a channel, all you need to do is click the gray Subscribed button, then click Unsubscribe from the pop-up window that appears.

>> **Description:** The video description field should provide all sorts of helpful information about the video and a way for viewers to find additional information, which may include links to make a purchase or support a political candidate, for example. Only part of the description is shown, so a viewer can click the Show More bar under the description summary to see the rest of the information. Chapter 9 shows you how to best organize the description field.

>> **Comments:** Comments about the video are placed just below the description field and can be sorted according to popularity or recency. Regular YouTubers know that comments can range from highly informative to occasionally pretty rude. Remember that YouTube is a social media platform and with it comes the good, the bad, and the ugly — especially in the Comments section. As a creator, you definitely want to attract comments, but keep in mind that you can filter out inappropriate ones or ban specific viewers who only cause trouble. (We tell you more about comments management in Chapter 10.)

Working with a YouTube Account

There are a number of reasons you'd want to open a YouTube account. Though the logged-out experience is interesting, you need an account to subscribe to channels, create playlists, comment on videos, and generally become part of the YouTube community. Not to mention, you need an account to launch your channel, where you upload videos, run ads on those videos, and generate some revenue.

REMEMBER

Be aware that signing up for a YouTube account means signing up for a Google account. Google owns YouTube, and recently Google has been busy unifying its products under a single login, allowing you to use one username and password to log in to its complementary services — like Gmail, Google Drive, Calendar, and Maps — in addition to your new YouTube account.

One of the first things you notice when you arrive on the YouTube home page is the Sign In button in the top right of the screen. Google and YouTube want you logged in so that they can monitor your viewing habits and provide more focused video recommendations and — ultimately — relevant advertising. If you already have a Google account and you want to use it to house your channel, you can. If you're creating a new channel, it may make sense to create a new Google account to go with it.

WARNING

You'll use this channel as your business, and you should, as the popular idiom goes, "never mix business with pleasure." Though not always 100 percent true — many people have jobs they truly enjoy — this statement definitely applies in this case. If you take to heart all the principles in this book and have a bit of luck, your channel could become quite popular. You'll then be in the unenviable position of running your new online video business in your personal email account, and you'll be stuck with the job of sifting through the guilt-inducing emails from your mother, the advertisement for the big sale at the store where you bought a gift for your ex once (like 12 years ago), and, of course, messages that might actually be important. Rather than deal with that hassle, just go ahead and start a new account. It's free.

Follow these steps to get a Google account you can use on YouTube:

1. **Click the blue Sign In button.**

Doing so takes you to the Google login screen, shown in Figure 2-8, where you can log in or create a new account.

REMEMBER

Last time we checked, the big blue Sign In button was in the top right of the screen, but be aware that YouTube, like all other websites, tends to redesign things and move buttons around from time to time.

If you already have a Google account, you may already be logged in. If you're creating a new account to go with a new channel, it may help to use a private browsing mode in your web browser to avoid confusing Google.

TIP

2. **Click the Create Account link, below the Username and Password fields.**

Doing so yields a pop-up with two options, shown in Figure 2-9: For Myself and To Manage My Business. Though the account-making process is identical for both, the latter enables the Business Personalization setting, allowing Google to target ads toward you that it thinks will help your business. Unless you want to receive marketing tailored toward your business, going with For Myself is just fine.

FIGURE 2-8:
The Google login
screen.

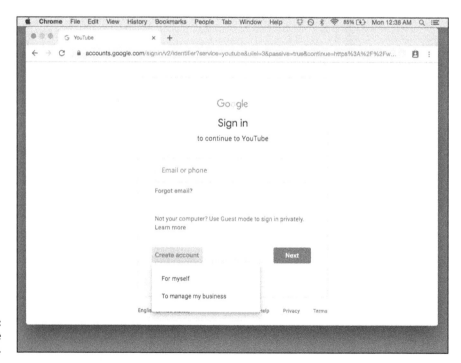

FIGURE 2-9:
Choosing the type
of account.

3. **Fill in the necessary information.**

The fields shown in Figure 2-10 are much like what you'd expect, but here's a description of each item anyway:

- *Your name:* This is the name associated with your account. You can use either your real name or a made-up name that reflects your account. Just be aware that the name functions as the public face of your channel, so sophomoric attempts at humor are probably not the way to go.

- *Your current email address:* We like Gmail, so create a new Gmail address when setting a new account, instead of using your current email address. It makes all your YouTube work easier. Below this field is a link that offers the option to create a new Gmail account.

- *Password:* You've probably done the Create a Password and Confirm Your Password song-and-dance a thousand times before, so we don't offer any advice other than to recommend that you follow the sound password tips that Google offers during this process.

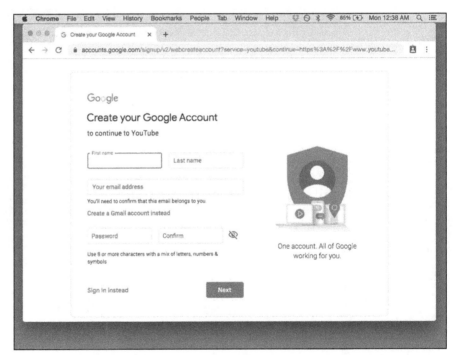

FIGURE 2-10:
Creating your
Google account.

4. **Click Next.**

5. **In the new dialog box that appears (see Figure 2-11), enter the following personal details:**

- *Verify your phone number:* A mobile phone number is required for identity confirmation and account recovery processes. (You use account recovery when you've forgotten your password.) So go ahead and enter your phone number.

- *Add a recovery email address:* Though adding one is optional, we recommend that you enter a recovery email. Like your phone number, it can be used for account recovery and serves as a good backup if you're unable to reach your phone.

- *Birthday:* No ifs, ands, or buts — you need to choose a birthdate. You may not want to show your real age, what with YouTube largely being a young person's game, but we won't encourage you to lie.

TIP

If you're going to be a smart-aleck and decide to give the age of your channel rather than your own age, make the age at least 18. Some content on YouTube has age restrictions, and giving your channel a birthdate that makes it less than 18 years old can come back to bite you.

- *Gender:* Gender is truly up to you. It's a sensitive subject these days, so we won't joke about it here. Personally, when we're creating business accounts, we usually choose Rather Not Say because we think of the channels as an inanimate object.

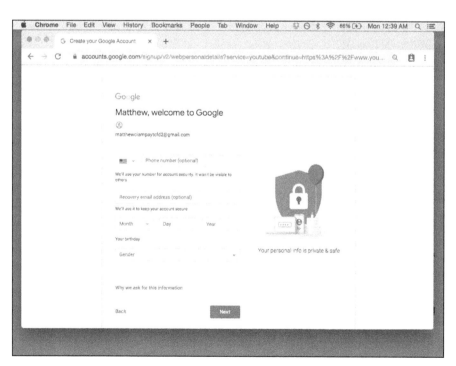
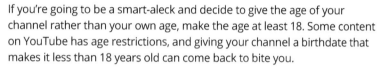

FIGURE 2-11:
Enter your personal details.

6. **Click Next.**

7. **In the next dialog box that appears (see Figure 2-12), verify your phone number and then click Send.**

   You should receive a text containing a code; if you don't, click the Call Instead button to receive an automated voice message.

8. **Enter the code, as shown in Figure 2-13, and then click Verify.**

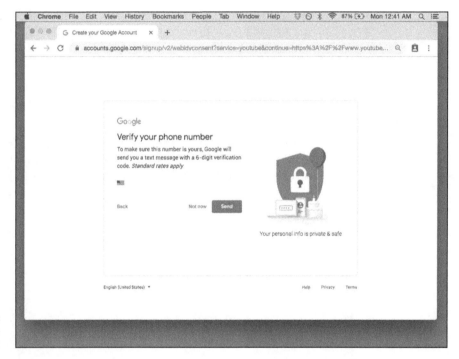

FIGURE 2-12:
Verify your phone
number.

You're asked whether you want to enable web phone usage, as shown in Figure 2-14. This allows calls made to your phone number to be received while using your Google account. It also allows Google to use your number for ad targeting.

9. **Choose either Skip or Yes, I'm In.**

10. **In the new dialog box that appears (see Figure 2-15), click the I Agree button to agree to Google's terms-and-services agreement.**

    This is the requisite "fine print." We'll leave it to you and your legal representation to decide whether you're comfortable with it.

FIGURE 2-13:
Enter your
verification code.

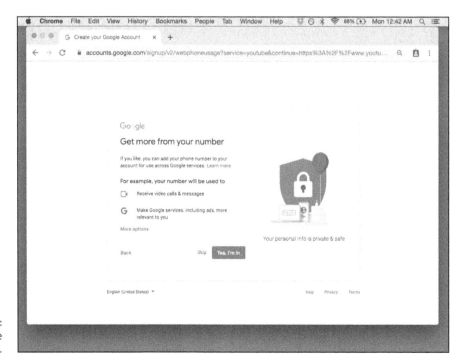

FIGURE 2-14:
The web phone
usage agreement.

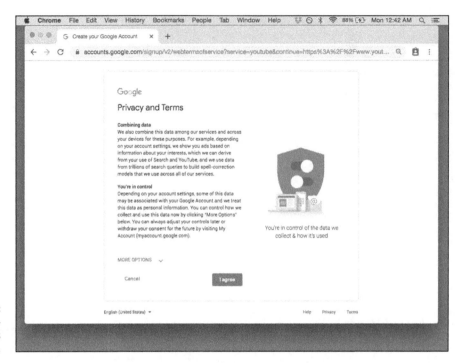

FIGURE 2-15:
YouTube's terms-
and-services
agreement.

Logging On to Your YouTube Account

If you have completed all the steps to set up your YouTube account, you should be logged on to the YouTube site automatically. (You may need to click the Sign In button to be automatically logged in). If that doesn't happen, the first thing to do is follow these steps to log in with the account you created:

1. **Click the Sign In button at the top of the YouTube main screen.**

   You're taken once again to the Google Sign In screen (refer to Figure 2-8) and prompted to enter your account details.

2. **Sign in with the email address and password you used when creating your account.**

At this point, you're logged in to YouTube but don't yet have your channel set up. We cover that topic in the next section.

Creating a YouTube Channel

Building a channel is what you came here to do, and now it's time to get to it. You can do the work to establish your channel after you've logged on to YouTube with a Google account. After that's done, follow these steps to get your channel off the ground:

1. **Log on to YouTube, and click the Channel icon in the top right to bring up the YouTube Studio and YouTube Settings pull-down menu, as shown in Figure 2-16.**

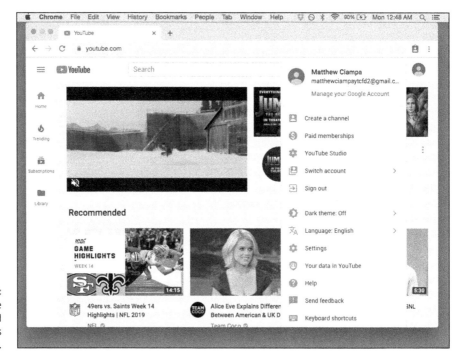

FIGURE 2-16:
The YouTube Studio and YouTube Settings pull-down menu.

2. **Choose the Create a Channel option from the pull-down menu.**

   A dialog box appears, with "Your creator journey begins" across the top, as shown in Figure 2-17.

3. **Click the Get Started link.**

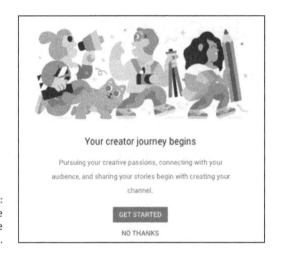

FIGURE 2-17:
Starting to create
a YouTube
channel.

4. **In the new dialog box that appears, choose the name you want to use for your channel.**

   You're given two options, as shown in Figure 2-18: to use your name or to create a custom name. Sometimes it's okay to use your real name for your channel. If your content is personality-based (a vlog based around you, for example), this can work just fine. If that's the way you want to go, just click Select under that option and be done with it. However, if you want to go by a different name or are creating a channel for your business, we recommend creating a custom name.

5. **To create a custom name, click Select under that option, enter a custom name in the new dialog box that appears (see Figure 2-19), and then click Create.**

   This name can be anything you want and isn't set in stone. You can change your channel name at any time, though it isn't to be confused with your custom URL, which we get to later.

6. **In the new dialog box that appears (see Figure 2-20), start setting up your new channel.**

   At this point, whether you've decided to stick with your own name or come up with an original one, you have the option to set up some crucial details about your channel. Don't skip this task — it makes your channel more visible and accessible to others:

   - *Upload a profile picture, as shown in Figure 2-21:* This is the avatar for your channel. Whether someone is on your page or reading a comment you've made, this is who they'll see. As long as it adheres to the correct dimensions and community guidelines, it can be anything you want.

FIGURE 2-18:
Choosing how
you create your
channel.

FIGURE 2-19:
Creating your
channel name.

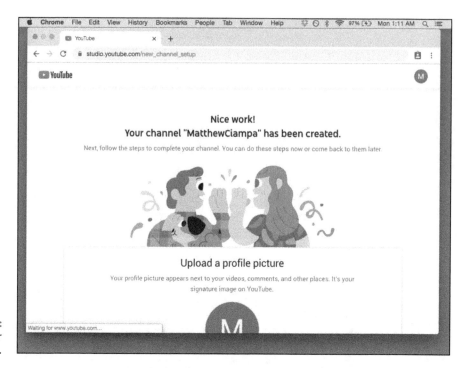

FIGURE 2-20:
Setting up your
new channel.

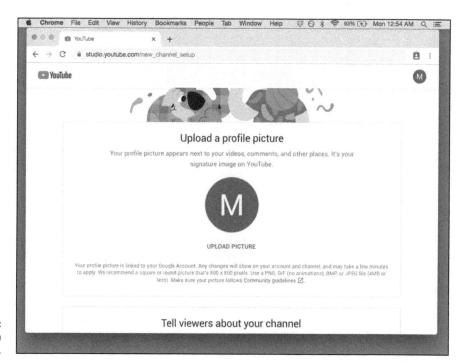

FIGURE 2-21:
Uploading a
profile picture.

- *Add a channel description, as shown in Figure 2-22:* This is the elevator pitch people see when searching your channel. It's a good way of introducing who you are and what kind of content you make. It's also a way of making your channel more visible when searched online (also known as search engine optimization, or SEO). Don't skimp on this; the more descriptive words and phrases you use, the better off you are.

- *Link your websites, as shown in Figure 2-23:* Whether it's a website or a social media page, link them here. This enables you to easily drive traffic to whatever page you're trying to promote.

7. **When you finish setting up your channel, click the Save and Continue button. (Refer to Figure 2-23.)**

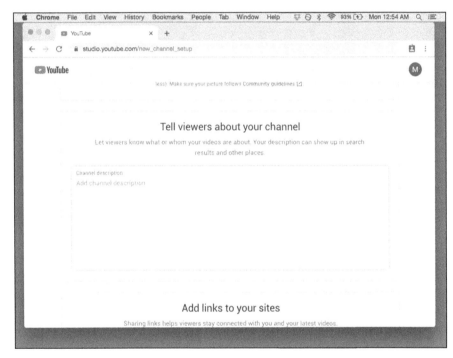

FIGURE 2-22:
Adding a channel
description.

You are now the proud owner of a channel with no content and a boring default layout. (Check out Figure 2-24 to see what we mean.) If you gave your channel a new name, by clicking your avatar in the top right, you'll notice that your name has changed from your Google account name to your brand-spanking-new channel name. But all that is covered in Chapter 3. You have even *more* account setup tasks to complete.

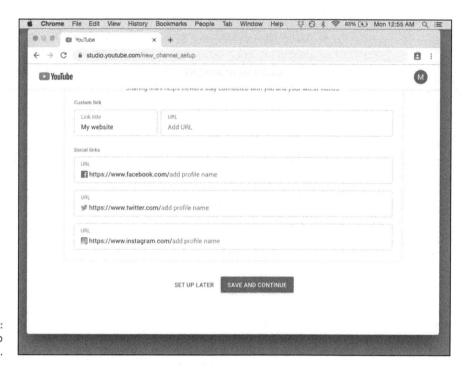

FIGURE 2-23:
Adding links to
your websites.

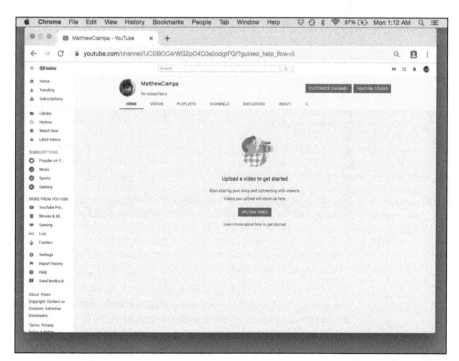

FIGURE 2-24:
The default
channel layout,
which is boring.

CHOOSING A CHANNEL NAME

Take a reflective pause before you choose a username or channel name or another identifying criterion you want as your public face for the whole YouTube world. An over-hasty decision here could end up being one you regret later. Many a creator has made the mistake of beginning to upload videos to what they thought would remain a low-key, personal channel, only to have that channel take off in popularity, at which point they begin to feel trapped in a channel named after their cat. (Okay, just to be clear, this wouldn't be a problem if the channel is actually about your cat). The channel URL, however, is a different story, and you can learn about that topic later in this chapter, in the section "Setting Up a Custom Channel URL."

Keep the following advice in mind when making your reflections:

- **Avoid rushing into anything.** You should think hard about this decision. Though it seems like a light one, it can truly impact the success of your channel in the long run if you choose a bad name.

- **Relate the name to your content, if possible.** Are you creating a channel about video games? Try to work a gaming term into your title. If you plan to create fitness-related content, try to integrate workout or sports terms.

- **Steer clear of profanity, vulgarity, and inside jokes.** Though you may find it hilarious to name your channel Dadfarts, a name like this one necessarily limits your market. It's hard to predict what path your videos might take on their way out into the world, and a sophomoric name (or a downright obscene one) might deter your viewers from sharing your video. ***Note:*** *You want people to share your videos!*

- **Come up with a catchy name.** Your channel name needs to be memorable. People love puns, rhyming, and alliteration, but don't try to integrate all three. That's a little much.

- **Make the name easy to spell.** People need to be able to find your channel, and choosing a word that's difficult to spell can prevent people from finding you. Do *not* see this as a felicitous opportunity to create a recondite channel name thronged with abstruse vocabulary that will confuse and confound your potential viewers.

- **Provide a name that's easy for people to talk about.** When you think you've hit on the perfect name, try reading it aloud a few times, and make sure you can pronounce it. You want to have a channel name that people can talk about and make themselves understood. The best test for this is to call a friend on the phone and direct them to your channel. If you can tell your friend the channel name and they can get there without your having to spell it, you have a usable name on your hands.

(continued)

(continued)

- **Ensure that the name is available and that you won't be confused with another business on YouTube or elsewhere.** You should search the web in general, and YouTube specifically, to make sure your brilliant channel name isn't already in use elsewhere. You should also ensure that the URL you prefer is available. YouTube's allocation of URLs isn't automatic, and you choose your custom URL in a later step. So, even if your channel name is available, your custom URL may not be available. Check this in advance or else it can turn into a real problem.

Verifying Your YouTube Channel

Before you get around to beautifying your channel and making it your own, you need to verify your channel to prove that you're a real human being and not some kind of Internet robot who has created this channel for nefarious purposes. Several steps are involved in verifying your account:

1. **Log on to YouTube and click the Channel icon in the top right to open the YouTube Studio and YouTube Settings pull-down menu. (Refer to Figure 2-16.)**

2. **Choose the Settings option from the pull-down menu.**

   Doing so takes you to the Account Settings Overview page.

   In most Google products, the Gear icon implies "settings."

REMEMBER

3. **On the new page that appears, click the Channel Status and Features link. (See Figure 2-25).**

   A long list of features appears, as shown in Figure 2-26, but you're interested in the Verify feature — you need to verify again before you can move on.

4. **Click the Verify button.**

   The Account Verification page appears, spelling out that account verification is a 2-step process. The first step of the verification asks for your country location and asks you to specify how you want to receive a verification code, as shown in Figure 2-27.

5. **Specify your country location, choose a verification method, and then click Next.**

   You can receive a verification code by text message or voice call. Just pick an option, enter your phone number, and click Submit, which takes you to Step 2, as shown in Figure 2-28. Whichever delivery method you choose, you'll soon receive a numeric code.

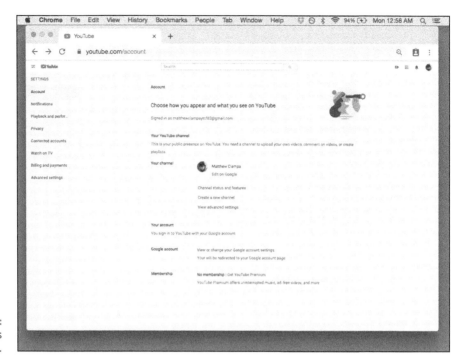

FIGURE 2-25:
The Settings
page.

FIGURE 2-26:
The Status and
Features page.

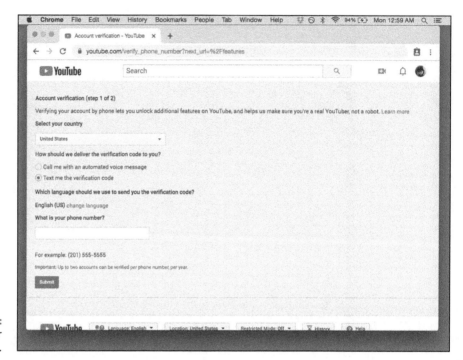

FIGURE 2-27:
Verifying your account, Step 1.

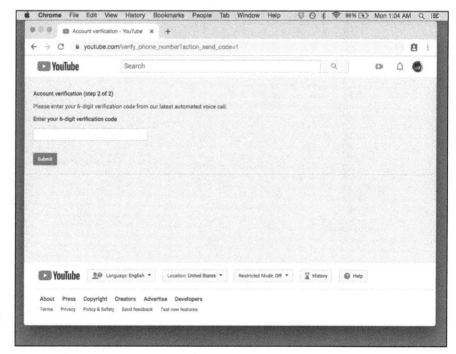

FIGURE 2-28:
Verifying your account, Step 2.

6. **Enter your verification code and then click Submit.**

   You move on to a screen with a satisfying check mark that informs you that you're verified.

7. **Click Continue.**

   You are now verified! You're returned to the Additional Features page, where this whole verification thing began.

This simple verification unlocks a number of features within your YouTube account, many of which now have green underlines on the Additional Features page, as shown in Figure 2-29.

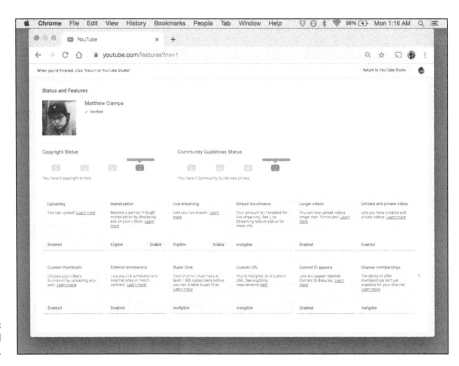

FIGURE 2-29:
Your enabled
features.

We list only a few of the new abilities you've just unlocked for your channel:

>> **Longer videos:** You can now upload videos more than 15 minutes long.

>> **Custom thumbnails:** You can now upload a custom image to act as the thumbnail for your video. (Chapter 9 also has more on custom thumbnails.)

>> **External annotations:** Links to websites outside YouTube can now be placed in your videos. (For more on how to do this, check out Chapter 10.)

>> **Unlisted and private videos:** Ever wanted to grant limited access to your videos to a chosen few? Now you can. (More on this neat feature in — you guessed it — Chapter 9.)

You may also notice that the Monetization feature has an Enable button next to it. Though seeing it may seem exciting, at this stage you aren't eligible to make money from your videos. This is a benefit of being a part of the YouTube Partner Program, which we briefly discuss later in this chapter (in the section "Joining the YouTube Partner Program") and thoroughly explain in Chapter 14.

Setting Up a Custom Channel URL

By default, YouTube assigns your channel an ugly, random, and completely unmemorable URL. (URL, short for Uniform Resource Locator, is a fancy name for a web address.) You'd do well to replace this ugly URL with one that supports your branding and helps viewers remember your channel. Just note that, to update the URL, you must meet some eligibility requirements. More specifically, you must have at least 100 subscribers, at least 30 days of channel management under your belt, a Channel icon, and a piece of channel art. (We go over how to do this in Chapter 3, in the "Customizing and Branding Your Channel" section.)

Anyway, here's how you get the customizing process started:

1. **Log on to YouTube and click your Channel icon in the top right to open the YouTube Studio and YouTube Settings pulldown menu. (Refer to Figure 2-16.)**

2. **Choose the Settings option from the pull-down menu.**

    You're taken straight to the Account Settings Overview screen.

3. **Click Advanced Settings, located at the bottom of the list on the left side of the page. (Refer to Figure 2-25.)**

    You progress to the advanced channel settings, which you can see in Figure 2-30.

4. **Click Create Custom URL.**

    Doing so takes you to a page that prompts you to choose a new, custom channel URL.

5. **Choose a custom channel URL.**

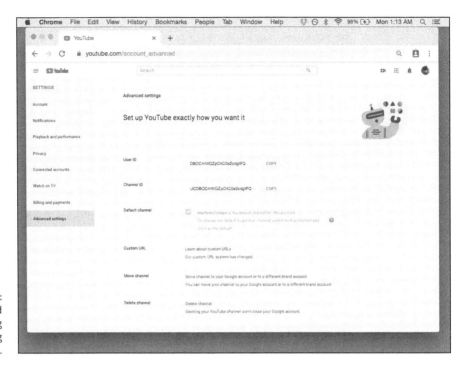

FIGURE 2-30:
Advanced
settings, featuring
the confusing
random URL.

WARNING

You get only one chance at this, so get it right. If you screw it up and choose a channel URL you hate, you need to delete your channel and start over.

Because you followed the advice earlier in this chapter and checked to make sure your URL was available before you chose your channel name (Right? *Right?*), you can just enter the name of your channel and you'll be all set up with a nice, clean URL that matches your channel — something like this:

```
www.youtube.com/user/mychannelname
```

Joining the YouTube Partner Program

It's possible to make money on YouTube. If you're really successful, producing content for YouTube can be your full-time, exciting job. But don't run to the bank yet, because you'll need to create a great channel, fill it with wickedly good content, build a passionate community of fans — and join the YouTube Partner Program.

The YouTube Partner Program is a formalized way of helping content creators (which usually goes hand in hand with channel owners because they're often one and the same) make money in several ways:

>> **Advertising revenue:** You can allow Google and YouTube to place ads against your content and receive a share of the ad revenue. You can learn all the details about this in Chapter 14.

>> **Channel memberships:** You can offer paid subscriptions with viewers paying a monthly fee for access. This option isn't for everyone, and you'll need some unique content. Viewers on YouTube usually don't like to pay.

>> **Merchandise shelf:** You can use your content to help sell your product and actually provide special links where viewers can go buy your stuff. You can sell up to 12 items on your channel, and superimpose products on livestreams or at the end of videos.

>> **Live fan engagement:** Subscribers can pay to have comments or stickers stand out from others during live events on your channel.

>> **YouTube Premium:** Though YouTube Premium viewers don't see ads, creators can still receive revenue if their content gets viewed.

>> **Super Chat and Super Stickers:** Subscribers can pay to have comments or stickers stand out from others during live events on your channel.

Though the monetary aspect of the YouTube Partner Program is the primary driver for most creators, YouTube also provides some support for content generation though places like YouTube Spaces, which are special studios built just for YouTube creators and advertisers around the world. Check it out here:

```
www.youtube.com/yt/space
```

Our recommendation is to not rush into the partner program right away. Focus on your channel, content, and community, which you can learn about in detail in this book. With all that in place, you can check out Chapter 14 to start the revenue engine humming.

Chapter **3**

Building Your Channel from the Ground Up

A YouTube *channel* is where the creator can track activity, maintain account settings, and — most importantly for a creator like you — upload videos. The ability to find your way around your channel and understand the different features that YouTube offers is essential to building your audience, and [drumroll, please] obtaining revenue.

Navigating Your Channel

A YouTube channel has two primary purposes. For most users, YouTube is for watching videos. When you log in to your YouTube account, you're met with a page offering a lot of videos for you to watch. You also see a large ad — no surprise there — as well as suggestions from YouTube for what you should watch. You see sections for some of the channels you subscribe to, and some guesses at stuff you might like. A lot of the logged-in experience is covered in Chapter 2, but now it's time to dig a little deeper and look at what you can do with your channel.

The Your Channel menu item

The value of making your channel stand out can't be overestimated. Though your videos are ultimately the most important tool you have for attracting viewers and subscribers, the look of your channel is a big deal, too. YouTube wants viewers to spend more time watching content. What better way to do this than by giving users, like you, the tools to make an awesome YouTube channel experience?

When you're logged in on YouTube, clicking the circular icon in the top right with the first initial of the name on your account — or your picture, if you added it while setting up your Google account — reveals a dropdown menu. Selecting the Your Channel menu item at the top of the list brings you straight to your channel. Click the Customize Channel button to enter Edit mode, as shown in Figure 3-1.

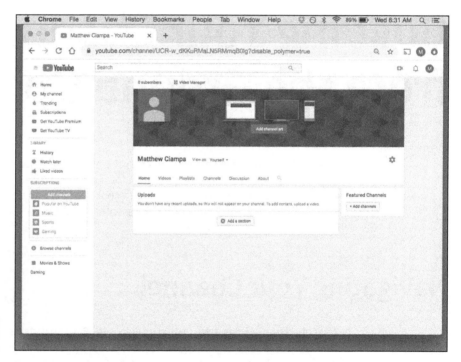

FIGURE 3-1:
Your YouTube
Channel's page.

Note the following elements:

>> **The header bar:** This element runs across the top of your My Channel page and gives you access to some pretty important information:

- *Subscribers:* Your channel may be new, so you probably have zero subscribers — the link on the header that reads 0 subscribers is at the top to point that out. Hopefully, that number won't be 0 for long.

When you click the Subscribers link, you see a list of your subscribers, which you can use to see who is currently subscribed to your channel and review the information they share publicly.

- *Video Manager:* Clicking the Video Manager link leads you straight to YouTube Studio, which is the most useful place to manage the settings for your individual video uploads, track analytics, explore monetization, and more.

» **Channel art:** The large, gray box with all the gray triangles as background is the default channel art for your channel. It shows images of a computer screen, TV screen, and phone screen, plus the colorful Add Channel Art button. Adding channel art is something you'll want to do as soon as you can. (Before you do, though, check out the "Customizing and Branding Your Channel" section, later in this chapter.) You can also add links to websites, links to social networks, and an email-contact button to this area. (We show you how later in this chapter, in the section "The Channel tabs.")

» **Channel icon:** Overlaying your channel art on the left side is the *Channel icon.* The default Channel icon is a light blue square with a nondescript dark blue icon in the middle. This element is an important one because it acts as your channel's identifying mark on YouTube and Google; it appears next to your channel's name all over both sites; it shows up in subscription lists; and it appears next to every comment you make. If your channel art is the face of your My Channel page, this icon is your face everywhere else on YouTube. A Channel icon is typically a brand logo or a picture of the channel's content creator.

REMEMBER

When you roll the mouse pointer over the different elements on your Channel's page, a small, gray box with a Pencil icon in it appears. This is the Edit button. When you get around to customizing your channel later in this chapter, the Edit button is what you'll use to access the controls for each of these elements.

Figure 3-1 shows the basics of your YouTube Channel, but you can add more. Here's a list of the kinds of items you can display there:

» **Channel trailer:** You can add a channel trailer for unsubscribed viewers. (Think "trailer" as in movie trailer, not "trailer" as in trailer park.) This is a perfect opportunity to show your audience what your channel is all about, what content you cover, what days you publish, and anything else you think might help viewers subscribe to your channel and watch tons of your content.

» **Sections:** These are groups of videos that help viewers explore your content. Create sections to make it easy for your viewers to browse and find content that interests them. Think of sections as bookshelves that hold content of similar types. There can be up to 10 sections containing your playlists, your most recent videos, your most popular videos, or other collections of content that you want your viewers to see. The default section on a new channel is Uploads — that's just the list of your most recently published videos. It's best practice to use as many sections as you can.

>> **Featured Channels:** This area is blank until you add in channels that are related to your channel. This is optional, but also a good opportunity to highlight any partnerships you may have formed with other YouTube creators. You can highlight your partners, and your partners can highlight your channel to help drive traffic between the pages.

>> **View As:** Whenever you've made some changes to your channel, you'll want to see how it will look to your viewers. Next to your channel's name in the middle of the page is a dropdown menu that allows you to toggle between two viewing modes: New Visitor and Returning Subscriber. To go back to Edit mode, simply click the blue Customize Channel button.

TIP

Create sections with multiple playlists in addition to just shelves with individual videos. This strategy helps your Playlist tab appear more organized, making it easier for viewers to find more content quickly. Be sure to have an eye-catching thumbnail image for every video in a section and every playlist.

The Channel tabs

Just like a web browser, YouTube channels have tabs. Tabs are helpful for viewers looking to navigate your channel quickly and efficiently. Each tab has a different functionality, intended to help the viewing experience:

>> **Home:** Viewers see this tab by default when they click on your channel from a YouTube search or when they manually type your channel address in their web browser. Your channel trailer and sections all appear here, on the Home tab.

>> **Videos:** The Videos tab contains exactly what you'd expect — all public videos on the channel. The default view is Newest Videos First — the videos that were added to the channel most recently. The viewer can always sort by Oldest Videos First or Most Popular instead.

>> **Playlists:** The Playlists tab is where all your channel's public playlists can be found. As a creator, you can fill up playlists with your own content. You can also curate content from other YouTube channels for your playlists.

REMEMBER

Playlists also come up in YouTube search results, so always use descriptive thumbnails for your videos, as well as compelling playlist titles and descriptions. A playlist is a great way to extend your viewers' session time on your channel. (Session time directly supports your channel ranking and discoverability on a YouTube search.)

Though we recommend making and sharing playlists, you may hide them from others by clicking the channel settings, denoted by the Gear icon on the right side of your channel, and turning privacy on. You can do the same with the visibility of the channels you're subscribed to.

>> **Store:** The Store tab is a part of YouTube's Merchandise Shelf feature, where users can sell featured merchandise on their videos and channels. This feature is not available for everyone. Users are eligible to apply for this feature if their channel is monetized, if they have over 10,000 subscribers, if they're in a country where the feature is allowed, and if children are not the target audience.

>> **Channels:** If you have partnerships, this tab is the place to add all those channels you associate with. If your brand owns many channels, you'll want to make sure all your channels are listed here, for easy discoverability and reference for the viewers. This is a quick way to get interested viewers to consume more related content.

>> **Discussion:** Viewers are sure to comment on your channel and videos if you're creating engaging content. You can follow along with all the channel comments on this tab. When logged in, you can remove inappropriate comments or report spam comments directly.

If you want to disable comments on your channel, click the channel settings and toggle the Show Discussion tab to Off. You can also allow comments to display automatically or — if you want to monitor what's posted — you can change the setting so that they don't display until approved by you.

>> **Community:** This feature, available only to channels with over 1,000 subscribers, replaces the Discussion tab. If it's unlocked, you're able to use this tab to post images, videos, and polls to drastically increase and enhance how you interact with your audience.

>> **About:** This tab acts as your opportunity to tell your viewers all about yourself and/or your business. It is important that you maximize this space (up to 1,000 characters) to improve your channel's discoverability. You can talk about your brand, the videos people should expect, and include an email address for viewers to contact you outside of YouTube. You can also include any relevant social network sites that you might be active on. Your viewers can come here to see some quick stats on your channel, such as your total view count, number of subscribers, and the date you created your YouTube channel.

TIP

YouTube's global reach means that many people who don't speak the same language as you may see your channel. To improve your channel's accessibility, click the Translating Channel Info link at the bottom of the Channel Settings list (accessed via the gear icon to the right) to create and save various translations of your channel's name and description.

Customizing and Branding Your Channel

If you're on your My Channel page (see the previous section for more info about that page), clicking the blue Customize Channel button in the top right of your channel puts it in Edit mode, which is where you do the bulk of the customization of your channel. This is an important series of decisions you're about to make, so pay attention to what you're doing. Lots of viewers make decisions about the quality of a channel based on a glance at the My Channel page. If there's one stereotype that pretty much holds true for YouTube viewers, it's that they're highly distractible. A professional-looking front page that holds a viewer's interest indicates to potential viewers that you've put a lot of thought, time, and effort into creating your channel. So get to it!

Creating channel art

The channel art section is in the large gray box at the top of the My Channel page when viewed on a computer. (It will look differently on other devices, like mobile phones and TVs, but a computer is the only device you can use to change your channel art, so start there.) By default, it has a few items in it, and you'll change pretty much all those items. Before getting into the steps of creating your channel art, though, you should keep some important guidelines in mind. YouTube is available on a lot of different devices. Your audience may be watching on a TV, a computer, or a mobile device. Given that fact, YouTube has gone to a lot of effort to create a system that allows your channel to look good across all kinds of delivery platforms. It has come up with some guidelines for artwork that you would be wise to follow. If you pay attention to the size of the graphics needed, you should have no trouble with your channel looking good, no matter how your audience is looking at it.

TIP

Channel art is most effective when it is representative of the channel's content. For example, if your channel is about the hottest new shoes, your channel art should include images of shoes.

REMEMBER

Before you get around to adding the channel art, you need to *create* your channel art. This process requires some kind of image creation software. We recommend software like Adobe Photoshop to create custom channel art, but it's an expensive option. If you're investing in the Adobe ecosystem for editing, Photoshop is probably a good option for you. If you're more interested in free tools, something like GIMP, an open source photo editor (available for download at `www.gimp.org`) might be more up your alley.

YouTube has created a template (see Figure 3-2) that makes the creation of channel art that works across platforms much simpler. The template calls for a 2560 x

1440-pixel image that is no larger than 6MB and provides you with guidance on how to place text and logos to allow the image to work pretty much everywhere.

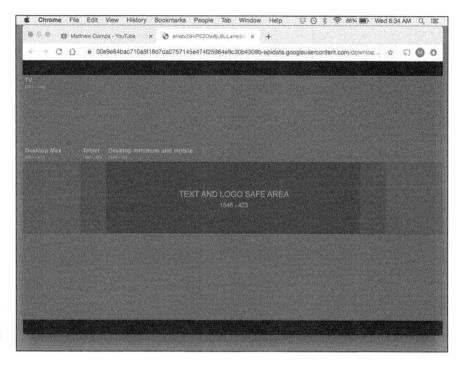

FIGURE 3-2:
The YouTube
Channel Art
template.

REMEMBER

When creating art destined for use in the YouTube channel art template, it's important to adhere to the advice it provides. You need to ensure that your text lands in the sections of the template that will not be covered up by your Channel icon or channel links after you upload this image. If you edge too close to the top left corner, you'll have a hard time maintaining the continuity of the image across devices and operating systems. Your text and logos might be cut off or unreadable on some devices, and that will contribute to viewers dismissing your channel and moving on to something else. Channel art is an opportunity to make a first impression, and the cold truth is that bad channel art can drive away viewers. Be sure to check how your channel art looks on several different devices.

TIP

If you find all this talk of pixels and formats confusing, it might be a good idea to consult with someone who has some graphic design experience. Even tracking down a graphic design student to help you tailor an image to the YouTube specifications can be helpful. If you don't feel comfortable doing the art yourself, and finding help isn't possible, YouTube does provide some stock options, which aren't great, but are a far better choice than the placeholder pattern of gray diamonds. If you do ask someone for help with your channel art, remember that creative professionals like to be paid for their work. Just because your friend is a graphic designer or your nephew is an art student doesn't mean that they want to work for you for free. Even if you don't pay them the market rate, paying them *something* is the decent thing to do.

Managing channel art

After you've created the art for your channel (or received art from the nice person you convinced to help you), it's time to add that art to your channel. YouTube has made this a pretty straightforward process; here are the steps:

1. **With your Channel in Edit mode, click the Add Channel Art button.**

   You shouldn't have any trouble spotting this button. It's the blue button that says Add Channel Art in the center of the placeholder banner.

   TIP

   If you've already set your channel art and want to change it, the Add Channel Art button is no longer an option. In this case, roll the mouse pointer over the banner, and a small box with the familiar Pencil icon appears. Click this icon to edit your channel art and open the Artwork dialog box.

2. **In the dialog box that appears (see Figure 3-3), choose from one of the following options to add new channel art:**

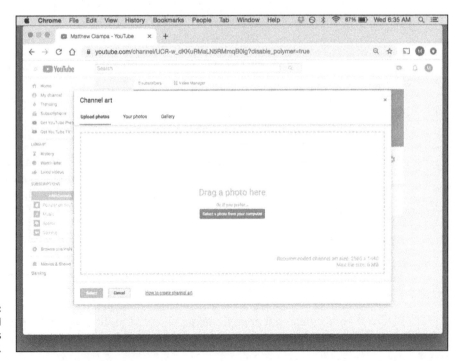

FIGURE 3-3:
The Upload Photos dialog box.

- *Upload Photos:* This is the default option for adding photos to your channel. If you've created your own artwork as spelled out in the previous section, more likely than not your artwork is somewhere on your computer. To upload that artwork, click the Select a Photo from Your Computer button, use the dialog box that appears to navigate to the file's location, and then select it. Alternatively, you can just drag-and-drop the file onto this window, and it should start the upload.

- *Your Photos:* Selecting this option allows you to choose a photo from your Google Photos album. Because you've probably just created this account, you're unlikely to have photos in any Google Photos albums — the Your Photos option probably won't be the option you choose. You can safely ignore this.

- *Gallery:* If you haven't created your own channel art, the Gallery section shown in Figure 3-4 provides you with some stock images that YouTube furnishes for free. Though none of them is great-looking, and they're unlikely to be excellent branding choices for your channel, they're miles better than leaving the default placeholder image as your channels banner.

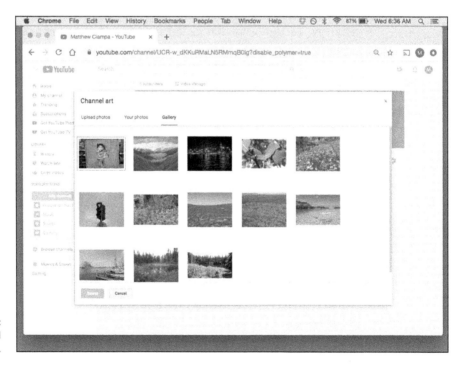

FIGURE 3-4:
The Channel Art gallery.

TIP

As you complete each step in the process of branding your channel, it's a good idea to click on either of the options on the View As menu next to your channel's name (accessible when your channel is in Edit mode). Clicking here lets you look at your channel as the public would see it, without all the controls you see as the owner of the channel. This is the best way to understand how the changes you're making will affect the look of your channel.

3. **(Optional) Crop your photo.**

   After you select a photo, you see a preview of your channel art across various devices. If you decide that you want to crop your photo, click the Adjust the Crop button to move the cropping mask around to select the portion of the photo you want to use. Click the Device Preview button to return to the preview of the art on different devices.

4. **After the size and placement of the image are to your satisfaction, click Select, and your channel art is in place!**

Creating the Channel icon

The Channel icon is an important aspect of your overall channel art and branding strategy. Though your channel art is the most prominent face directly on your channel's page, the Channel icon is the face of your channel everywhere else. It's also the icon associated with your Google account, which means that this icon appears pretty much any time your channel is listed on YouTube, and it appears next to all the comments you make on the site. So, creating an icon that works for you is important.

Creating a good icon can be tricky. You want something that is simple and easily recognizable — one that allows viewers to quickly recognize your content as *your* content, in other words. As usual, if you can't pull all that off, at least don't use an icon that will drive away viewers. Don't use an offensive or obscene image, and definitely avoid foul language. Not only will that stuff alienate potential subscribers, it will get you in trouble with the powers-that-be at YouTube. Keeping things simple is probably the best bet, and even a simple-colored background with the first letter or initials of your channel goes a long way toward adding a degree of professionalism. If you can add a little bit of themed art to that simple layout, all the better.

When creating an icon that will work with your channel, follow a couple of basic guidelines:

» **Image size:** Your icon appears on the site at 98 x 98 pixels most of the time, but you should create your icon as an 800 x 800 pixel square and upload that size. Let the site scale the image down for you because it results in the best possible image quality for your icon.

>> **File format:** YouTube recommends that you upload your files in JPG, GIF (no animated GIFs are allowed), BMP, or PNG format. All these formats should be available in your image editor, so choose the one that works best for you.

Uploading the channel icon

The default Channel icon is the purple box overlaying the left side of your banner art. It's marginally okay, but nothing to write home about, so you'll definitely want to replace it. When you have your icon all designed and ready, follow these easy steps to add it to your channel:

1. **With your channel in Edit mode, roll the mouse pointer over the large icon placeholder at the top of your page to make the Pencil icon appear.**

    Technically, the Pencil icon is referred to as the Edit Channel Icon button.

2. **Click the Edit Channel Icon button.**

    Doing so brings up a dialog box informing you that your Channel icon is also the icon for your Google account and that it may take some time to reflect the change.

3. **Click the Edit button.**

    This button brings you immediately to the Upload page. (See Figure 3-5.)

4. **Click the Upload Photo link, and then select a photo using the dialog box that appears.**

    You're given the option to adjust the crop, scale, and rotation of the image.

TIP

    We don't recommend using a casual selfie as your icon if you're just starting out. A nicely designed logo looks more professional than a selfie. An exception is if your channel is a personality-based vlog.

5. **After making your adjustments, click Done.**

    You'll be notified that it may take some time for the change to reflect across all associated Google accounts.

6. **To return to YouTube, click the 3-by-3 grid in the top right, and then select the YouTube icon.**

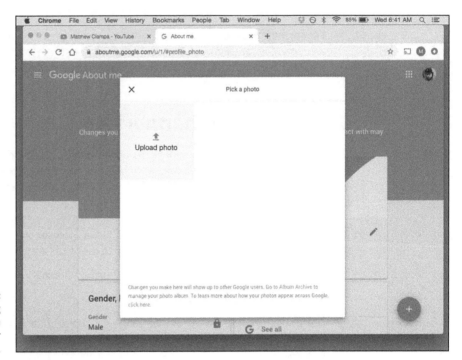

FIGURE 3-5:
The Google dialog box for adding an icon to your channel.

Managing your links

The last part of the channel art setup involves placing *link overlays* — the custom links on your channel art pointing to your website or social media pages. You can add links to many social networks, merchandise providers, and even iTunes. You can also add a link to an email address or even your personal website. Adding links is, like many of the tasks in this chapter, accomplished in a few simple steps:

1. **With your channel in Edit mode, roll the mouse pointer over the channel art banner, click the Edit button (the Pencil icon on the far right) when it appears, and then select Edit Links.**

Doing so takes you to a dialog box for adding and/or editing your links, as shown in Figure 3-6.

2. **Enter an email address in the For Business Inquiries field.**

Okay, the vast majority of email you'll receive in this context will be spam, but you never know. A legitimate offer may pop up. Stranger things have happened.

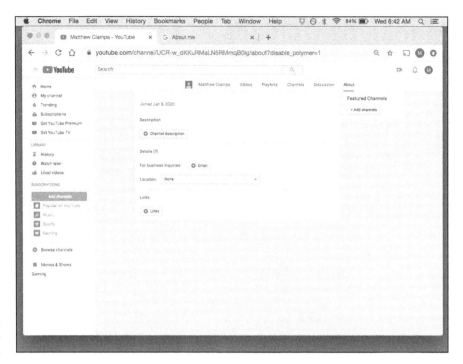

FIGURE 3-6:
Adding links to
your channel art.

3. **Select the country you're in from the Location dropdown.**

   This step shows viewers where you're based. You can also select None if you'd prefer to keep that private.

4. **In the Links section, click the Links button to begin adding your custom links to your website and social media pages.**

   The dialog box that appears lets you overlay links on your artwork. YouTube allows channel managers to link external websites and social media profiles from their channel, which means that you can send your viewers to your own site, where they can get more information about you; any social media or e-commerce sites, including Twitter, Facebook, and Instagram; and even sites like iTunes, Google Play, and Etsy, where you can sell stuff to your audience.

   A maximum of five links can be displayed on the channel banner. We recommend adding your personal website first because the corresponding link displays its full name. All subsequent links are compressed to display the corresponding site's logo.

REMEMBER

   You can add more than five links to your channel; they will simply be visible only in the About section of your channel.

Managing Uploads

Arguably, the most important part of building your channel is adding video content. That is, after all, why YouTube was created. We talk more about the nuts-and-bolts of uploading a video in Chapter 9, but we want to close out this chapter by at least giving you the big picture.

Before you upload anything to YouTube, it's a good idea to familiarize yourself with the kinds of things you can't upload to the site. YouTube disallows several types of content, and uploading content that violates these guidelines can get you in trouble. You can even lose your account. YouTube reserves the right to remove any video at any time, but these types of videos are explicitly banned and will get you in trouble with the YouTube authorities:

» **Pornography:** YouTube doesn't tolerate pornography or any sort of sexually explicit content. YouTube also points out that the company will report any videos of child exploitation to law enforcement if they are uploaded to the site.

» **Illegal behavior:** YouTube removes videos that show drug abuse, underage drinking or smoking, animal abuse, bomb-making, and a host of other illegal behaviors that people might (foolishly) want to document and share.

» **Gratuitous violence:** Videos that show people being attacked, hurt, or humiliated are also banned from the site.

» **Hate speech:** Videos that demean a group based on race, ethnic origin, disability, gender, age, or sexual orientation are removed if flagged by the community.

» **Threats or harassment:** Neither is YouTube a place for stalking, harassing, bullying, or predatory behavior. Content of this type will be removed.

» **Spam:** Videos with misleading titles, descriptions, thumbnails, or other metadata will be removed. *Misleading* means that the title doesn't match the content of the video. A good example of a misleading title is "Miley Cyrus at my house," when the video is actually about a cat riding a skateboard. It's also unacceptable to post spam comments on videos — for example, asking people to subscribe to your channel or to visit your website if it has nothing to do with the video you're commenting on. This typically leads to the comment being flagged as spam, and this makes it invisible to other viewers.

>> **Copyrighted material:** You should only upload content that you own or have the appropriate licensing rights to use. Though the other community guidelines are important to the smooth functioning of the YouTube community, the copyright restriction is hugely important to YouTube as a business. (See Chapter 16 for more information on copyright.)

>> **Private information:** Do not post anyone's personal information without their consent and explicit approval. Content featuring personal information will be removed at the request of the affected individual.

>> **Impersonating others:** Copying another channel's layout/appearance or uploading content with the intent of making it look like someone else's are both against the rules and will result in the removal of videos and/or disciplinary action being taken against your account.

>> **Exploitation of children/minors:** YouTube takes content involving minors very seriously. Bullying, harassing, sexualizing, exploiting, misleading, or making any other any other attempt to harm children is explicitly forbidden from YouTube and will be removed.

2

Making a Great YouTube Video

Chapter **4**

What Makes a Good Video a Good Video?

Not that long ago, video was a far cruder, much simpler medium. At home, people had more fingers than television channels, and, for those making their own movies, consumer-level video came in two varieties: bad and worse. Maybe that's a bit unfair, but the quality lagged far behind commercial productions.

Clunky cameras that captured low-resolution video were no match for the broadcast-quality content found on television. And the quality of television was inferior to the look of a feature film. Not sure about that last one? Just watch a music video from the early days of MTV, circa 1982.

Since that time, technology has evolved to the point where you can now watch thousands of channels and where most anyone who wants to has the ability to make a broadcast-quality movie that can be seen by potentially a global audience. Consumer-level cameras not only come close to broadcast quality but can also even rival it. That means your YouTube video can look truly professional. Of course, *can* is the operative word here.

Clearly, technological advancements have allowed online video to change the rules of consumer-level moviemaking. Yet because of the relative adolescence of online video, there's some confusion about what makes a good video. Understandably, that criterion depends on the particular genre of video. For example, a music video has a different set of standards than an instructional video on techniques for giving your date a goodnight kiss. And that differs significantly from the standards you'd apply to a video showing your cat chasing a red dot. Though diverse in content, there are still some fundamentals that every video should adhere to.

But what fundamentals are we talking about here? What makes a good video, in other words? Given the nature of human taste, coming up with clear criteria for defining a good video may be a fool's errand, so it might be better to concentrate on avoiding those factors that make a video nearly unwatchable. As a video producer, that makes your job relatively easy. Just eliminate the negatives — such as shaky camera work, distorted audio, or bad exposure — while providing entertaining content.

It sounds easy, but you're right to suspect that it may be a little more complex than that, due in part to some false conceptions that folks still hold about online videos. Some people still believe that an online video, or one destined for YouTube in this case, doesn't require the same quality as any other production destined for broadcast. That's simply no longer true. The way things have shaken out, more and more viewers are watching content online rather than on broadcast TV, and they are demanding better and better quality. This demand means that, with more people watching video on sharing sites like YouTube, the bar continues to rise when it comes to production value and content.

We talk a bit more about fundamentals later in this chapter, but right now we want to take a look at the *most fundamental* one out there — your choice for capturing video.

Picking the Right Camera for Your Needs

Once upon a time, a video camera was that bulky device you bought to capture moving images on video tape. Over the years, the cameras got smaller and tape formats evolved from analog to DV and from HD to 4K, with corresponding increases in the ease-of-use and quality categories. Not only that, but the prices dropped precipitously, which means that you can now buy a decent camera at an affordable price.

The only difference now is that there's a wider — some might even say "bewilderingly wide" — selection of cameras. The following list describes the major categories:

» **DSLR:** The digital single-lens reflex camera (digital SLR or DSLR, for short) is a jack-of-all-trades, as seen in Figure 4-1. This camera rightly dominates the still-photography market, but is also extremely capable of providing excellent high-resolution video (as high as 4K on some makes and models.) That's a great thing because the image sensor (when compared to conventional camcorders and other digital cameras) is significantly larger, and therefore captures better quality. The camera can take advantage of all lenses that fit its mount, so you can capture movies using a wide range of lenses, from extreme telephoto to ultrawide-angle to anything in between. Many accessories are available to further enhance your camera's shooting capabilities, from mounting rigs to external microphones to LED lighting. On the downside, the camera controls and handheld ergonomics favor still photography over moviemaking, and the accessories can be expensive.

FIGURE 4-1:
This Canon DSLR
is a versatile
jack-of-all-trades.

» **Point-and-shoot:** Though nowhere near as capable or as powerful as a DSLR, point-and-shoot cameras (or compact cameras) are still impressively capable devices and are extremely popular among many YouTubers. Lighter, simpler to use, and comparatively cheaper, these cameras are a great option for any first-time videographer. You do sacrifice some capabilities compared to a DSLR; you don't have the ability to swap out lenses, because most use an adjustable, fixed lens. Few are capable of capturing video as high-resolution as DSLRs are capable of, though some newer models are making it possible. These cameras also lack many of the fine-tuned internal controls that most DSLRs allow you to augment. That being said, whether you're a professional vlogger or just starting to dip your toes into things, point-and-shoot cameras are extremely impressive and useful.

>> **Action:** You may not have heard of the term, but you have heard of its biggest player: GoPro. These mini marvels are rugged, waterproof, relatively inexpensive, and mountable on just about anything to capture amazing quality from a unique perspective — from skydiver views to the rider's view on a BMX bike, as shown in Figure 4-2. Boasting features aplenty, these cameras are capable of capturing up to 4K (the new standard for ultra-high-definition television), stabilizing extremely shaky videos, and, on some models, even shooting 360-degree video. On the downside, many action cameras are limited to shooting wide-angle views.

FIGURE 4-2: Mounted directly on the bike with a handlebar mount, the GoPro provides a view that wasn't possible just a few years ago.

>> **Smartphone:** Just a few short years ago, considering a cellphone as a means of capturing a serious video would earn you an eyeroll because the results were often dismal. Not any more, because serious works have been captured on a phone, including the Oscar-winning documentary *Waiting for Sugarman*. And they keep getting better and better. Some phones are now capable of shooting 4K and capturing extremely slow-motion videos. Accessories are becoming more and more prolific as well, including mountable lenses and stabilizers. And, to top it all off, almost everyone has a smartphone now. Why not put it to good use?

- **Webcam:** A webcam is inexpensive to purchase, on the off chance that you don't already have one built into your computer. That makes it perfect for situations where you sit down in front of the computer. Just plop yourself down, check the lighting, and start talking. Because most capture in HD (some are even capable of shooting 4K), you're good to go. The downside is that you need to stay put or else you might position yourself out of the frame. The audio can sound "thin" if you're not using an external microphone. And worse than that, if the lighting is too harsh, you can look *bad*.

- **Dedicated camcorder:** Once it was the only way to capture video, but now the trusty dedicated camcorder is becoming increasingly obsolete. Yes, camcorders are designed for shooting videos: They're comfortable to use and have dedicated features and controls specific to moviemaking. But most other camera options, DSLR or other, are capable of many of the same features and more. Another dilemma is its monomaniacal devotion to a single task — making movies. That means some users may pass on a camcorder simply because they can't use it to send a text or make a call.

REMEMBER

Purchasing a top-quality model and instantly expecting to make great movies isn't much different from thinking you can purchase a Gibson Les Paul and become a great guitarist without knowing how to strum a single chord.

Both guitar-playing and videography depend on understanding technique. Gone are the days of haphazardly handholding the camera while randomly shooting a movie on the fly. It will not only lack cohesion but can also make the audience feel like they're having a seizure. As much as we like talking, thinking, and writing about cool cameras, we want to stress the fact that technique is crucial. That's why we focus much more on technique in this chapter than on fancy hardware.

Knowing What Makes a Good Video

An immediate side effect of watching bad video is that you no longer want to watch it. But that still begs the question of what makes a YouTube video truly good. Sometimes, that answer is a little harder to figure out. The more obvious indicators of a good YouTube video are that it's informative, depicts compelling situations, and, of course, makes people laugh. All these factors certainly contribute to the success of a YouTube video, but you have more pertinent issues to consider that deal with the technical aspects of making these videos enjoyable.

Keeping the camera steady provides a good start, as does making sure the lighting effectively represents the scene and that the audio is clear and pristine for the viewer to understand. It's also important to have a variety of shots to keep things visually interesting — in an interview, for example, cut between the subject and a scene of what the subject is discussing. Though these attributes are somewhat "below the radar" when people are enjoying the video, they lie nonetheless at the core of an enjoyable experience.

Here are a few of the components that make a good video:

>> **Good lighting:** "Let there be light" remains one of the oldest phrases ever. And for good reason. Without light of any kind, people clearly wouldn't be able to see anything — though good video depends on more than just seeing the subject. Good lighting — as opposed to merely adequate lighting — needs to bathe the subject in a flattering way, as shown in Figure 4-3. It doesn't matter if you're using a sophisticated light kit or ambient illumination or depending on the sun, as long as the final product looks good.

FIGURE 4-3: The peppers come to life as the sun bathes this outdoor market in late afternoon light.

>> **Steady camera:** Using a tripod (shown in Figure 4-4) or another means of stabilization clearly makes it easier to maintain a steady shot, but if you're stuck without a tripod, at least try to keep your handheld camera as steady as possible so that you can avoid that annoying herky-jerky motion.

>> **Top-quality audio:** The better a video sounds, the better it looks. Less-than-stellar visual elements can easily be accepted when the sound is clear. But the opposite statement rarely applies.

>> **Shot structure:** If you're editing video, you should strive for a nice selection of shot types and angles in order to keep your viewers engaged. Think about it: Nobody wants to see the same exact shot and angle for 10 minutes.

Mastering the Genres in Your YouTube Videos

YouTube videos cover a wide range of subject matter that appeals to a wide range of viewers. Though each requires its own, special finesse to make it effective, all share the same need for quality.

The following few sections take a look at the different types of video and the special needs for each type.

Mastering music videos

Music as a subject pervades the YouTube landscape in many forms. These include everything from the official video for the song from a recording artist to live concert performances to high school musicals and musicians seeking viral exposure. When it comes to musicians creating those "breakout" videos, consider the South Korean pop star Psy. He became an international sensation with his "Gangnam Style" video back in 2012. To date, that song has been viewed more than 3.5 billion times, and counting. Of course, music videos, official or otherwise, represent a large share of YouTube's content, so you'll have to be creative to stand out.

REMEMBER

With any type of music comes copyright concerns about either the song or the band performing it. See Chapter 16 for more details on copyright.

When it comes to making your music-based video, here are a couple of suggestions to consider:

>> **Get the audio right.** If the music doesn't sound good, the picture won't look good. That statement applies to just about any video, but when the subject is music, it takes on an even greater purpose.

>> **Keep it visually interesting.** Conventional wisdom suggests that some situations require compelling visuals, like in an MTV-style music video, whereas in other situations, the performances are more straightforward and may work well with merely a limited number of camera angles. Just be sure that the visuals work with the music — just because you have a great tune doesn't mean that you should skimp on the camera work. Remember that it's an audiovisual experience, so take advantage of it, as shown in Figure 4-5.

FIGURE 4-5: Still frame from the "Beautiful Eyes" video, by Alice Ripley (video produced by John Carucci).

If you're making a music video, here are a few tips to follow:

>> **Listen to the song.** Do it over and over. That's the only way you can get a true feel for the most effective way to visually depict it.

>> **Create a concept.** After listening to the song, you should have a better sense of what it would take to write an effective script. Just don't let your vision exceed your capabilities. If you're not careful, you can run out of time, exhaust your budget, or maybe embark on something you're not ready to accomplish.

>> **Find your locations.** You have to shoot your video someplace, so why not find the best place possible? Uncovering the best spots to shoot the video, obtaining the necessary permissions, and planning lighting and set decoration are all tasks you'll want to do well in advance. For the music video shown in Figure 4-6, the area was scouted for proper lighting and setting.

>> **Communicate with the artist.** A music video is a collaboration between the artist and you. That's why it's a good idea to make sure everyone is on the same page regarding concept and ideas. If a disagreement crops up during production, you may find yourself majorly frustrated.

FIGURE 4-6:
Still frame from a shoot in California's Muir Woods.

Producing your very own vlog

Ever hear of a *portmanteau?* It's when two different words are combined to form a new one that best describes the situation. Think about *Brangelina*, the couple known separately as Brad Pitt and Angelina Jolie, or *staycation*, the stay-at-home vacation, though it's generally more home than vacation. In the video world, the portmanteau of choice is *vlog*, the strange blend of consonants that brings together the words *video* and *blog*.

Before the turn of the millennium, one might take the odd word *vlog* to mean something completely different. And since then, what constitutes a vlog has morphed immensely. But these days everyone knows about the vlog. Some of the most successful content creators are themselves vloggers. The vlog has, in fact, become a staple of YouTube. Some vlogs are quite funny, and others, truly informative; some are simple, and others are highly produced, yet way too many are simply not worth watching.

That's because vlogs are poorly produced, or they lack focus in their subject matter — or they suffer from a combination of both. Like most other staples, the bar has been raised on what's now acceptable.

Here are some suggestions to maximize your potential when it comes to your vlog:

>> **Use a good-quality camera.** Though a DSLR produces the best quality, a point-and-shoot camera or even a webcam — as long as it can capture HD — works pretty well, as shown in Figure 4-7. Plus, it's simple to use and requires little, if any, setup.

FIGURE 4-7:
The built-in webcam on a MacBook makes it easy to shoot the next installment of your vlog.

>> **Use a separate microphone.** It may not always be easy to work with a microphone, but trust us — it's often worth the aggravation. Why have your voice sound tinny, distorted, or muffled when all it takes is plugging in an external microphone? Even a cheap one makes your voice sound better than your camera's or computer's onboard microphone. You can even use a lavalier, as shown in Figure 4-8.

>> **Be consistent.** If you're looking for an audience, think of yourself as a brand. That means the format should remain consistent with each video. Be original and spontaneous. Here's an opportunity to show how unique, creative, funny, and talented you are.

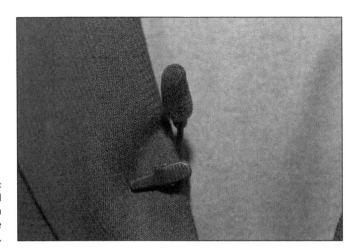

FIGURE 4-8:
A lavalier clipped to a lapel can greatly improve audio quality.

>> **Use good lighting.** These videos are about you, so if you think the overhead lamp and illumination from your monitor will suffice, think again. Whether you're outdoors or indoors, we strongly recommend making sure that there's ample light. If you don't want to use photo lighting, a plain household lamp (with shade) that's capable of providing bright, soft illumination is a good place to start. If you're out and about and can't set anything up, make sure your setting is one with a sufficient amount of ambient light, natural or otherwise.

>> **Don't ramble.** The difference between a great vlog and a terrible vlog depends on several factors — the host's sense of presence, the subject matter, and the length, for example — but it's the host not getting to the point that often acts as the deciding factor for the viewer to move on to another video. Don't be that person. Instead, plan in advance what you want to say or what you're going to do, and when the time comes to record it, manage your delivery effectively. Be sure to capture several takes so that you end up sounding as fluid as possible.

>> **Don't count on needing only a single take.** It's not a sport, nor is it something you need to do live, so always take your time and reshoot parts that aren't perfect — not just for getting your vocal delivery right but also to make the video visually more interesting. You can do that by shooting each take from a different angle or by framing your subject a bit differently.

Making an educational video

YouTube has become a great place for people of all ages, education levels, and interests to learn. And why not? It's a central location where viewers can find out about just about any topic; besides, though it's one thing to read about a subject, watching it on video provides a whole new perspective. You'll find history lessons, teaching aids, and coverage of current events all on YouTube.

Here are some tips for producing an educational video:

>> **Know your audience.** Before Goldilocks tells you that one video was too hard to understand and that another had information she already knew, it's up to you to make it just right. That starts with knowing your audience — knowing what they're capable of and also knowing what your audience most needs to know.

>> **Keep it simple.** There's no reason to show or tell any more information than necessary. In other words, stay on topic. Have a singular focus and be sure to use lots of strong visuals.

>> **Be concise in your introduction.** Potential viewers must have some idea of what they can learn. That's why it's important to have a clear description of the video. If you can't explain it in two lines, you should consider reworking your idea.

>> **Write a good script.** At its core, the educational video is still a movie. And like a great movie, its success begins with having a good script that both entertains and gets to the point. Be sure to write the narration as succinctly as possible, and make the visuals consistent with your time constraints and budget.

Making tutorial and how-to videos

Search on YouTube and you'll find endless videos that explain how to do everything from kissing your date after the prom and drawing a freehand circle to replacing an iPhone screen and making an epic movie trailer. YouTube even has videos on how to make a how-to video. Some of these how-to videos provide lessons that are quite informative; some are also quite entertaining, whereas others simply serve as examples of how not to make one.

If your goal is to make a good video rather than the typical not-so-good one that's too often found on YouTube, you'll need to heed the following advice:

>> **Know the subject.** It sounds obvious, but some of those less effective how-to videos suffer from a lack of understanding of the topic from the production side. Stick to what you know best and take it from there.

>> **Prepare a script.** A good script acts like a roadmap for making the movie, no matter what the subject matter. So, tutorials are no exception. Though everyone has their own method of tackling a topic, one idea is to create a skeleton of the entire process by writing down every step. After that, you can rewrite it as a script, taking into account video content and (of course) witty puns.

>> **Use title cards.** Simple text cards are not only cool in an old-school kind of way, they can also help viewers understand the topic. Using words in your video helps the lesson sink in. You can use title cards to introduce each step, and to provide a summary.

>> **Shoot cutaways.** A *cutaway* is one of the most effective components in a movie. It's basically a break in the current video by the insertion of another shot, one that's often related to the action at hand. Close-up and detail shots provide a clearer picture (pun intended) of the use of cutaways, but don't do them while shooting the actual video lesson. Instead, shoot them afterward, or before if that's the way you roll. Why? So that you have clean shots to edit later. It's often jarring for the camera to zoom in during the lesson.

>> **Shoot multiple takes.** Editing is your friend, so shoot several versions of the same scene to try out different approaches or simply to get it just right. These alternative shots give you enough content to work with while editing.

>> **Make sure the narration is clean.** *Clean* means speaking clearly and concisely — simple phrases and no jargon. And one more thing: Read the text many times to get as comfortable with it as possible.

Let's play (and make) gaming videos

Whether you're explaining how to find a settlement on Durotar in *World of Warcraft*, battling a Divine Beast in *Breath of the Wild*, or simply providing some tips in *Fortnite*, chances are good that lots of people are looking for these kinds of tips and more on YouTube. So, if video games are your thing and you want to share your exploits and advice with others or perhaps teach them something, why not make your own gaming video?

What's a gaming video without a real example from the game? Boring. So you want to be able to capture the action using a screen capture program. The simplest way is to have your game loaded on a computer rather than on a gaming system.

Here are a few choices that are inexpensive and work pretty well:

- » **Open Broadcaster Software, or OBS** (https://obsproject.com): This free, open source program is highly beloved amongst gamers, and it's available for both PC and Macintosh. You're given an extraordinary number of controls that allow you to both record and stream your adventures.

- » **Bandicam** (www.bandicam.com): You can capture ultra-high resolution footage at rates as high as 1,000 frames per second. The only downside is that this affordable program is available only to PC users.

Making animal videos

Take an informal survey, and you'll discover an insatiable fondness for videos that feature animals. People love to watch them over and over as well as share and share. That probably explains why the most viral content is content that features our four-legged friends. The recent "Cats vs. invisible wall" video has already attracted more than 35 million views. And the cats are not alone. Numerous videos are dedicated to canine accomplishments, whether they're playing with babies, pretending to talk, or just being cute.

But the animal video isn't dominated entirely by dogs and cats. In fact, you'll encounter every animal imaginable on YouTube. Horses, cows, monkeys, and even "lions and tigers and bears" are represented on YouTube.

So, if you think your pet has what it takes to be a YouTube sensation, it's time to break out the ol' camera and make Fido a star.

Follow these tips for making animal videos on YouTube:

- » **Find a willing participant.** Some dogs — and other animals, for that matter — are more inclined than others to ham it up for the camera, as shown in Figure 4-9. If you have one with the acting bug, consider taking out your camera because — who knows? — you may have a potential star on your hands.

- » **Nail down the right location.** That's what they say it *all* comes down to — why else would they repeat it three times? We're not sure whether that makes the saying triply true, but it does add value to the video when you find the right place. If it's a house pet, that can mean a tidy space in a part of your place that has sufficient lighting and is free of clutter. For outdoor situations, choose an area free of clutter, and make sure the sun is at your back.

- » **Reward the participants.** Dogs and cats work for treats, so when they do a good job, it's important to compensate them.

FIGURE 4-9:
Windee the
Airedale gets
ready to shoot
a scene.

Capturing sporting events

With the exception of professional sports leagues with a YouTube channel or a news organization granted rebroadcast consent by a professional league, most sports videos found on YouTube consist of extreme events and amateur sports. Because the latter often borders on boring for all but those connected to it (family members, participants, sadists), the former provides the best opportunity for the ambitious videographer.

These days, capturing extreme sporting events and activities has gotten easier, thanks to the GoPro. This durable little camera helps provide a fresh perspective by putting the viewer directly in the middle of the action, making GoPro videos some of the most compelling videos on YouTube. Besides, the GoPro is water-proof, captures amazing quality, and can mount to just about anything.

Here are some (extreme) ideas:

>> **Skateboarding:** Because it's a popular sport among young people, chances are good that there's a good audience for your skateboarding video, as long as it's compelling to watch. You can shoot with anything, from a dedicated camera to your iPhone, or mount a GoPro to the board itself, as shown in Figure 4-10.

>> **Skydiving:** Here's another situation that was changed by the GoPro camera. Just mount the camera to your helmet and capture a perspective that has rarely been seen until now.

FIGURE 4-10:
You can easily
attach a GoPro to
a skateboard to
get a board's-eye
view of the scene.

>> **Skiing:** Wow, it seems like a lot of extreme sports begin with the letters *sk,* and although skiing is more common, it can be every bit as extreme, especially when a parachute's involved, and you're skiing off a cliff. You can provide your audience with the skier's perspective by mounting your GoPro in a variety of places, including on your helmet, on a chest harness, or directly on your ski pole.

>> **Aquatic sports:** Attaching a waterproof video camera to your surfboard or raft or on your person while waterskiing can result in some compelling video content of places that a camera dared to tread — assuming, of course, that you don't wipe out after the first three seconds.

>> **BMX:** The possibilities are endless because you can mount cameras anywhere — from the bike itself to your helmet to strategically placing cameras on the course and from the crowd.

Film and animation

YouTube has liberated the stage or, more appropriately, the screen for filmmakers of all levels by allowing them to reach a global audience. Not that long ago, you would make a short film and then physically show it to your friends and colleagues in a dank screening room, a classroom, or (more than likely) your own basement.

On a good day, the screening may have been seen by scores of people. That would mean you would need dozens of showings, if not hundreds, to duplicate the reach of your YouTube channel moments after you upload a movie. Besides gaining exposure to a large audience, you can also enter your film in various online film competitions.

Here are a few types of movies you can find on YouTube:

>> **Short films:** One traditional gateway to directing a feature film comes from making a short film. But how a person actually ended up seeing one of these films remained one of the great mysteries in filmmaking. We all hear whenever they're nominated for an Oscar, but never knew where you could see one. Nowadays you can view short films of all genres on YouTube, and maybe even see a future Oscar nominee.

>> **Web series:** These series — both scripted and unscripted — are the YouTube version of a television show. And, just like their broadcast cousins, they cover a wide range of topics, situations, and subject matter, while not having to adhere to the standard 30- or 60-minute episode blocks. Popular web series include *Bon Appetit*'s cooking show *Gourmet Makes;* the variety show *Good Mythical Morning;* and the Emmy-nominated series *Cobra Kai*.

>> **Animated:** If you're a fan of animation or you want a place to show it off, YouTube can help you reach your audience. Whether you're going old-school with cell animation, doing stop-motion with objects, or venturing into computer-generated imagery, YouTube provides a great place to share your work with the world. You can even create an animated web series.

Entertainment

Most videos should entertain the viewer in some way, and that includes the ones that are about entertainment. Content that covers celebrities, movies, music, theater, and television should entertain the viewer beyond its subject matter. So, although *all* video should be entertaining, videos on areas associated with the entertainment industry should be doubly entertaining.

Though entertainment covers a wide ranges of topics, here are some of the areas you're likely to see:

>> **Celebrity interviews:** These can cover a wide range of subjects, including comments on specific projects, opinions on current events, and human interest stories.

>> **Red carpet coverage:** Stars attending their movie premieres, arriving at award ceremonies, or supporting their favorite charities are popular subject matter, as shown in Figure 4-11. Many make comments to the press, and some show off their fashion sense.

>> **Entertainment news:** This one covers the news side of the industry, with coverage of areas like obituaries, divorces, babies, and impaired driving arrests.

FIGURE 4-11:
Red carpet action, captured at the Toronto International Film Festival.

News and information

YouTube offers far more content for viewers than perusing the latest music videos, marveling at people doing truly weird stuff, or looking at dogs dressed in costumes. Though these provide a pleasant escape, you can also use YouTube to stay informed when it comes to news and current events. You can find coverage of newscasts, editorials on every imaginable topic, news segments and packages that cover anything from business and national news to entertainment and health issues, and even livestreams of events and breaking news. That's why almost every major news outlet has a YouTube channel where you can look at clips and watch video segments.

Here's a brief list of news organizations represented on YouTube:

» Associated Press Television

» ABC News

» BBC News

» NBC News

Autos and vehicles

Whether you're in the market for a new ride or just want to see something go fast, videos about cars dominate on YouTube. This content covers everything from reviews and test drives to maintenance and customizations. Not an automotive enthusiast? You'll find content on every other method of transportation, whether it's a motorcycle, boat, plane, or anything in between.

Want to break into the scene? Here are a few things to keep in mind:

» **Be safe:** Whether you're behind the handlebars of a motorcycle or beneath the undercarriage of a jacked-up off-roader, safety is a priority. Make sure you're obeying traffic laws and demonstrating proper etiquette with your machines and tools. This will not only keep you out of trouble but also keep both you, your viewers, and your fellow commuters safe.

» **Be respectful:** You may love the rumbling exhaust on your customized ride, but that doesn't mean everyone else in your neighborhood does. Plus, if you're trying to explain to your audience how and why something works, it's probably worth it to cut the engine first.

» **Be knowledgeable:** Sure, you don't necessarily need to be an expert to review the latest sedan, but it's worth it to do your research so that you can give an educated, nuanced perspective. By knowing the ins, outs, features, and even quirks of the vehicle you're talking about, your audience will find you more credible and set you apart from the pack.

Comedy

Do you have a gift for making people laugh? YouTube is a great place for comedians, both up-and-coming and well-established. Whether you're making a one-off skit or a humorous commentary or recording your latest stand-up set, you can likely find the perfect audience.

If you think you have what it takes to cut it as a comedian, be aware of this advice:

- **>> Understand your audience:** Humor on YouTube comes in a variety of shapes, sizes, and genres. Some of it appeals to a broader audience, and at other times it can be quite niche. Make sure you know which subset you fit into before trying to carve your way; otherwise, your wit may fall flat.

- **>> Be kind:** Simply stated, don't be a jerk. There's a fine line between teasing and bullying, and it's never a good idea to cross it. Jokes at the expense of others are not only hurtful but also, depending on their severity, may violate YouTube's terms of service.

Travel and events

Nothing expands your horizons quite as much as traveling, and with its global reach, YouTube puts the world at people's fingertips. The world is big and diverse, meaning that the possibilities for what you can share are virtually endless. Maybe you know the best places to eat in Japan, or maybe you're a fiend for festivals, or maybe you just want to share a little bit about all your adventures around the globe — whatever your take may be, there's always an audience for you.

Travel videos are a great way to grow your online presence; just be conscious of these tips:

- **>> Be a good tourist:** The world is an incredibly vast place, with countless people and cultures. It's imperative that you be respectful of other countries' rules and traditions. Your videos not only inform your audience, they also act as a reflection of both you and where you come from. Make sure that when you're visiting a region, you're being cognizant and respectful of how your host country goes about things. No one likes a bad tourist, so don't ruin it for everyone else.

- **>> Be curious:** The world is your oyster! A great way to stand out from the crowd of travel channels is by truly immersing yourself in wherever you're going. Get out of your comfort zone! Eat like a local. See the sights. Let loose and experience wherever you are to the fullest (while also being respectful). You only get one life.

Science and technology

What we know about the world is constantly changing and expanding, and so is the science community on YouTube. The range of knowledge and technology you can find is incredibly vast: everything from explanations of intricate mathematical formulas to theories about the origins of the universe to robots that will try their hardest — and not really succeed — to apply lipstick to someone's face. If you're curious about a scientific topic, odds are that you can find countless videos explaining it. And, because things are constantly evolving, there are always opportunities for you to contribute.

If you want to share some of your knowledge with the world, consider this advice:

>> **Cite your sources:** Though there's no doubt that you're a smarty-pants, odds are that your understanding of the universe is composed of an amalgamation of other people's theories and ideas. It's always a good idea to cite these and other sources of information. This not only lends you credibility but also gives your viewers a map to expanding their own knowledge.

>> **Stay on topic:** When discussing complicated subjects, especially dense theoretical ones, it's easy to become tangled in a mess of information. Make sure to script out your talking points. It keeps you focused, makes it easier to vet for accuracy, and helps your viewers follow along more easily.

Nonprofits and activism

YouTube is an excellent resource for those attempting to raise awareness about a cause they're passionate about. The world is a tumultuous, complicated, and sometimes unjust place, and YouTube can be the perfect avenue for raising awareness. Whether you're trying to raise funds for the local animal shelter where you volunteer or to increase awareness about climate change and the environment, YouTube can be an incredibly important platform.

If you're trying to bring about change, keep this advice in mind:

>> **Be honest:** We live in the age of "fake news" and hard-to-discern truths. It's important that the information you're conveying and advocating is truthful and transparent. Misinformation not only makes you look bad but can also negatively impact the cause you're advocating for.

- » **Be cautious:** Politics and Internet culture don't always co-exist peacefully. YouTube is an incredibly large website utilized by people with varying stances, both politically and socially. Just because you believe in something doesn't mean that others will agree with you and stay silent about it. The age old Internet adage "Don't feed trolls" stands true. Getting in arguments with people who disagree with you never leads to anything good. Sometimes you can't change people's minds, no matter how hard you try. Choose your battles wisely; invest your energy in helping others.

- » **Call others to action:** Simply talking about a subject, no matter how compelling, is not always enough. Directly calling out to your audience about which steps they should take next, whether it's online or in the real world, is a great way of encouraging interaction and follow-through.

Viral Videos versus Evergreen Content

One phenomenon created by the Internet is the spread of viral video. Just like a virus (except that it's the good kind that won't make you sick), a *viral* video spreads rapidly online and can garner millions of views in a relatively short time.

On the opposite side of the spectrum lies the *evergreen* video: As its name implies, a video with this distinction usually remains fresh and vibrant for longer periods, providing a timeless quality to the content.

Your channel's objective depends on being able to bring as many viewers as possible to your content. Sometimes that comes from a single, albeit extremely popular video, whereas at other times it's more about having a healthy lineup of relevant content.

Creating a single viral video can bring a great deal of attention to your channel, and those visits can quickly monetize into big bucks, especially with a video that garners a couple of million views. On the other hand, evergreen videos (see the later section "Evergreen content") lend themselves to less dynamic, though more steady buildup through a variety of content that keeps people coming back.

REMEMBER

Don't bet your YouTube strategy on trying to create a viral video. When it comes to viral videos, there's a random element to their success that cannot always be duplicated the next time around. Nevertheless, you can do some things to make success just a tad less random — we tell you more on that topic in the later sidebar "What makes a video go viral?"

Viral content

Viral videos usually consist of some trendy or contemporary aspect that allows it to build a huge audience quite quickly. For example, a new dance craze or music video sometimes makes for the most watched video, but it can also consist of a dramatic news event or wild stunt that people can't stop talking about. Sometimes it fades away as quickly as it started, whereas at other times it sticks around.

Evergreen content

Like a tree of shrubbery that never turns brown, the evergreen video remains popular with its niche audience for a long time. That's because it consists of content that people will search for often and over an extended period. If YouTube videos were gallons of milk, comparing the two, a viral video would have a shorter expiration date to more evergreen content. Though there's less pressure to creating a successful evergreen video, it still requires a lot of work to gain a following. You have to let people know that it's out there while keeping it relevant for them to venture out and find you.

The types of content that may have (potential) evergreen value include

>> Instructional videos

>> Educational videos

>> Travel videos

>> Overviews of holiday traditions

>> Biographies of famous people

REMEMBER

Most evergreen content — instructional videos or content associated with a historical event, for example — doesn't usually go viral but can enjoy a longer run of popularity because the content will continue to attract a steady stream of viewers.

WHAT MAKES A VIDEO GO VIRAL?

Viral videos usually have a humorous or quirky feel to them, and though most of the time they unintentionally gather a mass following, some corporations have managed to produce successful viral videos quite intentionally. But there's no guarantee that your video will find success, even if it's a promotional video with big money behind it.

Like the countless grains of sand, millions of videos are uploaded to YouTube — but only a few become viral sensations. As with winning the lottery, the success of a viral video is more "hoped for" than "planned for." Still, you can improve your chances by considering some attributes that other viral videos have displayed.

Consider these suggestions:

- **Engage the viewer.** You have to grab their attention before they know what hit them.
- **Be relevant.** Trends and pop culture references have a wide appeal to audiences, so why not integrate them into your video?
- **Add humor.** Make 'em laugh, and they'll keep coming.
- **Make it brief.** After grabbing viewers' attention and holding their interest, don't take a chance on losing them by droning on too long or having a lull in the action.
- **Use popular subjects.** The biggest YouTube video of 2019 was *Con Calma*, a music video by Daddy Yankee & Snow. It was, viewed over 1.5 billion times. Consider music as one popular subject.

After completing and uploading your video, here are some aspects that will help it along its viral path:

- **Spread the news over social media.** Tweet out your video link, post it on Facebook, and ask friends to share it.
- **Send out emails.** Send out an email blast with the YouTube link.
- **Blog about it.** If you have a blog, then blog about your video. Also reach out to other bloggers and ask them to do the same.
- **Listen to feedback.** It's no secret that comments found on YouTube can be hurtful, but some are actually helpful. Try to sift through them to find what people like about your video.

Chapter 5

Making Plans Both Large and Small

YouTube is a truly massive online community, with more than 500 hours of new video content uploaded every minute and where millions of new subscribers are added every day and a significant proportion of subscribers (both new and old) not only engage with YouTube creators but also frequently take some sort of action while on YouTube, such as buying a product. With so much content to choose from, you need to be authentic, well organized, and consistently active for your channel to attract a growing fan base. Effective planning and a continual review against your goals is critical to success on YouTube. Fortunately, putting your plan together is straightforward, but your goals need to be measured and adjusted on an ongoing basis.

Proper planning is about looking at the big picture first and then working your way through the details in a methodical way. YouTube audiences know the difference between great channels and mediocre channels because the best ones are always well planned. Planning makes all your other YouTube and marketing activities more efficient. You may feel the need to rush out and produce some videos, but you'll be better served — and achieve better results — if you step back and think about how audiences, channels, and content all come together. This chapter is about planning your YouTube strategy.

TIP

Go back to the basics if your existing channel isn't attracting or engaging viewers. Effective planning isn't only about creating new YouTube channels and uploading more videos — it's also about laying the groundwork for some cool marketing strategies. Fortunately, planning ahead goes a long way toward getting your present channel moving and your audience excited about your work. Don't be surprised if some of your viewers want to collaborate and offer to help you out.

Establishing Your Channel's Mission

Your YouTube channel is a great way for you to present yourself and your brand to an audience (that's potentially massive). You may balk at considering yourself a "brand," but we're here to tell you that it doesn't matter whether you're an independent creator, a Fortune 500 company, a cutting-edge digital agency, or a local business — every organization and YouTube creator has its own brand, whether they know it or not. Your brand's value is tied to its uniqueness and how it appeals to your viewers. That's why YouTube is so important and effective for showing what you or your company represent — far better than words can ever do, as a matter of fact.

Successful YouTube strategies incorporate a channel presence well beyond simply uploading your videos for free. Your channel is a place where viewers should visit regularly to discover and consume content. This is an opportunity to grow, engage, and inspire communities of passion.

Upon arriving on your YouTube channel, viewers should quickly understand what you and your channel are all about. The success of your channel is tied to making your brand and channel mission resonate loud and clear. Khan Academy, shown in Figure 5-1, is an excellent example of YouTube integration with its brand. Visit the channel at www.youtube.com/khanacademy to see a live example of a YouTube channel with a clear mission.

REMEMBER

If you have other online properties, such as a website, a Facebook page, an Instagram channel, or a Twitter account, make sure your YouTube channel has consistent branding and messaging that aligns with all your social networks and websites. Viewers commonly move across these properties as they engage with you, so your mission must be unified and clear.

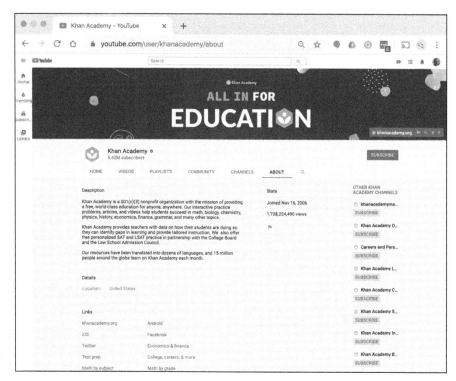

FIGURE 5-1:
Khan Academy's
mission aligns
with its YouTube
content.

Determining your goals

Your YouTube channel showcases something you're passionate about. What drives you to create a YouTube channel and content isn't so different from what motivates you to do other things in life, such as

>> Host a fundraiser

>> Write a blog

>> Support a cause

>> Give something back to society

>> Earn some income

>> Learn a new hobby

REMEMBER

The reason that YouTube is such a great place for you to share your passion is because video is a supremely effective medium for getting your audience to engage with you. Learn to put that medium to use for you.

Though building your channel is one major goal, you likely have additional goals. Here are some other reasons for creating your YouTube channel and its content:

>> **Build a brand.** There's no better way to show who you are, either as an independent creator or as an organization, than by way of a video or series of videos on your channel. The content might include different types of videos — something you've created, straight news, information about you, or a combination. Your motivation for brand building might be to obtain a new job, attract attention from industry luminaries, or make people feel good about your products.

>> **Educate your target audience.** Most people love to learn, and much of the successful content on YouTube revolves around education and tutorials. Educational content includes home repair, product configuration, justification for social causes, and many more topics. Educational content also helps drive brand awareness.

>> **Entertain the crowd.** People love to laugh, enjoy music, and become engrossed in a good story. These genres are all forms of entertainment, and all work especially well on YouTube.

Many forms of entertainment are highly subjective, so be sure to tailor your content so that it connects with the specific audience you're trying to reach.

>> **Sell something.** It doesn't matter whether you have a product to sell, a subscription to offer, or a candidate to elect, your YouTube channel is a great way to demonstrate to your audience that they want what you're offering. People are turning to YouTube to make buying decisions about future purchases. Make sure you understand that YouTube is now a primary source of information used to influence a sale. According to Tubular Lab, 64 percent of consumers use YouTube to review electronics when making a purchase decision.

>> **Earn a living.** We've explained that your videos can make money by driving and influencing sales. You can also earn a living from people watching your YouTube videos by monetizing your channel (as explained in Chapter 14).

Don't quit your day job — at least not yet. Making money from YouTube takes time, creativity, and persistence. Even the best-laid plans can't guarantee results if you don't (or your content doesn't) resonate with your target audience. Don't fret: Your YouTube channel may be a nice source of supplemental income, eventually.

Don't feel that you have to keep your goals separate. Donut Media's popular automotive channel (www.youtube.com/channel/UCL6JmiMXKoXS6bpP1D3bk8g) does a great job of combining educational goals with entertainment to keep its audience (almost 3 million subscribers) coming back for more.

EMBRACE DISCOVERABILITY

At the end of the day, YouTube is about one thing: getting people to watch your content. Simple, right? In theory, yes, but your challenge is to help viewers find your channel and your content. That's what discoverability is all about: placing your content in front of the right viewers so that they can watch. Unfortunately, YouTube doesn't share the secret sauce for getting found, though you can help improve the odds of your videos showing up in YouTube and Google Search as well as in Suggested Videos on the Watch page. What can you do in the planning phase for aiding discoverability? Make watch time an important goal.

Watch time is one of the most important factors that triggers YouTube to place your content in front of viewers. Several years ago, YouTube made watch time more important to discoverability than the number of views the video received. So, what exactly *is* watch time? In its simplest form, *watch time* is the total amount of time viewers spend watching your videos. People who watch your content are telling YouTube, "Hey, this is important stuff — make sure similar viewers know."

Watch time doesn't indicate whether your viewers watch the *entire* video (although that's a good thing, too) — it indicates that a relatively high percentage of the video is being viewed. How much? Again, YouTube isn't specific. Note that it doesn't matter whether your videos are short or long; what's important is that viewers are engaged. The secret is to make legitimately good content. Good content increases watch time, which increases discoverability.

WARNING

Creating viral videos shouldn't be your goal. Betting your YouTube strategy on producing viral videos is like betting your entire retirement savings on winning the lottery. Attain your goals by proper planning and execution, not by chance.

Being different, being valuable, being authentic

YouTube has 2 billion logged-in unique visitors every month, and this number continues to grow. Now, that might sound intimidating, as in "How can I get anyone to notice *me?*" but our advice to you is to jump right in. The trick is that you simply have to be different enough and interesting enough for people to care. Your content (or the content of those videos you choose to curate) must connect with your audience while tying into your brand. In an increasingly congested space, you need to be authentic to establish credibility and aid discoverability.

WARNING

Yes, it's possible to make a little money in the YouTube world by hiring yourself out as a spokesperson for a third party, but being a paid spokesperson is a risky strategy. You'll find that your YouTube audience is rather astute and will quickly weed out from their subscriptions and playlists any channels that lack authenticity. If you get paid to include product placements in your videos, be sure to notify YouTube when updating your monetization settings. You *must* follow all of YouTube's ad policies if you're paid to include product placement in your editorial content. For more on monetization settings, see Chapter 14.

Surveying the YouTube landscape

Your channel-planning blueprint must include a clear understanding of the community you're aiming to reach. Ask yourself these questions:

» **Who are the influencers and thought leaders?** Discover spokespeople who share your passion to determine their tone, style, and content approach. Determine how they engage with their fan base and with whom they collaborate.

» **Which channels are popular?** Use YouTube Search to determine which channels are the most popular with the subject matter planned for your own channel. Enter keywords into the search bar to discover popular channels and videos. Look at the number of subscribers, views, likes, and comments. Find out why these channels resonate by looking at style, branding, publishing, scheduling, collaboration level, and personality. See how the channels organize videos and playlists, repurpose content, and promote new videos.

» **How engaged is the community?** You need to gauge how viewers are reacting to the content they watch. Determine what normal levels of likes/ dislikes and comments are for your target audience. Identify the vocal members of the community and capture their constructive criticism and content recommendations. Comments are a great source for telegraphing audience needs.

» **Is my idea different enough?** Figure out whether there are gaps in the content being produced. Assess whether your approach covers some of the fan base content recommendations now unfulfilled by existing channels.

REMEMBER

The YouTube community is quite collaborative, especially among better channels and viewers. If you're in a competitive market, your audience will provide a competitive advantage by promoting your channel and making content recommendations. If you have a product or service, don't be surprised if your audience gives you feedback on that as well.

With more than 500 hours of video now being uploaded to YouTube every minute, you'll realize that you have to search through, watch, and analyze a good deal of content so that you can determine whether your YouTube strategy is sound. YouTube is the second-largest search engine in the world, so take a reasoned and disciplined approach to determine where you fit — or where your organization fits.

TIP

We recommend visiting comparable channels, watching their videos, and then exploring the video recommendations to determine whether your channel will be unique enough to build a following. You can use YouTube Search to track down the competition, or you can try some nifty tools that we describe below.

YouTube provides some valuable options to discover content that is important to your target audience or relevant to your discovery. Working directly from the YouTube search bar can be helpful: Whenever you begin typing a search query into YouTube, you see a list of possible search results displayed — these are the high-volume searches that YouTube feels may be relevant to your current query.

TIP

YouTube's basic search feature is a good tool to use if you want to gauge whether you're creating content that is in high demand. Using the advanced search filters, however, is much more efficient if what you want to do is find specific channels and videos. Figure 5-2 shows an advanced search filter query for the term *monster trucks*. (Turns out that a search for *monster trucks* yields nearly 1.2 million relevant videos — who knew?)

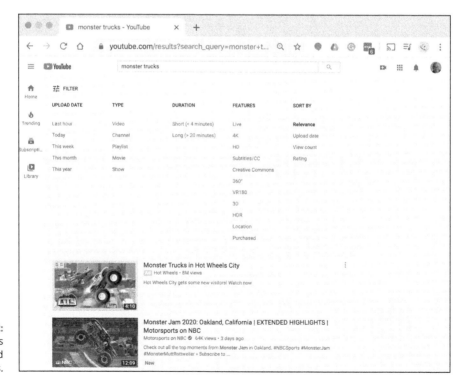

FIGURE 5-2:
Using YouTube's advanced search filters.

Mobile YouTube viewing and mobile search must be significant parts of your channel strategy. Understand that not all mobile apps have complete functionality, including the advanced search filters referenced.

Be sure to look at the recommended videos under the home page of YouTube we describe in Chapter 2. Your previous viewing and search patterns influence what shows up in your recommendations, so you may see a blend of content from different searches, both professional and personal.

Just as independent software tools, such as Adobe Creative Suite and Apple Final Cut, are important to the video production process, independent tools, including Pixability, (www.pixability.com), TubeBuddy (www.tubebuddy.com), and VidIQ (www.vidiq.com), are quite valuable to the channel discovery process on YouTube. These third-party products often combine YouTube data with information from social media sources in order to offer a more granular analysis of important channels, more detailed demographic information about your targeted fan base, and a closer look at what your audience watches and shares. Figure 5-3 shows the critical channels around a specific topic base.

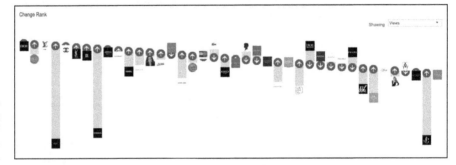

FIGURE 5-3:
Important YouTube channel identification using Pixability.

Understanding Your Target Audience

Your channel's success is linked to how well you know your audience. In Part 3 of this book, you can find out all about building your audience and determining whether they're finding (and hanging out on) your channel. Your core audience on YouTube is a community of passionate individuals who collectively care deeply about a specific subject.

To be truly effective on YouTube and get your audience to engage, you need to share their passion and be creative enough with your content, channel, and social interaction that your commitment comes through loud and clear to them. Your goals are to be either part of the community proper or an expert who provides value to the community.

Going narrow versus going broad

Sharing your passions most effectively often means focusing on your niche. Many aspiring YouTubers feel that going after the largest audience possible to start with is the clearest path to success. Not necessarily. In fact, we want you to consider a few factors that may make you reconsider your plans to try for the broadest audience possible:

» **Getting found:** It takes time for your channel and content to infiltrate a popular subject area. You're likely competing with millions of videos, some of which have proven immensely successful and will dominate search results for some time.

» **Producing unique content:** With so many videos in a popular category, you'll definitely have challenges standing out — at least initially. Channels that have been covering your topic space have also had time to refine their brands, another factor that makes their content stand out.

» **Reaching influencers:** Popular and important industry spokespeople and personalities are constantly bombarded by creators and viewers. You'll have a tough time attracting their attention at the beginning, no matter how insightful your vision or how creative your content.

» **Having help:** The channels at the top have lots of promotional help from subscribers or other advocates in social media. That didn't happen overnight. Invest time in developing relationships and proving that you bring value to the table.

TIP

Start off being the big fish in the small pond, and choose a specific topic space carefully. Your channel and your content will be more discoverable and will increase the likelihood of connecting with both key influencers and the fan base.

Knowing why your audience matters

Treat your audience as an adjunct to your marketing department, public relations firm, sales organization, and design group.

The right audience will

» **Spend time on your channel.** The length of time that your audience spends viewing your content is important. Videos that receive more watch time are more likely to appear in YouTube Search and watch recommendations.

» **Share your YouTube content with peers.** Everyone dreams of having a popular video with millions of views. A video becomes successful when it's unique and compelling enough to the target audience that one viewer eagerly shares it with peers who then just as eagerly share it with other peers, and so forth.

>> **Subscribe to your YouTube channel.** Subscribers watch twice as much of your content as nonsubscribers. They also receive updates about your channel activity (new videos, comments) in their subscription feeds, keeping them informed about all the exciting content on your channel. Ask your viewers to subscribe in the video, and, where appropriate, include annotations to subscribe to your channel.

>> **Engage with your channel.** Likes (or dislikes) and comments comprise the avenue for building a community around your channel. Motivated audience members may also include your content on their own channels or websites, expanding your reach and your opportunity to build your audience even further.

>> **Be your creative advocates.** An engaged audience truly cares about the channels they subscribe to and can be an important source of new ideas and content. Encourage your viewers to use the Comments section below the video to submit ideas — this strategy gives you more content ideas and helps engage viewer interest for the current video.

REMEMBER

Defining your target audience as precisely as possible is an important component of channel success. A target audience of "15- to 55-year-old men" is far too broad. Add a layer of detail to define a more targeted audience — for example, "people who like cooking" is a much more defined audience.

Finding out the nitty-gritty about your audience

If you haven't yet thought about your online audience, we recommend *Video Marketing For Dummies*, by Kevin Daum, Bettina Hein, Matt Scott, and Andreas Goeldi (Wiley). It provides a more in-depth look at audience needs and identification than we can offer here, but we do want to offer some food for thought. When planning your YouTube channel, have an image of your targeted fan base in mind at all times. Ask yourself these questions:

>> **Who are they?** Marketing people like to use the term *demographics* to describe some of the characteristics of their target audience. Think about your audience and attributes such as age, gender, and interest. If you're selling baby products, for example, your audience may be new mothers between 24 and 36 years old. Be specific.

YouTube now attracts more 18- to 49-year-olds than most cable networks. However, if you're seeking senior viewers, it may be a bit more difficult than if you were targeting a slightly younger audience. Fortunately, even some of your older friends are discovering YouTube as well!

>> **Where are they?** YouTube works as well for small local businesses as it does for the big, international companies. Your social media efforts around your YouTube channel should involve influences in the geographic location you serve.

>> **How do they get their information?** Make an effort to understand what your audience reads, where they go on the web for information, and which events they attend. This will influence the direction of your channel and its contents.

>> **Who influences them?** Which bloggers or YouTubers do your targeted viewers connect with? Pay attention to the style of how these web celebrities communicate.

Be authentic. Don't feel that you need to mimic an influencer, because your audience will see right through it.

If you have other properties, such as a website, a Facebook page, an Instagram channel, or a Twitter account, you likely have much of the audience information you need for your YouTube planning process. As your channel grows in popularity, don't be surprised if your audience changes as well.

Defining Desired Actions

Your channel planning blueprint must spell out the type of action you want your audience to take, That's *activation*. It goes beyond just watching to include subscribing, commenting, collaborating, and so much more. You need clarity around the type of action you want, because it influences the type of content you create and the steps you want your audience to take. (We cover all of these topics in detail in Chapter 10, but you definitely should identify these actions during the planning phase.)

No matter how intelligent and independent your fan base, you need to guide them through the experience with your channel and its contents. Believe it or not, your viewers want you to tell them what to do. Some of that supervision may be as explicit as a Subscribe button, or more implicit with the automated viewing of a playlist.

This guidance is an area where many people and organizations struggle. Define what you want the viewer to do and determine how you'll help them do it. If your audience is aligned with your mission, they entrust you to guide them through your channel and give them a call to action (CTA, for short). Look at the following CTA options and determine which one sums up what you want your viewers to do:

>> **Subscribe to your channel.** Subscribers are much more valuable viewers because they statistically consume more content and engage more on YouTube and social media.

   Don't be shy! Always ask viewers to subscribe.

>> **Watch more of your videos.** Content is often related. If a viewer has just watched a video of yours on house painting, chances are good that they'll watch a video on paint options or brush selection *if you ask them to*. See how playlists (Chapter 3) and end screens (Chapter 9) can help you guide viewers to watch more.

>> **Do something.** What do you want your viewers to do? Vote? Volunteer? Run marathons? Cook Thai food from your recipes? Video is a strong motivator, so use that factor to drive your viewers to take action.

>> **Make a purchase.** YouTube is now one of the places that people go to make buying decisions. If you're selling something, ask them to buy what you're selling, and be sure to let them know where they can close the sale — whether it's a physical location or a "virtual" store on the web.

>> **Follow you on social media channels.** Once a viewer becomes a fan, he or she will likely want to see what you're doing on your other digital destinations.

>> **Share their experience.** If a viewer enjoyed your channel or content, help them tell others about it in person, through email, or on social media. It's another helpful way to attract subscribers and views.

Planning an Outstanding YouTube Channel

YouTube rewards you with higher search rankings and supplementary video recommendations based first and foremost on your channel and individual video watch times. In addition, YouTube looks at factors such as viewer engagement and video sharing rates. Your job in the planning process is to identify and coordinate each component so that you're in a position to keep your channel active.

Having a spokesperson

Okay, you've analyzed your target fan base and figured out what motivates them on YouTube. Now you need to determine whether a specific channel spokesperson would be the right fit for your target fan base. This is a critical decision for both independent creators and organizations.

REMEMBER

Typically, an audience gravitates toward either a personality or content, but not toward any old personality or content. Whatever you choose to prioritize, it has to have a high level of authenticity. If the viewers in your topic area engage more with personality, for example, be sure to choose a spokesperson with credibility and appeal. This might be you, the creator and channel owner, or someone you hire to be a part of your YouTube production team for a small business or large brand.

TIP

Aim for the style or content across your channel to be consistent. Make it all high end or all vlogger style, for example. You choose what is right for your audience and stay authentic in whatever you choose.

A good example of a brand with a consistent voice throughout its entire channel is Aveda (www.youtube.com/user/aveda), a hair care company focused on beauty, wellness, and the environment. Every video the company creates for each segment of its audience has a specific look and feel. For example, it makes high-quality, polished ad spots to introduce new products, and it creates vlogger-hosted content with popular YouTube creators using their favorite Aveda products. This gives the company a nice variety of content on the channel and appeals to customers and beauty professionals alike.

Branding

Branding can be a large and complex topic, but we keep it simple: *Branding* is all about coming up with a name and design that are unique to you. Need an example? Think about Apple. You see consistency in all its products, its naming conventions, its website, and its packaging. Over time, that branding symbolism — the look and feel — becomes synonymous with who you are. Want to learn more? Check out *Branding For Dummies*, by Bill Chiaravalle and Barbara Findlay Schenck (Wiley).

REMEMBER

Your YouTube channel and videos are powerful extensions of your brand. If you have an existing website, logo, or color pattern, bring it over to your YouTube channel, and use it for the branded elements of your videos as well. If you give your viewers a great experience on YouTube, chances are good that they'll end up on your website, too. Keep the branding consistent. Your viewers will appreciate it.

Planning the channel layout

Your channel must be visually representative of the video content you create. When viewers first visit your channel, it's important that they understand what kind of videos you produce or curate. You also want viewers to be in a position to quickly find out when new content is expected from your channel. A helpful design layout makes these tasks a lot easier. Figure 5-4 shows a terrific YouTube home page and a great use of branding by Khan Academy.

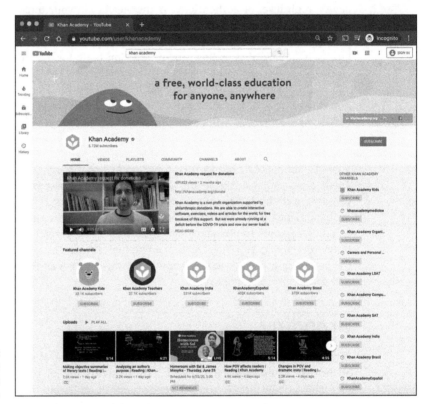

FIGURE 5-4:
YouTube home page for Kahn Academy.

When coming up with a design layout, keep these elements in mind:

>> **Channel art:** The banner you see across the top of your YouTube channel's home page is the welcome mat for your viewer, so make it as appealing as possible. A good channel art design is *device agnostic* — it looks good on mobile devices, desktops, smart TVs, or what-have-you. To help you make the

creation of your channel art easier, you can download a customized graphical template for your YouTube channel at https://support.google.com/youtube.

» **Channel trailer:** The channel trailer is the first video that visitors see when viewing your channel. This is where you need to captivate your new viewers and get them to subscribe to your channel. You can customize the channel trailer for subscribers or nonsubscribers.

» **Channel and social media links:** The small icons that live in the lower right corner of your channel art direct viewers to your other digital properties, such as Facebook, Twitter, or Pinterest. The complete list of digital properties is under the About section of your YouTube channel, and you can choose whether to display icons for some or all of your properties.

» **Custom sections:** Visually dividing your channel page into sections is a great way to help your viewers find the most relevant content on your channel. One way to customize your sections is to create unique playlists or groupings of videos per section.

» **Custom thumbnails:** Thumbnails are visual snapshots of your video, similar to a poster for a movie. They are chosen by default by YouTube — three optional frames from the beginning, middle, and end of your video are provided for every video asset that's uploaded. You can, however, create a custom thumbnail (see Chapter 9) for each video. If you do so, choose a thumbnail that is illustrative of the content in the video.

TIP

Thumbnails have a tremendous impact on a video's view rate. With that fact in mind, always choose or create a good thumbnail, especially for videos shown in sections.

» **Featured channels:** Channels that you own or like or that are simply relevant for your audience are best included in the Featured Channels section on the right side of your channel page.

TIP

Under Featured Channels, you control the additional section **Related Channels**, which YouTube populates with channels that it considers to be like yours. Though YouTube doesn't disclose the exact criteria, it's likely based on content type and what viewers search for. You can turn off this feature, but by doing so, YouTube won't put your channel on the Related Channel feeds of other users. You benefit only by keeping it on.

REMEMBER

With so many channels on YouTube, viewers may think they're viewing the appropriate channel for an organization or famous personality. The verification badge shows up to the right of the channel name and helps alleviate any viewer concerns about the legitimacy of the channel.

Crafting a Content Strategy

Coming up with a mission for your channel is important, as is defining your audience and planning how your channel could best serve your target audience's needs, but at some point you have to define the content that brings it all together. Well, there's no time like the present, so get ready to tackle that task.

Recognizing that content includes video and more

When establishing a content plan, consider these factors that influence how your audience discovers your content and what action viewers take as a result of watching:

>> **Video:** The *channel trailer* is the first video visitors see when viewing your channel. This is where you need to captivate your new viewers and get them to subscribe to your channel. It is important to make a compelling channel trailer to drive subscriptions; you never know where a new subscriber is coming from. Viewers can click your channel icon from any of your videos' watch pages and jump to your channel.

>> **Intros and outros:** Create consistent intro and outro styles for your videos. Think of intros and outros as what you see at the beginning and end of your favorite television show. In the first five seconds, a viewer should know that this is one of your videos; this consistency can be something as simple as the way you say hello and greet your viewers or as complex as an animated logo. Outros should be similar across your channel as well — a goodbye ritual or recommendations for what they should watch next from your channel, and maybe end screens. (End screens, which are covered in Chapter 9, are screen overlays that allow you to direct your viewers to another video or playlist, ask them to subscribe, visit other YouTube channels, or visit an approved website.)

>> **Metadata:** *Metadata* are the words you use to describe your video —the video title, your keyword tags, and the video description, for example. The more specific and precise your metadata, the better. The goal is to help viewers find the exact content they are looking for. Keep in mind that, if you stuff non-relevant keywords into your metadata, it's not going to help anyone. You'll only end up losing viewers when they realize the content you're showing them is not what they wanted. In Chapter 9, you can see how to add and modify your metadata content.

Metadata is important for discovery and YouTube Search. Viewers can also find more information about the video or links back to your website if they want more information.

>> **Thumbnails:** Thumbnails need to be descriptive of the content that viewers can find in your video. Make custom thumbnails (see Chapter 9) to help viewers discover your content above the rest, and don't hesitate to update thumbnails whenever a video's performance is lacking. You can change a video's thumbnail at any time — it doesn't have to be a new video.

>> **End screens:** An end screen is the best way to keep a viewer engaged after watching your video. If your video is longer than 25 seconds, you can customize an interactive screen where viewers can click on videos you want to promote, subscribe to your channel, and more. You can even reference the end screen when you're shooting the video, to encourage viewers to take action.

>> **Links:** Use clickable links in your video description to drive viewers to a specific location on the web or somewhere within YouTube.

Your planning process should consider the viewer who wants more information from a specific video. Providing links in the video description or end screens is a helpful way to give the audience more information when they want it.

Looking at content formats

If you've been mulling over jumping into the YouTube world for a while, we're pretty sure that you've spent a lot of time wrestling with how to produce all that content you need to keep your channel fresh and active. With YouTube, you have several options for your content strategy:

>> **Creation:** Regularly produce your own content. You can certainly build a channel without a stitch of your own content, but if you're going to stand out, your viewers need to see your genuine stuff.

>> **Curation:** Mine the YouTube universe for content that complements your channel, and organize it in a logical way, using sections and playlists for the viewer.

Think of curation in terms of what a museum does: Collect all this great art *(content),* and then pull it together into a themed exhibit. The YouTube playlist serves as the museum's exhibit. That's why museums place French Impressionist paintings together: It's all about the viewer/visitor experience. Would you want to see an impressionist painting together with contemporary pottery? Probably not.

Channel owners generally love having their videos included in playlists, because it helps promote their channels and attracts viewers to watch their content. Done right, your curation favor will be returned many times over.

>> **Collaboration:** You don't have to do everything yourself! Team up with other channel owners and create joint content. It's a popular and effective way to grow an audience and gain subscribers. A YouTube video can be associated with only one channel, so your collaboration planning should take into account content that you'll own (create) and content that you'll help share (collaborate).

Here are some examples of different types of content you can add to your channel:

>> **Episodic content:** The idea here is to have recurring content that creates a series or a body of work on a specific topic. This is great content to produce for your channel because it's highly attractive to channel subscribers. Subscribers can choose to be notified every time you release a video.

>> **Short- and long-form content:** Creating a mixture of short- and long-form content can help you understand the sweet spot for your viewers. YouTube Analytics (described in Chapter 11) helps you plan better by identifying the optimal total runtime for your videos. If you're creating 10-minute videos with short watch times, consider making an alternative video cut that is shorter to see whether watch times improve.

>> **Create new edits, and recycle footage:** Don't be afraid to think outside the box when it comes to content creation. Reuse video outtakes, behind-the-scenes shots, and additional footage (called *B-roll*) to make new edits. Recycle your content when it makes sense for your viewers.

>> **Playlists:** Reengage viewers with old videos in new playlists. Highlight videos that are still relevant on your channel page and in new playlists. You can include your playlist updates in your custom channel sections to update your fans.

>> **Plan for mobile:** Mobile viewership accounts for 70 percent of global YouTube video consumption. Make your content easy to consume on mobile devices. Easy-to-see thumbnails and text onscreen are important for your mobile audience. Shorter titles are easier to read and understand on mobile devices as well. In Chapter 11, you can see how to use YouTube Analytics to check your channel traffic sources and understand what percentage of views are from mobile.

REMEMBER

Just because viewers are watching video on their mobile phones doesn't mean that they want shorter clips. Create both long- and short-form content whenever you can, and watch your channel analytics closely to develop a strategy that is right for your audience.

Curation recycling

A *multichannel network* (MCN) aggregates many similarly themed YouTube channels and personalities and then makes them available in one place. Frequently, they help promote their managed channels' content on a single primary channel. To see what we mean, check out Tastemade (www.youtube.com/user/tastemade/channels), which is a great example of an MCN *curating* its channels' content — it groups videos from different channels into a unified theme and makes it much easier for viewers to watch them.

You don't have to own or be affiliated with a YouTube video to include it in your own channel playlist lineup. If you really like hunting down recipes, for example, you can collect and curate them from your audience. There are no limits to what you can curate, although some content will resonate better with your audience.

TIP

Create sections and playlists on your channel that include videos from other creators. As long as it makes sense for your channel to include outside content, curating content is an excellent way to expand your channel's appeal and keep it active even if you aren't creating unique content.

Adidas, for example, has a ton of channels. Company leaders made a conscious decision to link many of its subchannels to sections and playlists on its primary channel, at www.youtube.com/user/adidas. Adidas has also subscribed to its own channels, to highlight even more of its content. Doing so encourages cross-promotion of its other assets and channels.

Programming for Success

Suppose that you create a good channel and produce ten excellent videos that your audience would likely watch, share, like, and comment on. Uploading those ten videos all at one time translates into only one measly real event for your audience — meaning that you've left nine marketing opportunities unexploited.

REMEMBER

The moral of the story? Don't rush to upload all your content to YouTube at one time. You draw better audience engagement if you space out your uploads — in essence, delivering your content on a regular basis. Programming dictates how best to deliver your content to your fan base.

TIP

Keeping your subscriber feeds active is an important part of your programming strategy. It helps keep viewers coming back to your channel frequently. Not all subscribers will choose to receive every last notification from your channel. The default is personalized notifications, where users can choose to receive updates whenever your channel uploads a new video or any updates you share.

REMEMBER

Subscription feeds show only your recently uploaded videos to subscribers — no other activity gets your channel highlighted in anyone's subscription feed. Keep in mind that after you designate a video as content made for children, subscribers don't get notifications about that upload. If your entire channel is content made for children, the notification bells for your viewers are grayed-out.

Delivering content consistently

A famous philosopher once spoke rather disparagingly about foolish consistencies being the hobgoblins of little minds. That may be a good philosophy for your branding and content, but not for your YouTube channel programming. Though YouTube differs significantly from broadcast television and cable networks, your viewers will want consistency and predictability of content scheduling.

The better YouTube creators post content on their channels regularly. That's what a publishing schedule is: the day you make your videos public. Best practice is to upload your videos as private while you work on the descriptive information — also known as metadata, a topic we discuss in great detail in Chapter 9. Figure 5-5 shows some publishing statistics and more from the beauty industry. The day-and-time that you make your videos public is when your subscribers are notified.

TIP

Upload content weekly. Don't hide it. Let the audience know your publishing schedule on YouTube, and use social media to alert them when your content is live.

FIGURE 5-5:
An analysis of beauty videos on YouTube including top content types, keywords, average video length, and publishing calendar.

Courtesy of Pixability.

Being flexible and reactive

Just because you're producing regular, addictive, episodic content that amasses both subscribers and views doesn't mean that you can't generate some additional excitement around your channel. You may want to consider certain triggers:

>> **Tentpole events:** Significant cultural or industry events may play well into your channel-and-content strategy. If you sell zombie paraphernalia, Halloween is a perfect tentpole event for you. Identify regular events or happenings in your topic area. If your channel covers auto racing, consider certain events such as the Daytona 500 and Le Mans as tentpole events. Industry events may be a great way to capture footage with industry leaders and personalities.

TIP

Make sure you have important YouTube apps installed on your mobile devices, especially at tentpole events. Several apps are available on both Android and iOS that allow you to work on-the-fly. The Studio app, for example, lets you manage your channel from anywhere. Do you just want to watch some YouTube videos? The YouTube app is great for that.

» **Reactive:** You should be prepared to leverage nonplanned events for your channel, which should drive additional traffic and viewership. Nonplanned events are about news, but only if it's relevant to your channel. Marques Brownlee (www.youtube.com/user/marquesbrownlee), a major video reviewer, covers the consumer electronics business. If someone announces a new smartphone, you can be sure that Marques will have content on YouTube relatively fast.

TIP

Time-sensitive content may help you when it comes to showing up in searches or as recommended videos, because YouTube likes to put trending content recommendations in front of relevant viewers.

» **Momentum:** You can repackage your content into video trailers to help drive channel promotion. Just completed a livestream? Put together a highlight reel to keep your channel active and your subscribers' channel feeds flowing. Don't be afraid to craft outtake videos, behind-the-scenes content, and more personal pieces to let your audience know that you're excited about this new content. This strategy helps personalize and enhance the authenticity of your channel.

Going live for more engagement

You can deliver a much more interactive experience with your most passionate viewers by taking advantage of YouTube livestreaming. You can livestream any number of events, but remember that they should align with your channel's mission.

WARNING

You have to heed channel restrictions and some technical requirements for livestreaming. Ensure that your account is in good standing with no strikes and that you meet the technical requirements. Don't forget to test sufficiently before using this service.

Consider the following statements before adding livestreaming to your YouTube programming mix:

» **Promotion is important:** YouTube livestreaming is clearly different from regular YouTube video — your viewers must show up for the live event to experience it as it happens. If they don't know about it, they won't show up, and all your prep work may be for naught. Be sure to get the word out, and don't be shy about asking your YouTube subscribers to help.

>> **Adjust in-flight:** Your audience provides feedback on-the-fly as your event occurs, so be sure to watch the comments and respond accordingly.

>> **Repurpose event content:** A livestream event is a great way to capture rich and engaging content for use on your channel. Figure out how it fits into your channel after the event is over, and make several videos from the stream to create multiple pieces of follow-up content to live on.

REMEMBER

To livestream from your mobile device, you need at least 1,000 subscribers.

Before you use content derived from a live event on your channel, you will, in some circumstances, need the legal right to use the content. Don't worry: You don't need to hire a lawyer, because you can read all about it in Chapter 16, when you learn all about copyright. Stay away from copyrighted music while livestreaming, and you'll probably be fine.

Planning Never Ends

Your channel is live. You created great content. You have views. Your audience is engaged. It's all smooth sailing, right? Hopefully, yes, but as the saying goes, "You have to inspect what you expect." Look to see whether your audience

>> Watches your videos all the way to the end

>> Stays on your channel and views more content

>> Comments and provides creative suggestions

>> Shares your work on social media

>> Includes your videos in their playlists

"Well, how do I do all that?" you may ask. Fear not: You can find the answers to all these questions (and to a few others) when we help you explore YouTube Analytics in Chapter 11.

REMEMBER

The YouTube world constantly changes, with new channels, new content, new personalities, and new trends. Your channel makes you part of this world, and you're responsible for adapting to changes in order to stay relevant. Pay attention to what your viewers are telling you, and feed it into your ongoing planning process.

Chapter **6**

Acquiring the Tools of the Trade

et's face it: Making video is easier now than it has ever been, and that trend is growing. Cameras, editing software, and computers that can edit video are now relatively cheap and available, which means that, after following a few best practices, almost anyone can make a decent YouTube video with equipment they may already own. This chapter looks at a few of those best practices and helps you make a decision about price versus quality by examining the advantages of new camera and recording formats. To close out the chapter, we also take a look at the production tools you need in order to produce great video for YouTube.

Checking Out Your Camera Options

Let's get the good news out of the way right off the bat: There's a good chance that you already own a high-definition (HD) camera. Video cameras are everywhere. According to the Pew Research Center, as of June 2019, 81 percent of American adults own smartphones. Most modern smartphones have an HD camera, as do most modern laptops and all-in-one desktop computers. But just because access to cameras is easy doesn't mean that choosing the right camera is simple. Quality varies widely, and some tools and techniques can help even a basic camera shoot good video. We talk about several types of cameras specifically, but you have to take a few (mostly universal) features into account when shopping for cameras. For the most part, we talk about these three types of cameras:

» **DSLR:** DSLRs have exploded in popularity in recent years. DSLRs have traditionally been used for still photography, but they now all include an array of video features and settings. You can capture great-quality video and easily stay under a $1,000 budget for your camera gear.

» **Camera phone:** We use the term *camera phone* as a catchall term for a camera built into a mobile device. (So don't write in to tell us that your tablet isn't a phone — we're well aware of that fact.) When we say *camera phone,* you should see in your mind "a camera that is built into your iPhone or Android or Kindle or whatever." Camera phones have come pretty far, with resolutions, frame rates, and features that can rival their more dedicated counterparts. When the moment comes to capture the footage of one of your dogs sitting on your other dog and howling the tune to "Total Eclipse of the Heart," the best camera is the one in your pocket that you can start shooting with immediately.

» **Point-and-shoot:** These compact, easy-to-use little cameras aren't to be messed with. Sure, they lack the bells and whistles that come with their bigger DSLR-siblings, but they are extremely capable and affordable. Plus, they're easy to use and quite portable, making them helpful in a pinch.

Working through the (camera) basics

Before getting into a detailed discussion of the pros and cons of the different camera types out there, we want to talk a bit about a few features and elements that *all* cameras share. That way, we can get some terminology out of the way that may prove helpful when you're comparing cameras:

» **The sensor:** The heart of any digital video camera is its sensor. The larger the sensor, the better the image quality. That's because a larger sensor has larger pixels, which capture more light, resulting in higher image quality. Currently, a "big" sensor is a full-frame sensor measuring in at 36 x 24mm, the same size as a 35mm film negative.

REMEMBER

When people talk about megapixels, that's something of a red herring. A 10-megapixel camera with a larger sensor can likely capture better-looking video than a 12-megapixel camera with a smaller sensor. Though this description can be confusing and technical, the important thing to note is that a larger sensor is generally better.

>> **The lens:** The pros will tell you that it's all about the glass. The lens in a camera is a huge factor in image quality, and it's a factor that can be difficult to understand. The most important feature of any lens is its aperture capability. The *aperture* of a lens controls how much light enters the camera body and hits the sensor. Basically, along with shutter speed (how long the image is exposed) and ISO (the sensor's sensitivity to light), this is the control that makes the picture brighter or darker.

The aperture is also called the *f-stop* (or *t-stop,* on cinema lenses), and aperture ranges are denoted as f1.4–f32 or similar language.

The most popular look on YouTube now is an f-stop of 5.6. It draws the viewers' attention to the foreground, keeping it in sharp focus while leaving the background soft.

Try to use lenses that have a fixed f-stop, not a variable f-stop. Such lenses often are of a much higher quality — with a price tag that reflects that fact. A Canon 50mm 1.8 is a great starter lens and usually costs around $100.

>> **Resolution and format:** The YouTube player supports 4K video, and you really should have an HD camera to take advantage of that support. Most modern cameras are capable of shooting full 1080p HD (1920 x 1080 resolution) and higher (many are capable of 4K), and that is what you should look for. Some cameras have variable frame rates, but as long as they can shoot the standard rates — such as 24p, 30p, and 60i — you should be able to find something you like. Look for all these numbers in the specs when shopping for cameras.

The numbers in front of the letters indicate how many fields per second are shown. As for the *P,* it stands for *progressive,* where the video image is drawn progressively, line after line. In 30p, to take one example, one whole frame is typically shown every $\frac{1}{30}$ of a second. The *I* stands for *interlaced,* meaning the odd or even rows in the picture show every $\frac{1}{60}$ of a second; 60i is typically used for sports or fast-paced videos because it results in less of a flicker feel; 30p is often perceived as higher quality for less action-based footage because its resolution brings with it a clearer image; 24p is the frame rate of film — but getting that "film look" also depends on lighting and composition.

Many of the latest-and-greatest DSLRs can shoot in the format 4K (*4K* is short for 4,000-pixel resolution), which is a much higher resolution than 1080p HD. Though footage shot in 4K is beautiful, many cameras that shoot 4K tend to be expensive. The reality of shooting video for YouTube is that 4K resolution is often overkill. The site can display 4K, but the vast majority of views are on computer screens or mobile devices incapable of displaying 4K or 8K content.

>> **Codecs:** Most cameras compress the captured video to save space on whatever recording media you're using. The compression software the

camera uses is a *codec*. In the past, different codecs could result in wildly variable performance when the time came to edit. Often, footage would need to be transcoded to a different format in order for the editing suite to understand it. Thanks to improvements in editing software and hardware, transcoding is largely a thing of the past. All the major editing packages these days can handle just about any codec you care to throw at them. Just be sure to record in the highest-quality codec for your device — which generally means the least-compressed video.

» **Monitoring:** You need to be able to see your video as you shoot it. Most modern cameras have an LCD screen for monitoring video. Usually, manufacturers talk about these screens in terms of pixels. When choosing a camera, make sure you can tell whether the image is in focus from the view on the LCD. Built-in focus assist options also help when using a smaller LCD. If you cannot tell whether an image is in focus, you may need an external HD monitor, or you may want to add an electronic viewfinder (EVF) from a third party for monitoring.

» **Zoom:** To zoom is to change the focal length of the lens to make it seem as though the camera is closer to its subject. Though zoom is a somewhat familiar concept, one important fact to remember about it is the difference between optical and digital zoom:

 • *Optical zoom* is the actual telephoto effect produced by the physical change in the focal length of the lens, and it's the only zoom you would ever want to use. It allows you to zoom in on the subject with no significant degradation of picture quality.

 • *Digital zoom* is usually a very high, seemingly impressive number, but it's a feature to avoid. Digital zoom doesn't actually change the optics of the camera; it simply scales the image up, which produces a lot of static in the picture. Stated simply, it does nothing but make your footage look bad.

» **Memory cards:** It is important that you have the right memory card for your camera. Most cameras take one of two types (or both): Secure Digital High Capacity (SDHC or SD, the more common title) and Compact Flash (CF). Both are excellent. They're relatively cheap, reliable, and ubiquitous. You can buy them just about everywhere.

TIP

When it comes to memory, our recommendation is to choose your camera first — that decision often determines what kind of memory card you need to purchase. When purchasing a memory card, either SD or CF, choose one that can read and write data as quickly as your camera can. An example of write speed is 1000x: This means that the card reads and writes at approximately 150 megabytes per second.

>> **Image stabilization:** Higher-quality cameras and lenses often offer image stabilization, a feature that does just what it says — it stabilizes images. One hallmark of footage from people who are new to videography is shaky footage. Image stabilization can help with this problem, and it comes in a couple of different flavors:

TIP

- *Optical image stabilization:* This type of correction features gyroscopes and moving elements inside the lens itself. When the camera shakes, the lens detects the movement, and the lens elements roll with the punches, so to speak. The lens parts move to correct for the motion, and the sensor captures a stable image.

  Internal gyroscopes can be noisy, so be sure to use an off-camera audio recording device when using optical image stabilization. (An internal camera mic is sure to pick up the noisy gyroscope sounds.)

- *Digital image stabilization:* This correction uses various software algorithms to reduce the impact of shaky hands on your video. Unfortunately, some of the tricks it comes up with aren't that aesthetically pleasing. For example, the most common way digital image stabilization corrects an issue is by removing the edges of the frame. More often than not, you end up with a degraded image that's just not worth keeping. Yes, you may be able to correct in post-production, but your best bet is to collect the highest-quality image while recording in the field.

>> **Manual controls:** An important feature to look for in a camera is easily accessible manual controls. Though at first you'll probably want the camera to manage most aspects of image capture for you, as your skills as a videographer develop, you'll inevitably want to take control of the camera's controls. The manual controls have to be easily accessible — ideally assignable to physical buttons on the outside of the camera. These physical buttons allow you to change settings quickly, which can be important when you're trying to capture a moment. Controls that are buried deep in the camera's settings menus aren't truly useful.

Looking at DSLRs

DSLR stands for *digital single-lens reflex*, but its initials aren't the key concept to understand here. The big reason that DSLRs are massively popular these days is that they can produce great image quality for a relatively low price; the many happy DSLR owners out there probably don't know — and don't care — what the initials stand for.

As with any camera, the DSLR has both upsides and downsides. The upsides are clear:

>> **The big picture:** By a large margin, the most important advantage that the DSLR affords a filmmaker, is its large sensor. Some DSLRs even have a sensor that's roughly the same area as a traditional frame of 35mm film — these are *full-frame* sensors. Without getting too technical, the larger the sensor, the better the image quality. Also, the large sensor, when combined with the right lens settings, produces a shallow depth of field, which is desirable if you want your video to have that sheen of professionalism. This depth-of-field effect is, put simply, the phenomenon in which the subject of the video is in focus, but the background is out of focus, which makes the subject feel separate from the background. This out-of-focus background — called *bokeh* by all the arty film school types — is an important trick to have in your repertoire.

>> **The lenses:** Another useful feature of the DSLR is its interchangeable lenses. A DSLR allows the operator to choose the type of lens that's required for the shot. Some lenses are better for action shots, and some lenses are helpful in low light; macro lenses shoot subjects in extreme close-up, and zoom lenses allow you to capture distant subjects. This sort of flexibility, which is crucial in higher-end filmmaking, can greatly improve your videos' visual quality. A nice bonus is that each manufacturer has a standard lens mount that most of its cameras use. For example, if you start with an entry-level Canon camera and obtain several lenses for it, those lenses should also fit the fancier Canon camera if and when you decide to upgrade.

>> **Continuous autofocus:** More and more DSLRs are capable of automatically focusing while recording video. This feature is extremely helpful if your subject is moving frequently throughout the frame. Some are even equipped with face-tracking, which allows the camera to keep constant focus on your subject's face. This feature isn't without its problems, though: If your subject is moving too quickly or if the space is too dark, your camera may have a difficult time adjusting its focus.

>> **Manual settings:** Most serious videographers will tell you that capturing the best image requires understanding and using the camera's manual settings and setting characteristics such as ISO, aperture, and shutter speed. We don't get into explaining all the details of how to use a camera in this chapter. The important point here is that even entry-level DSLRs have robust manual controls that are usually easy to use and understand. Advanced videographers want to make changes to these settings quickly and easily, and most DSLRs have dedicated buttons on the camera body to change each of these settings quickly.

As proof that not everything is hunky-dory in DSLR-ville, check out these things that folks love to hate about DSLRs:

>> **The sound:** Though this situation is slowly changing, DSLRs have traditionally been reviled for their inability to capture sound well. Audio is extremely important to making a watchable video, so this is kind of a big deal. We will say up front that no DSLR on the market today has an acceptable built-in microphone. We believe that you should not use the built-in mic on the camera when you can avoid it — we recommend that you buy more stuff to accompany your camera. You can find a couple of ways around this problem.

- *An external microphone:* This is the simplest solution to the DSLR audio problem. Most DSLRs have a connection that allows the user to plug in a separate microphone. Because this audio problem is widespread in the DSLR market, quite a few options are available that are designed to work specifically with DSLRs. You have many choices in this space, but we find one solution to be the Rode VideoMic Pro; it has an excellent cost-to-value ratio.

- *An external audio recorder:* Even with an external microphone, many DSLRs still don't have a helpful way to monitor the audio you're recording. This is a very big deal. If you don't know what the audio sounds like as you're recording the footage, you can quickly ruin the shoot and waste a lot of time and resources. A number of digital recorders on the market are designed for this very purpose. These recorders come in a wide variety of price points, but they do confer a lot of advantages. Going down the list, they offer balanced inputs (eliminating hiss and hum noises), phantom power for professional mics (using the audio cable to power the mike instead of batteries), more control of audio levels, and compressors and limiters for keeping levels from clipping (exceeding what your device can capture). We recommend the Sennheiser MKH416.

REMEMBER

Recording the audio externally does mean that you have to synchronize the footage and the audio recording in editing, which introduces more work and an opportunity for problems to arise. Just because you're using an external audio recorder doesn't mean you should turn off the in-camera audio recording. You'll want audio from both devices captured for reference when syncing in post-production.

>> **Manual settings:** Extensive manual controls can be both a blessing and a curse. The best part about shooting manually is the amount of control you have over the quality of light in every shot. You can choose how bright you want the shot to feel based on the emotion of the scene, whereas if you use an automatic setting, you may lose some of the mood you could have created with your lighting setup. The sheer number of settings and the fine gradations of adjustment can be overwhelming to an inexperienced user. Though DSLRs generally have a full automatic mode that allows you to point-and-shoot quickly, we recommend working in the manual controls and maintaining control over the quality of each shot, even if it takes more time.

>> **Record time limitations:** One long-standing complaint about DSLRs is that almost all of them have some kind of record-time limitation. Admittedly, popular cameras like the Panasonic GH4 or the Sony a7s iii have no duration limits, but in some cases, a camera can shoot only 29 minutes of continuous video.

TIP

Before planning a long video, make sure your channel is verified. (See Chapter 2 for how to verify your channel.) Unverified channels are capped at 15-minute maximum uploads. Neither does YouTube allow uploads over 12 hours long.

>> **Manual zoom only:** The only way to zoom on most DSLRs is to manually adjust the zoom ring on the lens barrel. This can cause a number of problems while shooting video. Touching the lens will more than likely produce a shaky image — it takes a steady hand to make a smooth manual zoom. If you're planning to do lots of zoom shots, a DSLR may not be the right choice for you.

>> **The expensive aftermarket:** A lot of the issues we've described with DSLRs *do* have solutions, but you have to pay a pretty penny for them — or try to build them yourself.

If you're a YouTube video creator just starting out, a DSLR may be just the ticket for you. If you have no experience with video production or photography, be patient — the DSLR has a learning curve. The inexperienced creator often can use a simple point-and-shoot or webcam to get started. If you do have experience creating video and you're making content that requires the best image quality for your buck, a DSLR is the way to go.

Several manufacturers are in the DSLR market, including Canon, Sony, Nikon, and Panasonic. Though all these companies make good DSLRs for still images, we generally recommend the Canon DSLRs for shooting video. In our estimation, they offer good features for the price. Start by looking at some entries in the Canon line:

>> **Canon EOS 5D Mark IV:** Though this option is a bit pricey, around $3,300 for the camera without a lens, it's a truly excellent camera choice for shooting video. The 5D Mark IV has made huge improvements to its video capture capabilities, and its full 35mm sensor gives you the ability to capture beautiful video. As with any DSLR, you need to have at least an external microphone and maybe even an external audio recorder; but as far as image quality goes, the 5D is hard to beat. The latest Canon DSLR cameras have done a lot to improve the onboard audio capture quality.

>> **Canon EOS 90D:** Much more affordable than the 5D, the SL3 is widely available for around $1,200, and it delivers excellent image quality. It features a somewhat smaller sensor than the full-frame 5D, but it's still extremely capable.

THE MIGHTY, MINIATURE GoPro

Many specialty cameras are available in addition to the types we discuss in this chapter. One that is hugely popular for making YouTube videos is the GoPro, often used in extreme sports videos. It's extremely small, durable, affordable, and waterproof. It also happens to deliver excellent HD and UHD video, considering its miniature size and miniature price. The GoPro isn't only for sports, though. It can be useful for capturing risky shots for which you may not be willing to use your fancy DSLR. This can provide you with some freedom to try interesting cinematographic techniques. Check out the features of the GoPro at http://gopro.com/cameras.

Settling for smartphones

We won't argue that the camera on your phone should be your primary camera. Though they are quickly improving, smartphones aren't the best video cameras; they can be difficult to stabilize, and the footage files they produce can often be difficult to work with. Still, sometimes in the heat of an amazing moment unfolding in front of you, the best camera is the one in your pocket. It may not have much in the way of manual control, and it may not produce the most beautiful image, but in a lot of cases, being quick on the draw is more important.

The specs for smartphone cameras are a moving target. Smartphone manufacturers are constantly trying to outdo each other by packing more powerful cameras into phones. We don't make a specific recommendation, but we know that pretty much any high-end or flagship smartphone has a camera that can shoot exceptional HD video.

TIP

In many ways, choosing the camera that works for you is a matter of personal taste. If you're just getting into videography, you should watch a lot of videos. Find the stuff you like on YouTube, and then find out how those videos were made. The beauty of YouTube and social media is that the barrier is much lower for reaching out to creators. Find creators that make stuff you think looks good, and then ask them nicely how they shot it. Though you may not get a response from a creator with millions of subscribers, smaller creators are often happy to help out. Give it a try.

Stabilizing the Shot

One of the most important things you can do to give your video an air of profes-sionalism is to stabilize your shot. Nothing says amateur video like extremely shaky handheld video. We've all watched home videos that induce motion sick-ness as the camera whips around. Many tools can help you lock down your shot:

>> **Tripod:** The most useful stabilizing tool is the simple tripod. It has three legs; you attach your camera to the top, and your shot is as stable as stable can be. Tripods are readily available online, at camera stores, and at electronics stores, and they have a wide variety of price points. We recommend investing at least $50 here. It can be helpful to get one that has a built-in level to keep your shots from being crooked.

TIP

When you're shopping for a tripod, choose a model that has a fluid panning head, meaning you can turn it smoothly from side-to-side (known as panning) and that it's built to resist bumps and vibrations. At some point, you'll want to add a few camera moves to your repertoire, and you'll need that fluid head when that time comes. A basic still photography tripod may be cheaper, but you'll regret it when you need to move the camera during a shot. Tripods with nonfluid heads cannot replicate the smooth motion that a fluid head can provide.

>> **Monopod:** This is the one-legged cousin of the aforementioned stabilizer. No, this one doesn't give you a perfectly stable shot, but it's a great tool for reducing a majority of unwanted shake and movement. It's also much more portable and compact, because you're working with only one leg versus three!

>> **Dolly:** A dolly is simply a set of wheels for the camera. The simplest dollies attach to the bottom of the tripod, and — voila! — your camera is now on the move, allowing you to create interesting motion and following shots.

>> **Stabilizer:** A number of handheld stabilizer rigs are available these days, but they can be a little expensive. They also require a great deal of skill to use effectively. That means practice. If you want to get good handheld shots using a stabilizer rig, you have to practice, practice, practice to get the hang of using the thing. If you do put in the time and get good at it, you can create some cool shots with these devices.

>> **Sliders/cranes/jibs:** A wide variety of devices are also on the market to create moving shots. Sliders allow the camera to move on rails, providing a sense of smooth motion in the shot. Cranes/jibs allow the camera to move from side to side *and* up and down in space, creating a smooth sensation of flight. Many of

these are available as add-ons to tripods. Though they aren't absolutely necessary, a few nice moving shots do provide a feeling of high production value to almost any project. Sliders start at around $200; if you're ready to build something in order to save money, search YouTube for some DIY slider videos.

Seeing Your Way with Light

Another important aspect of creating a video with some level of professionalism is lighting. You don't need to win any lighting awards, but decent lighting goes a long way toward making a watchable video. You can approach lighting in a couple of ways: You can buy specialized lights, which will probably produce the best results, or work with the lights you already have. Just using lamps from around the house isn't ideal, but it can get you started, and there are ways to improve your video's look just by putting some thought into light placement.

Setting up 3-point lighting

The simplest, and generally most useful, lighting setup for shooting a person inside is *3-point lighting.* As its name implies, this lighting setup involves three lights, and it illuminates a subject in what is considered a traditionally pleasing way.

We describe the three lights that are involved (see Figure 6-1) in the following list:

>> **Key light:** The key light is the main (and brightest) light in a 3-point lighting setup. It's usually placed to the right or left of the camera, and it points directly at the subject from a 30- to 60-degree angle. The height of the light should be set, ideally, so that it points slightly downward on the subject's face, but not so high that it creates shadows on the face. It should point down from slightly above the subject's eye level.

>> **Fill light:** The fill light is a generally a softer light that should be pointed at the subject from the opposite side of the camera. The fill light shouldn't be as bright as the key light. It's there mainly to create a more even light on the subject. Using only a key light would usually result in creating dramatic shadows on the subject's face, and unless you're shooting a horror movie or a serious drama, you probably should stick with somewhat even lighting.

>> **Back light:** The back light (sometimes called a *hair light*) shines from behind the subject and casts a thin outline of light around the subject's head, almost like a halo. This is intended not to give the subject an angelic look — but rather to create depth and separate the subject from the background. The back light can be directly behind the subject, but it can also be placed at an angle to the subject. Be sure not to get the light in the shot if you're going to place it directly behind the person.

>> **Background light:** We know, it's confusing to add a fourth light to a section about 3-point lighting, but the reality is that most 3-point lighting setups also use a background light. This light does what its name implies — it lights the background. This is sometimes used to call attention to the background, but it's most often used to light the background separately from the subject. This can help create a sense of distance between the subject and the background, and can help enhance the separation between the two.

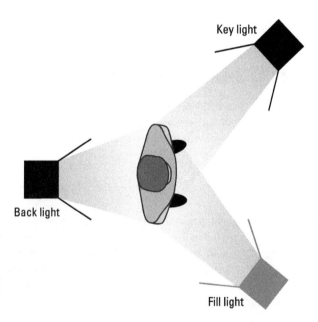

FIGURE 6-1:
Three-point lighting.

Setting up high-key lighting

Another viable, if less popular, lighting scheme is *high-key lighting.* This involves using multiple high-powered key lights and turning them all on very brightly. This setup basically floods the subject with light. Though this setup lacks subtlety, we recommend it because it's simple. It also allows for quick production, because pretty much all shots require the same lighting setup. No one will comment on your beautiful lighting if you use this setup, but it does make things easy.

WORKING WITH THE LIGHTS YOU HAVE

Your video will look best if you have actual video lights. The problem with this strategy is that video lights are expensive. Why can't you just use the lights you have in your home? The good news: You can. You can create a simple 3-point lighting system using lamps from around your house. If you use them, though, you should follow a few guidelines:

- **Move the lamps.** Using home lights is the easy way out, but it's usually not quite as easy as just turning on the lights and rolling the camera. You need to move the lights around into something resembling the 3-point setup. You also might have to move some lamps from other rooms because house lamps don't have the same brightness as video lights.

- **Standardize.** When possible, try to use the same type of bulb in all the lamps you're using to light the scene. Mixing fluorescent and incandescent lights can cause weird-looking results in your picture, so you should choose one or the other and make sure your bulbs are all the same color temperature (the color of light is measured in temperature). Each different type of light bulb emits a different temperature; mixing bulbs can make skin tones look unnatural, for example. LED lights are also a good option because you can adjust the color temperature of some.

- **Lose the shades.** Lampshades can cause uneven lighting, so you should take those things off while you're using your lamps as video lights. This also helps with maximizing the limited power of household lighting.

Capturing Sound

A crucial factor in creating an air of professionalism in a video is the sound. In this sense, audio is truly king. Capturing good audio to accompany your video is essential. Good sound is, in most cases, transparent. If you're able to record your talent's voice clearly and cleanly, the audience won't notice, which is exactly the reaction you're looking for here. If you record echo-laden bad audio, the audience will notice, and not in a good way.

Looking at microphones

The single biggest thing you can do to improve the audio in your videos is to obtain a decent external microphone. Though some camcorders do have a decent built-in microphone, you'll almost always obtain better results by using an external microphone. You can use a few different types of microphones:

>> **Lavalier:** The lavalier mic — or *lav mic,* for short — is also known as a *lapel mic.* A lav mic's primary advantage is that it's small. The microphone can be attached to the speaker's clothing, and it's small enough to be unobtrusive. Most viewers are accustomed to seeing newscasters and other video subjects with visible microphones, so it isn't generally off-putting for the audience. Lav mics are usually omnidirectional, which means that they pick up sound from every direction: You can hear not only your subject but also hear every sound in your recording environment.

Lavs work best in quiet environments or controlled studios. The nice thing about the lav mic is that it is, for the most part, a set-it-and-forget-it solution. After the lav mic is attached correctly to the talent and the levels are set, you need to check only periodically to ensure that the levels are maintained.

>> **Shotgun mic:** A shotgun microphone (or *boom mic*) is a highly directional mic that is often used to record voices in videos. The shotgun mic is designed to record audio from a single direction, and it's less sensitive to sound coming from behind the mic, to the sides, or elsewhere around the subject. This type of mic is especially useful for isolating sources in noisy situations, where background noise can overwhelm the subject's voice. Shotgun mics, which are a lot larger than lav mics, need to be pointed at the talent from just off camera, no more than a foot from the speaker's mouth. This is usually accomplished by a *boom operator,* a human who holds the shotgun mic attached to the end of a pole and points it at the talent. (One other option is to attach the boom mic to a stand with a clamp and then positon the mic over the talent.)

>> **Handheld:** You often see onscreen talent using a handheld microphone. A handheld mic can be a practical solution for capturing audio, but it's clear that the talent is using a microphone. This is completely acceptable in newsgathering situations, and it can be a great solution for videos of that type.

Capturing good audio

Capturing good audio is important, so it's worthwhile to look at a few factors that go into capturing it. You may already know that you need a decent mic, but here are a couple of other considerations:

>> **The recording environment:** Modern audio-editing software allows you to make quite a few changes and fixes to your audio after the fact, but the best way to end up with good audio is to *capture* good audio. A huge part of

capturing good audio is controlling the environment in which you shoot. If you shoot your video in a busy coffee shop, it's difficult to keep the sounds of the coffee shop out of your video. Make sure you've chosen a quiet place for your video recording, away from traffic, refrigerators, air conditioners, pets, crying children, televisions, and so on.

>> **Monitoring your audio:** Another key aspect to capturing good audio is to listen to what you're recording while you're recording it. Though a good camera will have an onscreen monitor visually representing the sound levels of audio you're capturing, it's essential to listen to the audio in headphones as you're recording. Ensuring that everything sounds good, and retaking shots marred by audio glitches or other noises, is much more time-effective than trying to fix all that stuff in post-production.

WIRED OR WIRELESS?

Most microphones for video can be purchased in either a wired or wireless version. The wired version is connected directly to the camera with a microphone cable, and the wireless version uses some kind of radio signal to send audio to the camera or audio recording device without wires. The wireless option can be quite useful, and it certainly feels futuristic, though it can be finnicky. As with any device that relies on radio transmission, interference can be a problem, especially in crowded urban areas. Wireless devices also use batteries, and dead batteries can be just one more thing to go wrong. Wireless mics are necessary for applications where the subject moves around a lot, or is far from the camera, but in other situations, it may be wise to consider wired mics. They may not have the same level of tech appeal, but they can remove a couple of layers of complexity from your shoot.

Chapter **7**

Putting It All Together to Capture Some Video

The big day has arrived, and it's time to shoot some video! You're ready to stride onto the set as the big-shot director or producer and yell "Action!" It's all a breeze from this point, right?

Not quite. A video shoot can be an incredibly high-pressure environment, with too much to do and too little time to get it done. You must perform an amazing juggling act that keeps the cast, crew, camera, script, set, props, costumes, and all those inevitable but unplanned events all moving forward to get your video "in the can" by the deadline.

The good news is that a video shoot can also be one of the most creative and rewarding experiences you'll ever have. When all the elements click and you see that outstanding performance or fantastic camera angle, you'll feel a sense of deep personal satisfaction and pride that you nailed it. When the shoot is going well, the payoff far outweighs the pain.

This chapter explains how to prepare for the shoot — from developing a checklist the night before to setting up on the big day. We lay out the steps involved in every good camera take, and we list the little details that every first-class director, like yourself, must keep an eye on in order to capture the outstanding footage you need.

Setting Up for a Shoot

Directing or producing a video is similar to running a marathon: You must be rested and ready before you can go the distance. The night before you run 26.2 miles, for example, you don't want to begin wondering whether you should have bought new running shoes. Similarly, the night before the big shoot, you want to be as prepared as possible. The more you prep, the smoother your shoot — and the better you sleep the night before.

Getting organized

TIP

Buy a production notebook to make your film or video production extremely well organized. We recommend a good old-fashioned 3-ring binder, the type often carried by schoolchildren. It's the perfect 1-stop spot to store all your shoot-related information, and it will soon become your new best friend.

Stock your production notebook with these items:

>> **Dividers:** They add instant organization and make the items you need during the shoot easy to find.

>> **Pens and pencils:** Pens are the first thing you lose, so be sure to have more than one.

>> **Blank paper:** You may need scratch paper or sheets of paper to illustrate shots.

>> **An envelope:** You need something to store the receipts from your expenditures, right?

Completing your checklists and shoot sack

After you have the basic items for your production notebook (as described in the preceding section), expand its contents by storing these items in it as well:

>> **Script:** Your copy of the dialogue to be used in the shoot should always stay with you so that you can make notes, change the dialogue, or stay abreast of scenes that have been shot.

>> **Call sheet:** This is a list of your cast and crew's arrival times on set. If you expect them to arrive at different times, keep track of their schedules.

- **Cast and crew contact sheet:** This list of contact information (such as email addresses and phone numbers) is the easiest way to ensure that participants can contact each other.

- **Schedule:** A schedule is useful when a number of cast or crew members are arriving on the same day and you want to better schedule the shoot, by determining which scenes to shoot and when, and when to let everyone take a break.

- **Storyboard:** This series of panels shows the individual shots within a scene. Keep the storyboard handy to show your crew the shots you want.

- **Shot list:** Similar to the storyboard, this lists all the shots you plan to capture during your shoot and any relevant details, including the type of shot or specific lens you intend to use.

- **Prop and costume list:** Double-check this list after the shooting day ends to ensure that all items are accounted for and returned to the appropriate person or place.

- **Script breakdown:** List cast members, props, costumes, and types of shots for every individual scene, and specify whether the scene is an interior or an exterior.

- **Cast breakdown:** This reverse version of the script breakdown lists actors and the scenes in which they appear. Creating this list helps you schedule the shooting order of scenes.

Though the script breakdown and cast breakdown may be unnecessary for a simple shoot, if you have multiple scenes and actors, consider the breakdowns as insurance against losing important elements of the shoot. (We've seen actors released from a shoot for the day only to find that they were still needed for another scene later the same day.)

The night before your shoot, complete these tasks:

- **Charge all batteries.** Charge up all related devices, such as your camera, lights, laptop, and cellphone.

- **Wipe any reusable media.** If your camera records video to SD or CF cards, format them (otherwise known as erasing them) and clear some space.

- **Double-check your equipment.** Quickly test your cameras, lenses, lights, and audio equipment. Ensure that every item works and that you know the exact location of all your equipment and accessories.

- **Pack props and costumes.** Don't wait until the morning of the shoot to pack everything!

>> **Make copies of the script.** While you're at it, take the extra step of labeling every copy individually for your cast and crew. Make sure you have extra copies of any important documents (schedules, contact sheets, and so on).

>> **Stock up on petty cash.** Withdraw cash from a nearby ATM so that you can purchase food, water, extra batteries, coffee, and any other necessities you may need for the shoot. This is where that receipt envelope comes in handy.

>> **Confirm call times.** Call, text, or email all participants to ensure that they know when and where to show up. Make sure you get a response guaranteeing their confirmation.

>> **Check the weather forecast.** Make sure that the atmospheric conditions won't affect you adversely. Pay attention to rain forecasts and storm warnings, and prepare for all conditions.

While you're charging batteries and anxiously awaiting the last of the cast to confirm their call times, turn your attention to another vital element of the shoot: the *shoot sack.* Simply fill a gym bag, large backpack, or (our favorite) rolling suitcase with the following essential items, and then you can take this film-production survival kit with you anywhere:

>> **Batteries and chargers:** Store any batteries that aren't already installed in your equipment, and add any extra AA or AAA batteries you may need.

>> **Extension cords:** Bring along at least two long heavy-duty cords.

>> **Power strips:** Bring two of these also.

>> **Gaffer and spike tape:** These heavy-duty tapes have millions of uses, from taping down equipment to labeling spent memory cards.

>> **Lights and mic:** As long as these items fit into your shoot sack, add them.

>> **Screwdriver and knife:** You never know when you'll need to tighten the bolt on a tripod plate or cut some rope on set.

>> **Work gloves:** The lights may become too hot to touch after being on for a while.

>> **Tripod and monopod:** Even if these items don't fit in the bag, pack them as part of your preparation ritual. (A monopod is a 1-legged tripod, typically used for shots requiring a more dynamic feel or a quick-paced live event or production.)

>> **Laptop (and optional external hard drive):** These devices are likely to have separate cases, but you should make them part of your preparation ritual, too. You may need them for transferring footage among cards on the set. Bring a card reader as well, if your laptop lacks a built-in one.

Take a moment to look over everything you've packed. You've created a production notebook, double-checked equipment, charged batteries, confirmed schedules and locations with your cast and crew, and made for yourself the world's best shoot sack. You're ready to go, so take a deep breath and get a good night's sleep.

Arriving on set

TIP

Whatever call time you've given your cast, plan for your crew to be on-site at least one hour earlier. Even if the hour is more time than you need to set up, having enough time to prepare without feeling pressured starts the shooting day on the right note. Besides, you'll quickly fill that hour.

Every shoot requires these three distinct spaces:

>> **Shooting area:** This area should be ready for use when you arrive on the set so that you can begin setting up camera angles and lighting. Be polite but firm about claiming your space, and remove any items that don't belong in the scene.

>> **Equipment area:** Designate a quiet corner in which to store equipment, props, and costumes and to serve as a charging station for batteries.

>> **Green room:** Give your cast and crew (and perhaps certain equipment) a place to relax — and stay out of the way — between takes. In an office space, for example, a conference room is the perfect spot, but you may have to take whatever you can get. The green room is also a good spot for setting up an alcove to serve coffee, water, and snacks to your cast and crew.

After you determine the boundaries of your space, you can set up the following equipment in it:

>> **Charging station:** Plug in a power strip, and set up your camera's battery charger (and the chargers for light batteries, if you're using them).

>> **Data station:** Plug in your laptop and external hard drive so that you can periodically "dump" footage.

>> **Camera, tripod, lights:** After you unpack these items, you can start setting up the first shot. Check the natural ambient light in the room by looking at the camera's viewfinder to see what adjustments you need to make. Experiment to find the camera angles that work best.

Planning a realistic shooting schedule

When you watch a short scene in a video, you may believe that creating the scene was a simple task. And if the video is no good, it probably was a simple task. Virtually anyone can flip a switch on a camera and ask an actor to speak. Finding a unique and memorable way to shoot a scene takes time to prepare and pull off — even for simple scenes — and this amount of time has to be figured into your shooting schedule.

Two forces are at work in every film and video shoot: the creative need to make the production special, and the technical need to complete the production as quickly and inexpensively as possible and still look good. These needs are equally important. If you can't complete the shoot on schedule, you'll have nothing to show, but if you rush to complete the video with no regard for creativity, what's the point in even making it?

We would love to boil down the standard schedule to the simple mathematical formula "x number of shots divided by y setup time equals z," but scheduling simply doesn't work that way. (Besides, math is not our forté.) To come up with a realistic estimate of the time you need, consider these factors:

>> The number of shots your production needs

>> The length of each shot

>> The amount of time you need to realistically set up, shoot several takes, and break down the set

Shooting usually takes longer (often, *much* longer) than most people anticipate. The technical setup can be complex, and actors may need a few takes to nail their performances. If you're working with non-actors, you may want to add an extra 30 to 60 minutes to their scenes, just in case it takes longer to get the performance you need.

These guidelines can help streamline the shoot:

>> **Spend no more than 5 minutes setting up a shot.** A 5-minute limit keeps the setup process lean and mean. You should have enough time to adjust the lights and position the camera. Obviously, some shots require more time than others, but when you're working on a deadline, time magically passes faster than normal.

>> **Shoot scenes out of order.** Few film productions shoot scenes in the exact order they'll appear in the finished product. Usually, the shooting schedule is created by determining which resources (such as locations, actors, props, or

lighting) can be reused in other scenes. Those scenes are then filmed consecutively.

By shooting out of order, you can schedule certain actors' scenes one after the other and then release the actors when they finish, leaving fewer people to manage as the day progresses.

» **Shoot "big" scenes first.** If you're shooting a crowd scene or another type of complicated shot, get it out of the way early in the day. Your cast and crew will be more energized, and you'll have that worry out of the way as the day wears on and pressure grows to wrap up the shoot.

» **Experiment.** Once, anyway. If you want (or a cast member wants) to try a radical idea, just to see whether it works, do it. But shoot the scene as specified in the script, too. Don't get *too* creative at the expense of the clock.

» **Cut freely.** If you find that your schedule is overstuffed, pull out the script, storyboard, and shot list and cut some of the shots. Not scenes, mind you, just shots. We generally encourage you to shoot scenes with multiple shots (called *coverage,* which we address later in this chapter, in the section "Determining the best shot"). If time is running out, be prepared to change the shot list.

REMEMBER

» **The fewer people who are on the set, the faster you can shoot.** The more people who watch a scene, the more your shoot can turn into a party rather than a production. When something strange or funny happens on the set (and suddenly everyone is laughing or chatting and no longer working), you have to play the role of benign dictator. Firmly, but with a friendly smile, ask all bystanders to clear out — pronto. When you have a camera, you wield power!

Practicing good habits before a shot

Your camera is set up, the actors are in place, and all eyes are on you. You're ready for the first take of the day. What do you say and when do you say it? You can actually set up a smooth, productive workflow by using a series of commands to move through each shot within a scene.

Draw from this handy list of words and phrases to communicate with your cast and crew — and to help them to communicate with you:

» **"Quiet on the set."** When you let everyone know that you're about to "roll camera," the only audible sound should come from whatever is happening in front of the camera. Side conversations, coughing, and mobile phones can all spoil a take, and you should have zero tolerance for them.

» **"Roll camera."** When your actors and crew are set, cue the cameraperson to start shooting.

- » **"Camera rolling."** The camera person should reply to "Roll camera" with this phrase after shooting begins. If you're doing the shooting, just say "Camera rolling."

- » **"Sound rolling."** Someone who is listening to sound separately on headphones says this phrase to indicate that the audio sounds good.

- » **"Action."** Finally! This famous cue tells actors to start the scene and lets everyone else know to remain quiet. Wait a few seconds after the camera and sound are rolling to say it.

- » **"Hold."** If a sudden event (such as a passing police siren) interrupts a shot, call "Hold" to let everyone know to stop what they're doing until the interruption ends. Then call "Action" again.

- » **"Cut."** After a scene ends, wait a few seconds to say this famous cue so that the crew continues shooting video and recording sound until the moment you say it.

After a few tries, your cast and crew will have the order and rhythm of these cues down pat, and your set will quickly sound professional (as long as an actor doesn't announce, "I'll be in my trailer").

TECHNICAL STUFF

Every take of a shot should have *handles* on it — a waiting period of a few seconds before you say "Action" and after you say "Cut." This way, an editor (who may be you) who works on the scene in postproduction has a clearly defined segment of video to work with. "Action" and "Cut" are also cues for them.

WARNING

Don't wait to press the Record button immediately after calling "Action" or "Cut" (a mistake typically made by novice filmmakers). This bad habit leaves the editor with a scene that is potentially missing its first and last seconds — a huge amount of editing time. (Applying a cool transition effect during the editing process — a dissolve or a fade-in, for example — is then impossible.) Also, actors shouldn't break character until you say "Cut." As they finish their lines, they should remain in place until you stop shooting.

Maintaining continuity

Continuity is the purely technical requirement of maintaining a consistent look and action in every shot, including the background and lighting of the set and the actors' costumes, hair, and (most frequently) movement. A mobile phone that's held in a character's right hand in one shot and shifts to the left hand in the next shot jars the audience out of the moment.

But don't stress; if continuity mistakes happen to you, you're in good company. Many successful Hollywood movies are full of continuity mistakes. Throughout *The Wizard of Oz*, for example, the length of Judy Garland's hair and dress changes several times. If that type of huge production can slip up, your video can, too.

REMEMBER

A simple way to keep an eye on actors' positions between shots is to call "Hold!" (refer to the list in the earlier section "Practicing good habits before a shot") and quickly set up for the next shot. You can also show actors an earlier take so that they can position themselves to match their own movements. If your characters are drinking from a glass, for example, make the liquid level consistent from shot to shot (to prevent the audience from wondering how the glass was seemingly refilled). If you're shooting over several days, take a photo of your actors in full costume so that they can match their looks for the next day.

Continuity has an additional meaning for actors. It refers to their characters' mental and emotional states from scene to scene. When you're shooting scenes out of order, matching these states from the previous scene can be challenging. As a director, it's your job to keep actors on track from scene to scene by reminding them of their previous circumstances, such as where they're coming from, what has just taken place, and where they're headed. You can even draw a timeline for reference. Actors should see the big-picture view of their entire performances *and* their scene-to-scene progress.

Shooting a Great-Looking Video

To say that camerawork is a technical process, and not a creative one, is a mistake. Film and video are visual media, and the camera resembles a paintbrush. A huge dose of creativity determines where to place the camera. If you look at the camerawork in the films of Alfred Hitchcock, Steven Spielberg, or Peter Jackson, for example, you see one stunning memorable image after another. This section tells you how to use your camera effectively, from choosing angles and specifying movement to framing scenes and capturing extraordinary imagery.

To illustrate the techniques we describe in this section, we use the following familiar scenario to show how to use the camera and the *frame* (the rectangular image you see on a movie, TV, or computer screen) to better tell a story: When a young child plays ball in the house and his mother warns him to move outside, he ignores her request and instead breaks an expensive vase. Oops! The child's unhappy mother confronts him.

Composing and dividing the screen

Composition is the process of creating a picture that helps to effectively tell a story within the camera frame for each shot. Just as a photo needs composition to possess more visual power, a moving picture needs composition to help tell the story more powerfully.

TECHNICAL STUFF

The *rule of thirds* (a visual arts composition guideline) divides a rectangular picture, such as a camera frame, into nine smaller rectangles of equal size — three across and three down. Though this concept originated in photography and painting, it has its place in film and video production.

Using the rule of thirds to position the subject one-third of the way from the edge of the frame (rather than in the center of the frame) makes the picture stronger and more interesting visually.

TIP

Because the rule of thirds also applies to framing the background of an image, you can create beautiful, symmetrical images in outdoor shoots by positioning the ground across the lower third of the frame and positioning buildings and trees and the sky in the upper two-thirds of the frame.

The rule of thirds is an artistic concept related to the way the human brain interprets imagery. It simply makes images "look better."

In the example, you can create tension in the shot (again, because of the way the brain processes images) by moving the camera so that the child is one-third of the way from the edge of the frame. When the child tosses the ball, you see the nearby empty living room, full of breakable objects, and you start to anticipate the ball flying from his hands and into Aunt Bertha's expensive Ming vase.

TIP

If you have a photo camera, try this experiment for capturing a better, stronger image. Frame the subject in the center of the shot, and take a picture. Then move the camera to frame the subject approximately one-third of the way from the edge of the shot, and compare the photos.

Determining the best shot

Your selection of camera angles, or *shots*, is limited, technically, only by your imagination, though you should master the basic principles before trying any fancy tricks. This section explains the building-block shots you see in most film and TV productions, and most scenes are built using a combination of these shots. In Hollywood, *coverage* is the practice of shooting a scene from various angles.

When you start shooting video, take these types of shots first:

>> **Master:** The master shot is the foundation of your coverage. It shows everything — every important element of your scene. Place the camera far enough away to capture all the action, and shoot the entire scene from beginning to end. You can always cut back to the master shot to remind the audience where the characters are located in relation to each other.

>> **Medium:** The medium shot moves in to show characters (or a single character) in an area from roughly just above their waists to a little over their heads. The medium shot is commonly used because it shows facial detail but still conveys a sense of the bigger picture.

>> **Close-up:** In the close-up shot, the camera moves in tightly on a subject's face or on an object, such as the bouncing ball in this section's running example. The close-up is a powerful tool to show lots of facial detail and to build tension and emotion in a scene.

>> **Extreme close-up:** In this type of shot, the camera (obviously) moves in even more tightly on a subject to show lots of detail. A shot of a character's eyes or of fingers drumming on a table or of a doorknob turning slowly shows an intimate level of detail to drive home a particular moment. Though an extreme close-up is rarely followed by a master shot (it's too much of a leap for viewers to make from small to large), you can follow it with a close-up or a medium shot.

These steps show one way to break down the scene in the bouncing-ball example:

1. The master shot shows a child tossing a ball in the living room. The shot is framed to show the child positioned one-third of the way from the edge of the frame. You can hear his mother say, "Don't play ball in the house!"

2. Cut to a medium shot of the child watching the ball move up and down. He smirks and says, "No problem, Mom."

3. In the master shot, the child throws the ball high into the air. Uh-oh.

4. A close-up shot of the child shows him watching the ball begin to descend.

5. Cut to a close-up of the child's hand reaching for the ball — and missing it.

6. An extreme close-up shot shows his eyes widening as you hear a vase shatter.

7. Cut back to a medium shot of the child looking at the floor, horrified.

8. A close-up shot of the broken vase shows the ball lying in the middle of the glass shards.

9. Cut to a close-up of the child as he gulps, and his mother scolds him.

10. Return to the master shot, as the child turns to face his mother and blurts, "It wasn't my fault!" while she crosses her arms angrily.

These steps break down a scene, moment by moment, into shots that underscore the emotion of every beat of the scene. We won't win an award for this scene, but we can probably make an audience feel tension (and make them laugh at the child's excuse). That's how you "paint" a scene with your camera and the camera frame.

WARNING

In any scene you shoot, keep your shots smooth and steady. In the age of point-and-shoot cameras, people have a tendency to start the camera rolling and then point it at various characters in a scene, in one long take. They often attempt this all-over-the-map approach with a shaky hand so that the scene ends up looking like an earthquake just occurred. Unless you're shooting *The Great Quake of the 21st Century*, we recommend that you simply place the camera on a tripod. If your scene involves a lot of camera movement, shoot it with a smooth, steady hand.

Moving and grooving the camera

Anyone can put a camera on a tripod, turn it on, and shoot the scene before them in a single shot. But this style amounts to simply recording a scene, which is boring, rather than true directing, which uses the different shot choices that are available to tell a story, controls what an audience is seeing from moment to moment, and moves the camera to achieve great-looking images.

You can choose from a few basic camera moves to spice up your storytelling:

>> **Pan:** Simply move the camera from side to side, along the horizon. If the child in the bouncing-ball example enters a room, spots the ball on a table, and walks to it, you can follow his movement by panning from the doorway to the table.

>> **Tilt:** Move the camera laterally, along a vertical plane. In the example, you would tilt the camera from the child's hand grabbing the ball and then lifting it to his chest as he looks at it mischievously.

>> **Track:** In this tricky-but-fun shot, you simply follow the subject throughout the scene. You can track the child from an outdoor starting point, keep him at a distance, and then follow him right up to the ball. The tracking shot, which is used in lots of Hollywood films, can be an effective way to show off. (A famous 3-minute tracking shot from Martin Scorsese's *Goodfellas* follows Ray Liotta's character through the hallways and kitchen of a nightclub.)

You can pan and tilt by either using a handheld camera or placing it on a tripod or monopod. Tracking shots are typically accomplished with the use of a steadicam or dolly. To add a slick touch to your video, work out a brief tracking shot of one character.

Matching your eyelines

TECHNICAL STUFF

An *eyeline* is the invisible line leading from the eyes of a character on camera to a person or an object that the character is looking at off-camera. When you cut to the next shot showing the off-camera person or object, it must be placed within the frame where the brain would expect it to be. If a character is looking upward, for example, you should then cut to the object that the viewer sees, placed above the camera. If the character's eyeline and the object's position don't match (if they look down at an object that you then see hanging over their heads, for example), the audience becomes disoriented and disconnects from the scene. The eyeline makes a subtle but crucial difference when cutting between two people who are speaking to each other within a scene.

In this section, we explain how to add two medium shots to the bouncing-ball example. One shows the mother furrowing her brow at her child, and the other shows the child lowering his head after being scolded. For these two shots, you can shoot the actors in this scene separately or even on different days because they don't appear in the frame together in this particular moment. Above all else, you have to match the eyelines of the mother and her child.

Suppose that the child looks up at his mother towering over him and then you cut to a shot of her face. Rather than look down at him, as your brain expects, she instead looks directly across the shot at an object at the height of her eyes. Your brain would automatically connect the two shots to make you wonder what she's looking at (another person in the room, for example). Because she's the taller of the two, her eyes should aim downward at him, at a spot that's as close to the same spot in the frame where his eyes were looking up in the previous shot.

A character who looks offscreen at another character should be looking at the spot where the other character would stand. If you *reverse* the shot (to show the other character), the second character's eyes should be focused on the spot where the first character is positioned. Any well-made TV show or film has examples of shooting proper eyelines. In one with incorrect eyelines, you cannot determine where characters are oriented in a scene.

TIP

To ensure matching eyelines, position an offscreen actor behind the camera so that the on-screen actor can look at that person and deliver her lines. Encourage actors to stand immediately off-camera, even when they aren't part of a shot, to help make eyelines match. It also helps a cast member with her performance to speak directly to her scene partner, even if the partner is standing off camera.

Following the 180-degree rule

The 180-degree rule is a critical guideline for how scenes are shot in a film or video. When you watch a movie in which two characters are speaking and the cut moves from one to the other, you're likely seeing the *180-degree rule* in action: It establishes the spatial relationship between characters or objects within a scene — specifically, when the scene cuts between shots of them. Most viewers are unaware of the 180-degree rule when it's followed; but when it isn't, viewers can become disoriented or confused about where characters are standing or sitting in relation to each other.

To use the 180-degree rule to construct a scene, imagine a straight line running down the middle of the characters, as shown in Figure 7-1. To avoid disorienting the audience, choose *one side* of the 180-degree line on which to shoot all your shots, and don't cross the line. Understanding this concept can be confusing, so we walk you through an example.

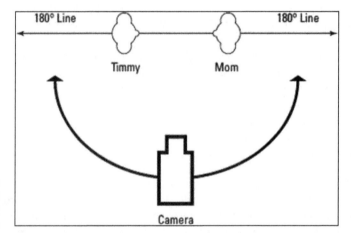

FIGURE 7-1:
The imaginary line of the 180-degree rule.

Rather than show each actor individually, such as in the bouncing-ball example, you can use the popular Hollywood technique known as the *over-the-shoulder* shot. For a shot of the child in the example looking up at his mother, you place the camera over her left shoulder and aim it at the child so that part of her left shoulder and hair frame the shot of his face.

Cut back to the mother looking crossly at her child. If you place the camera over his *right* shoulder, pointing up at the mother, who is towering over him, his right shoulder and hair frame the shot of his mother looking cross. Then you cut back to the first shot over her *left* shoulder, of the child looking remorseful.

In this example, you stay on one side of the line, over the mother's left shoulder and over the child's right shoulder. If we had moved from her left to his left, we would have crossed the line and confused the audience, because they wouldn't know where the characters were standing in relation to each other.

In another example, you see a shot of a train flying down the tracks, moving from right to left in the frame. Cut to a person waiting for the train, and then cut back to the same train, except that now you've crossed the tracks and you're shooting from an angle on the other side. The train is now moving from left to right! Your brain believes that it's another train, heading directly for the first train, and suddenly you've made a disaster film!

The 180-degree rule has one exception: If the camera is moving, you're allowed to cross the imaginary line if the shot itself moves across it. Then the audience will understand why you switch sides in the next shot.

Shooting an interview

Shooting an interview is a fairly easy task. In the world of marketing videos, you'll likely shoot a lot of sit-down interviews.

Follow these steps to shoot a simple but professional-looking interview:

1. **Set up two chairs.**

   One is for the subject and one is for the interviewer (who may be you). The subject should be seated.

2. **Set up your camera on a tripod.**

   Place the tripod to the side of your chair, facing your subject.

3. **Frame the subject.**

   Use a medium shot, moving upward from mid-torso or slightly closer.

4. **Light and mic your subject.**

   For more on this topic, see Chapter 6.

5. **Have your subject look at you, not at the camera.**

   Looking into a camera lens tends to make a person self-conscious. You can conduct an excellent interview that has a conversational flow by having the subject speak to you. The camera serves to record the conversation you're having. (The most common camera style on YouTube is to have the subject speak directly into the camera; we recommend this style only if the subject can appear natural.)

TIP

A person who is verbose the first time he answers an interview question may want to answer a question a second time, after having the opportunity to find the best wording for his answer. To avoid being heard asking the interview questions, you can edit yourself out, by having the subject rephrase your question within the answer, as in this example:

You:

> "How long have you been the president of Smith Industries?"

The subject:

> "I have been president of Smith Industries for 40 years."

Encourage your subject to answer as simply as possible, always including the crux of the question within the answer, and you'll have a professional-looking, easy-to-edit interview that you can replicate with different subjects.

Shooting extra footage and B-roll

B-roll footage is supplementary footage, traditionally used to accompany a documentary or TV news story. For example, in an interview with the president of Smith Industries, during an especially dry segment, you can *cut away* to show the Smith Industries factory floor or show workers picketing the president's office.

B-roll can be shot quickly and is a useful way to enhance your video's main storyline. The more footage you shoot (within reason), the more shots you'll find that can blend well with the main part of your video. Establishing shots of buildings or areas is a helpful way to indicate where scenes take place. *Intercutting* (cutting back and forth) between B-roll and your main storyline can heighten the drama or strengthen the message of your video.

Capturing the perfect take — several times

Whether you're shooting a scripted scene or an interview, you probably won't get the perfect take the first time every time. Someone may flub a line or slam a door offscreen, a dog may begin barking, or a sudden rainstorm may interrupt a romantic picnic scene. Or, the "magic" just isn't happening right away, and your actors need a few takes to warm up and discover the best way to play the scene. In any case, if you have to do it again, shrug your shoulders, yell "Cut," and prepare everyone for another take.

Shooting multiple takes can be demanding because actors have to repeatedly speak the same lines and hit the same marks. However many takes you shoot of a scene, the acting always has to seem fresh. One way to achieve this goal is to let the actors vary their line readings slightly on every take. You can always revert to an earlier take if you don't like the revised version.

TIP

After you capture an excellent take, shoot a *safety* take immediately afterward. This extra version ensures that your editor has two good takes to work with, just in case something goes wrong with the footage during the postproduction process.

Working with Voice

When you shoot video, it's easy to get caught up in the visual aspect of each shot. However, you must also keep audio quality in mind at all times. See Chapter 6 for details about audio, but aside from mics and audio capturing devices, you have another tool in your audio arsenal that is provided for free by your actors: their voices. Whether you're dealing with seasoned or first-time actors, you can get the most from the mouths of your talent in a few ways, as described in the following sections.

Practicing diction and dialects

William Shakespeare, no slouch himself in producing one or two quality scripts, had some good advice 500 years ago for video actors: to speak their lines "trippingly on the tongue." In other words, he suggested good *diction*, or the proper enunciation of the words in a script. Your actors need to practice diction in order to get your message across. Even unscripted interviewees can stand to use good diction.

TECHNICAL
STUFF

Diction is all about several distinct vocal areas:

>> **Volume:** Actors should speak loudly enough for the mic while still sounding believable. (Our experience tells us that nearly every actor can stand to be a bit louder.)

>> **Clarity:** Determine whether actors are speaking unclearly, such as pronouncing words incorrectly or dropping sounds off the ends of their words. Most of us do this when we're speaking casually. Make sure that actors practice pronouncing the trickier words in your script. No one should sound like Mary Poppins, but every word should be clearly understood.

>> **Pace:** Make sure that your actors aren't speaking too quickly or too slowly. Many people tend to rush through sentences when they're excited or stressed — which is exactly how actors will feel with the camera on them. Take time to rehearse the scene, and find an appropriate speaking pace.

>> **Vocal energy:** Not to be confused with volume, vocal energy refers to the quality of an actor's voice, such as whether he's speaking with passion and animation or in a tired monotone. Because the camera is fairly close, actors don't have to speak the way they would to a crowded auditorium, though their voices should possess energy and make the dialogue sound authentic and believable.

Everyone speaks in a *dialect,* or regional accent. There's no universal, unaccented way to speak. A dialect can add huge amounts of believability and variety to a performance and truly drive home the content of your video. A dialect that's too strong, however, especially if an actor seems to be struggling with the lines in a script, can also detract the audience from engaging in your video. The key is to ensure that the words in your script are striking the audience as clearly and effectively as you need.

The power of the pause

People who speak to large groups or, worse, in front of a camera tend to barrel through their lines in an effort to reach the end of the script as soon as possible and stop speaking. Because they simply forget to *pause,* they're missing out on the most powerful audio tool available.

A well-placed pause carries a lot of weight. For a brief moment, suspense hangs in the air. The words you've just heard settle for a second, and then you hear more. A pause used by actors can add drama, dimension, and structure to the words they're saying.

Work with actors to find two or three spots to pause the dialogue. Don't overdo it, and don't make a pause last forever. Make sure that the pause is real, however. You want the speaker to be able to take a breath and feel in control of her words, not the other way around.

Managing crowd audio

Keep this Hollywood secret between you and us (and everyone else reading this book). Watch a crowd scene in a movie or TV show — a restaurant or bar scene is perfect. Notice how you hear the main characters speaking clearly while the crowd around them is quiet. How do the creators *do* that? Yes, mics are being used, but the bigger trick is that the *crowd is completely silent during filming.* All their talking is pantomimed, and the sounds are later added by editing.

TIP

Hollywood uses stock crowd sounds, which is why (if you're paying attention to these sort of things) you sometimes hear the same voices on different TV shows. When you're shooting a crowd scene, stock crowd sounds are available for different group sizes, and you can find the one that best suits your scene.

You can also direct the crowd to simply speak more quietly than normal. Depending on how many people you're working with, this suggestion can be an easy solution or a tough one to manage. The key is to get a great sound level from your main actors while retaining a believable amount of background noise. Remind crowd members that they're adding to the authenticity of a scene and offer to throw a party after the shoot is complete.

IN THIS CHAPTER

» **Choosing editing software**

» **Getting started**

» **Editing and polishing your video**

» **Adding music and sound effects**

» **Exporting the final version of the video**

Chapter **8**

Fixing It in Post: The Edit

E ven the simplest modern editing tools are powerful applications. If you want to edit your own videos, expect to spend some time learning how to use your tool of choice. If you've ever worked with Word or PowerPoint, for example (from the Microsoft Office suite), you may recall that you spent some time learning how to use that program. Let's be honest: Most people discover new features and new ways of doing things in these programs all the time.

To edit a video, you need to get familiar with the software and some foundational editing techniques. In this chapter, we describe both of these and how to turn your footage into a polished video.

Picking the Right Software Package

Editing programs are sophisticated tools for content creation with a lot of powerful features. The best way to approach them is to first read about the basics, or you may take a class to get started. Then just dive in and complete a project. Most people become comfortable using their chosen editing tool during the first few days.

The first item to consider when choosing editing software is your existing operating system on your computer. In other words, if you use Windows, you need editing software for Windows; if you use a Mac, you need editing software for the Mac.

Mac tools

In the film and video industries, the Mac is widely considered to be the go-to operating system, despite the selection of available editing tools being somewhat smaller than on the PC. This isn't necessarily bad news, because of the high quality of Mac-based programs:

>> **Apple** itself provides two industry-leading editing applications:

- *iMovie:* Entry level

- *Final Cut Pro:* Professional level

>> **Adobe,** the market leader in creative software, offers a full line of tools for the Mac.

iMovie

If you have a Mac, you already have iMovie. This powerful little editing application comes preinstalled on every new Mac. We highly recommend this for your YouTube video editing because it's easy to use.

TIP

Upgrade to the latest version of iMovie, if you can. It's free to download and update straight from Apple's website: www.apple.com/imovie.

iMovie covers virtually everything you need for normal video editing, and it comes supplied with helpful templates for impressive titles and neat visual effects.

TIP

A good companion product for iMovie is Garage Band, which comes preinstalled on Macs as well. You can finish up your visual edits in iMovie and export directly into Garage Band. It lets you put together soundtracks for your videos and provides some useful background music tracks that you can use immediately. Be sure to check on the copyright for any existing or canned background music tracks you pull from Garage Band. Your video monetization may be affected when using tracks with existing copyrights.

Final Cut Pro

Final Cut Pro is the professional-grade editing application from Apple that covers most capabilities an editor needs. It's used by many professionals, including such legendary editors as Walter Murch *(The Godfather, Apocalypse Now)*.

Final Cut Pro is a major upgrade from iMovie. Its user interface is quite similar to iMovie, and old iMovie projects can be imported directly into Final Cut Pro. It offers much more flexibility, such as unlimited video and audio tracks, many more visual effects, a feature-rich footage management system, and sophisti-cated audio editing.

If you're going with Apple editing programs, start with iMovie (free for newer Mac users and $14.99 for older computers) and then upgrade to Final Cut Pro X when you run into limitations (a one time purchase of $299).

Adobe Premiere

Apple's primary competitor on the Mac platform is Adobe and its Premiere editing programs — note the plural form here. You have a choice between two Premiere products:

>> **Premiere Elements:** The entry-level Adobe editing program Premiere Elements is designed for consumers as well as business users.

The advantages of using Premiere Elements over the free Apple iMovie program are that it

- Supports multiple video and audio tracks

  (The additional power is useful if you edit more complex projects, such as footage shot with multiple cameras simultaneously.)

- Offers a more sophisticated way to organize large collections of raw footage

- Provides more flexibility in dealing with photos and other images

>> **Premiere Pro:** Premiere Pro, the Adobe program for professional video editors, offers all the same professional features of Final Cut Pro. Some editors like it better because

- Its user interface is optimized for a professional editor's typical workflow.

- It has broader support for the file formats that professional and consumer-level cameras produce. It allows you to work with files natively — no transcoding needed.

- It integrates the workflow as a one-stop — you can take a project entirely by way of the Adobe Creative Suite, including color correction, motion graphics, and audio finishing.

Windows tools

Dozens of editing programs of all sophistication levels are available on the Windows PC platform. The following five sections describe a few of the most popular.

Microsoft Photos

Similar to iMovie on the Mac, the free editing tool Microsoft Photos covers very basic video editing needs. It lets you quickly import footage and pictures, arrange and trim clips, add music, and apply basic visual effects and titles. If your Windows PC doesn't have Microsoft Photos installed, you can download it for free at

```
www.microsoft.com/en-us/p/microsoft-photos/9wzdncrfjbh4?
    activetab=pivot:overviewtab
```

TIP

Microsoft Photos is a helpful way to get your feet wet with video editing. Most people working on advanced video projects quickly run into its limitations, such as having only one background audio track, one video track, and limited visual effects. Furthermore, its particular way of handling the start and stop points of clips isn't ideal for precision editing.

Adobe Premiere

Like with Macs, both Premiere Elements and Premiere Pro are available for Windows users. These versions are largely identical to their Mac counterparts and are highly respected tools for professionals.

REMEMBER

Premiere can work with multiple video and audio tracks, which allows for the easy arrangement of footage and complex narrative structures. That's an important advantage over the free Microsoft Photos.

Vegas

The entry-level Vegas Movie Studio and the more advanced Vegas Pro are interesting alternatives to Adobe products. They offer features that are comparable to some of the best editing software on the market. If you're looking for the most bang for your buck, Vegas Movie Studio is affordably priced, and Vegas Pro will set you back considerably more.

Pinnacle Studio

This product is significantly more sophisticated than Premiere Elements. It boasts unlimited video and audio tracks, animated titles, broad format support, sophisticated audio editing, and a ton of professional-level special effects.

Pinnacle Studio is priced reasonably and is a good choice for people who want to do frequent, sophisticated editing and are willing to endure a bit of a learning curve.

CyberLink PowerDirector

Another tool competing with Premiere Elements is CyberLink PowerDirector, priced similarly to Premiere Elements. The PowerDirector feature set is comparable to other products in this market segment, but its performance tends to be somewhat faster, and its user interface is nice and clean.

The drawback to using PowerDirector is its somewhat weaker media organization functionality, which can be a problem for people with a lot of footage. But thanks to its speed, it's one of the best programs on the market.

Knowing Where to Get Started with Editing

At first, the task of editing video may seem confusing and somewhat scary. The process has many technical expressions to understand, many software features to use, and many concepts to grasp. The best way to deal with this complexity is to simply dive in.

Attempting a test project

After some preparation, there's no better way to get up to speed in video editing than to simply try it. Select a topic for a test project and put together a simple video about it. This gives you firsthand experience with the editing software before you create your first real video.

READING BOOKS AND WATCHING VIDEOS

As a starting point for editing video, you may want to read a book about your editing software of choice. A book can help you understand the basic concepts that your editing application is built on, and it can provide a quick overview of all its features. In addition, good books have step-by-step guides for more advanced features.

Several books in the *For Dummies* series explain how to use some of the most popular editing programs, and we highly recommend them.

Apple and Adobe products generally have the biggest selection of good instructional books available, though some of the less popular editing applications aren't covered as thoroughly. Before you decide on a particular editing program, look at what kind of information and support are available for it. Don't forget to check out YouTube for editing tutorials; many channels are dedicated to this topic.

If you have some video footage from your last vacation or family event, that's a good place to start, because your family can then enjoy a watchable, well-edited video. Or, if you want to dive right into marketing-oriented videos, shoot some quick footage about your business and use existing pictures.

Avoid overthinking your first project. Your goal isn't to produce a masterwork of cinematic storytelling — it's to explore the features of your editing tool and experience the basic process of editing.

Your first project should follow these guidelines because you find these elements in most serious video projects:

>> Import, view, and organize multiple clips of raw video footage.

>> Use pictures and graphical elements, such as a logo, in your video.

>> Experiment with different title styles.

>> Try variations of background music to see how music can influence the mood of a video.

>> Explore basic visual effects, such as transitions between scenes.

>> Record a voiceover narration track.

Make a short video first, maybe a couple of minutes long. Don't forget to share the video with a friend for feedback — you'll be surprised at what you notice when you're sharing a project.

Handling file formats, resolution, and conversion

Video used to be supplied on magnetic tape. Though it was available in several formats, such as VHS and Betacam, figuring out what you had was fairly simple. The digital world has brought about a dramatic cost reduction (video professionals no longer have to own a VCR for every cassette format), but it also brought about more complexity. Dozens of different digital video file formats are now used in the industry.

Fortunately, modern editing programs handle much of this mess for you. Almost all editing tools handle the most common dozen or so formats. But if you work with video footage shot by someone else, you still may occasionally encounter an exotic format. That's why you should understand the basic principles of using video file formats.

Sorting out the file formats

Digital video produces extremely large files. These files would be even larger if not for the heavy compression that's applied to the original video signal. Video compression uses some fancy calculations to squeeze high-quality moving pictures and sound into files that are as small as possible. To give you an idea, your video files would be between 5 and 50 times larger without compression.

The compression process is managed by a *coder/deco*der, or *codec.* This piece of software squeezes the video into a smaller digital format when it's recorded and decompresses it again when it's being watched. Because a codec typically isn't compatible with other codecs, you can't watch a video recorded via codec A on a device that supports only codec B.

Some of the most popular video codecs are

» Apple ProRes

» Digital Video (DV)

» H.264 (a more modern version of MPEG-4)

» MPEG-4

» Windows Media (WMV)

The data generated by these codecs is stored in a file that contains additional information, such as the title and description of the video, synchronization markers that sync audio and video, subtitles, and more.

You see these file formats, or *container* formats, on your PC or Mac. These container formats and their file endings are the most popular:

» Flash Video (.flv)

» MP4 (.mp4)

» MPEG (.mpg)

» QuickTime (.mov)

» Windows Media (.avi)

Don't let yourself become confused: Container files can contain several different codecs. For example, a QuickTime file can contain a video in Apple ProRes, DV, or H.264 format. Each format can be matched with a number of audio codec formats, such as AAC, AIFF, or MP3.

In other words, if someone asks you for the format of your video files and you respond "AVI" or "MOV," the person doesn't know much more about the format than before he asked. Any container file type can contain any of dozens of different codecs.

The only way to determine what you have is to open the video file in a player application, such as QuickTime Player or Windows Media Player. Then use the menu command that shows you details about the file. In QuickTime, it's Window ⇨ Show Movie Inspector. In Windows Media Player, it's File ⇨ Properties.

Converting formats

Modern editing programs can work with most widely used video file formats. However, if you use footage in a more exotic format — material provided by someone else, for example — you may encounter roadblocks. Your editing application may not be able to work with unusual formats directly.

In this case, convert these files to a more standard format by using a video conversion program. Your editing program may even have one already.

You can find many free or inexpensive conversion programs. If you have to deal with an exotic video file format, the time savings are definitely worth the price. On Windows PCs, AVS Video Converter (`www.avs4you.com/avs-free-video-converter.aspx`) and Any Video Converter Pro (`www.any-video-converter.com/products/for_video`) are good choices. On the Mac, AVCWare Video Converter (`www.avcware.com`) and Wondershare Mac Video Converter (`https://videoconverter.wondershare.com`) are recommended products. Another good option is HandBreak (`https://handbrake.fr`), a free, open source program that is available for all operating systems.

When it comes to downloading free software off the Internet: let the buyer beware. Many free programs can look legitimate but are actually malware in disguise. We recommend sticking with the above or doing thorough research.

Editing Your Video

Editing is the art of telling a story using video footage, pictures, and sound. Editing is often called *the invisible art* because the best editing isn't noticed by the viewer.

A well-edited video brings the viewer into the story; none of the elements of the actual edit should be seen, unless your goal is to show off a digital effect on the footage.

RECOGNIZING VIDEOS THAT NEED NO EDITING

Some types of video can stand on their own with no significant amount of editing. You can prepare the following types of videos for publishing with a minimal amount of trimming:

- **Talking head:** A talking head video shows a person simply speaking into the camera to make an announcement or to explain a concept or an issue. This technique isn't terribly interesting visually, but it can be effective if the speaker has interesting material. If your talent can complete the statement in one take, you typically don't even need to edit.

- **Speech and presentation:** Sometimes, you can tape a representative of your company or an outside expert presenting a relevant topic at an event. You can typically use this footage without editing if the presentation is brief. But remember that presentations on video tend to be less interesting than the ones you see in person.

- **Simple product demonstrations:** A salesperson, or even a CEO, may be able to give a killer product demonstration in only one take. Sometimes, a charismatic salesperson can be more convincing than a slickly produced product video. A competent camera operator can show details of the product by zooming in or moving the camera.

Even when you plan a video shoot meticulously, surprises and changes take place during editing. An idea that seems outstanding at first may not work in the final video. On the other hand, unexpected moments of excellence may show up in your footage to give your video an extra boost.

Editing can make or break your video. This section tells you how to approach this essential process. We use the Apple iMovie editing software in the examples, though other editing programs work similarly.

Logging your footage

After you return from a shooting location, follow these general steps to log your footage — the most important step in preparing for the editing process:

1. **Download the footage to your computer.**

    Using a modern camera, this process can be completed quickly — just copy the digital video files from the camera. Shooting on tape is more time-consuming because you have to let the tape run so that your editing program can capture all footage digitally. Refer to your camera's instruction manual to find out how.

2. Import the footage into your editing program.

You may already have completed this step if you downloaded the footage using your editing software, but in other cases you first have to import the footage manually.

TIP

If you captured your sound on an external audio recorder, now's the best time to synchronize it with your video. Some programs, such as Premiere Pro, easily allow you to match up audio and video directly on the timeline. If you're constantly pairing tons of footage, having a dedicated program might be worth the investment. PluralEyes (www.redgiant.com/products/shooter-pluraleyes) makes synchronizing footage and sound incredibly easy and allows you to export sequences directly to certain editing programs. Just make sure your camera is recording with its internal microphone or else it won't work!

3. Organize your clips.

After you have a bunch of clips that cover different parts of your project, start by organizing them to better see what you have. Group clips together that are related to the same scene. Editing programs offer different methods to help, such as

- Folders or bins in which you can store clips

- Labels and tags that you can assign to clips

- Events that group related clips

4. Watch your footage.

Review all your clips to determine what you have. If you have a lot of footage, there's no way to avoid this time-consuming step. But with practice, you can learn to shoot more efficiently, meaning you'll have less footage to pore over later.

5. Remove unwanted material.

If you have clips that are clearly unusable, remove them immediately. Don't delete them — just store them in a folder labeled Unusable in your editing program or in your computer's file system. Sometimes, a clip that looks unusable now can come in handy later.

6. Take notes.

The best way to find your footage quickly during editing is to take the time to record notes about every clip. Add a few simple words about the content of the clip and its level of quality. In most programs, notes can be recorded in the editing software directly in line with the clip you're referencing.

7. Mark the best clips.

If you have multiple takes of a scene, mark the one you think is best. Many editing programs let you use a special Favorites functionality, or you can simply make a mark in your notes. Also mark B-roll footage that you think looks good, and make notes of the best sound bites in interview clips.

REMEMBER

Logging your footage may seem like a tedious and time-consuming process, but investing time in it pays off later. During editing, you can waste a lot of time hunting for a particular clip that you somehow recall but didn't mark properly.

Trimming video clips

Clips often tend to be too long. If you want to use a one-take video, you can simply trim off unwanted pieces at the beginning and the end. Fortunately, trimming a clip on your computer is fairly easy. The best tool depends on the platform you use:

» **On the Mac:** Mac users already have QuickTime, a preinstalled media player that has basic editing features.

If you want to trim a clip, open the video file in QuickTime and then choose the Edit ➪ Trim command. A timeline showing the entire clip appears. Drag the yellow handles to mark the start and end of the clip, and then click the Trim button. The resulting clip can be saved or exported for use on YouTube or on your website. Figure 8-1 shows how to use the trim function in QuickTime.

FIGURE 8-1:
The trim function
in QuickTime
Player.

>> **On the PC:** PC users can select from a variety of video processing tools that provide the trimming function.

An easy way is to use Microsoft Photos (described earlier in this chapter). This simple editing application is free, and it works well if you want to trim only a few clips.

WARNING

Some simple video programs even let you assemble multiple clips into a longer clip. For example, QuickTime lets you add a clip to the end of the current clip by choosing the Edit ⇨ Add Clip to End command. On a PC, use Microsoft Photos and simply drag-and-drop the clips to the storyboard. This method works for assembling two or three clips, but don't expect it to replace an editing program. As soon as you want to move beyond the simplest trimming level (and save time in the end), invest in quality editing software.

Making a rough cut

The first step in determining what your video will look like is to make a *rough cut*, in which you line up all the good footage to figure out what works. A rough cut is typically much longer than the final product, and it lacks many of the elements from the final video, such as titles and visual effects.

To make a rough cut, first log your footage, as explained earlier in this chapter, in the section "Logging your footage." Then follow these steps:

1. **Review your storyline in sequence.**

   Tackle every scene separately.

2. **For every scene, find the best takes that you marked during logging.**

3. **Mark in points and out points for every clip to trim it to the part you want in the video.**

   In points and out points are indicators you set on the individual clips that make up the scene. An *in point* is the frame in the clip where you want to begin viewing, an *out point* is the frame with which you want to end the clip.

TIP

   Don't worry much about the exact timing. It comes later. In points and out points can easily be changed after the clip is in your timeline.

4. **Insert the clip in your editing program's timeline, in any order you want.**

   Figure 8-2 shows what a rough cut looks like in an editing program. It's just a sequence of clips with no further treatment.

5. **Repeat this process for all scenes to assemble a sequence of clips that tells your intended story.**

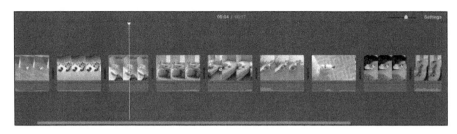

FIGURE 8-2:
A timeline with a
rough cut in an
editing program.

When you watch your rough cut for the first time, it probably looks bumpy, overly long, and <ahem> rough. Your goal is simply to figure out how well your material works when it's assembled.

TIP

If it's possible in your editing program, make a safety copy of your first rough cut — of either the timeline or the whole project. This copy may come in handy later in the editing process, when you don't see the forest for all the trees, and you need a fresh perspective. Making a copy can also be a helpful way to find raw clips quickly if you have a lot of footage.

Switching it around

The great thing about modern editing software is that you can experiment by moving clips and entire sequences to find the best combination of clips and scenes. Be careful: You can easily get lost in the experimentation process. First consider why you would want to change something, and if you have a truly good reason, do it.

Try some of these suggestions:

>> **Use different versions of the same take.** Sometimes, a take that you think is best when you watch it in isolation no longer works well with the rest of the material. If you're unhappy with a take, try using a different take of the same shot to see whether it improves the entire scene.

>> **Drop clips or entire scenes.** Shorter is typically better in editing. If you feel that a particular clip or an entire scene doesn't add much value to the video, drop the clip entirely and watch the video without it. If you don't miss it much, your audience will likely never miss it.

>> **Change the order of scenes.** Particularly in documentary-style and educational videos, scenes don't necessarily have a natural fixed order. You can also change the sequence completely for dramatic effect. For example, if you sell lawn mowers and you want to show how your latest model performs, you can grab your viewers' attention if you first show the pristine lawn that results from using your product and then demonstrate how your product was responsible.

Editing is storytelling, but stories don't always have to flow linearly. Early in your video, specify to the audience that you have something interesting to say. Learn from the pros: James Bond movies, for example, don't start with a boring explanation of the villain's latest evil plot, but rather with a high-octane action scene that grabs the audience's attention immediately.

Creating cuts

A rough cut is all about finding the right way to tell a story with your video. In a written document, the rough cut is the equivalent of the outline and first draft. But there's more to editing: Just as you would refine a written text for style and powerful language, refine your video edit with better timing, transitions, additional material, and refined cuts.

Working on these elements is the style aspect of video editing, and it makes all the difference between a video that's barely watchable and one that excites viewers.

A *cut* in film editing connects two shots. One shot ends and the next one begins, and between them is a cut. The word *cut* comes from the act of physically cutting celluloid film in traditional movie editing. Today, in the age of digital editing, no cutting is taking place, though the name stuck.

Different types of cuts serve different purposes. Depending on the effect you want to achieve, use one of these cut types:

>> **Hard:** This is the most basic (and by far the most frequently used) type of cut. One shot ends, and the next shot starts immediately. Both the picture track and the sound track are cut at the same time.

>> **Transition:** One shot flows into the next with some kind of visual effect. The simplest form of transition is the *fade,* which softly transitions one picture to the next. You can use many different types of other transitions, some of which can look quite elaborate. Use transitions with caution because the editing should be felt, not seen. You don't want to take away from the viewing experience with starburst transitions every minute.

TIP

Use transitions to suggest a special relationship between two shots, such as a scene transition.

>> **Cross fade:** This cut type can be used between shots as a softer replacement for hard cuts. If you want to edit to slow music and achieve a flowing pace, the fade is a useful technique.

Figure 8-3 shows what a cross fade between two shots looks like in the context of a video. On the bottom, you can see the timeline with the vertical bar that shows which part of the video is playing. On the top, the preview pane shows the two shots that the cross fade combines.

>> **Jump:** Cut from one view of a person or an object to another one that's only slightly different. You should generally avoid using the jump cut, but it can be used occasionally for dramatic effect. It's also used in interviews or talking head videos to shorten a statement or to add visual variety. For example, the person who's speaking can be shown in a medium shot while you cut to a slightly tighter shot for the next sentence.

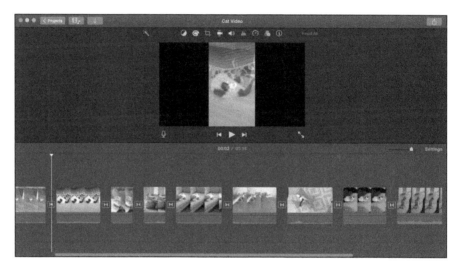

FIGURE 8-3:
A cross fade transition.

Your rough cut probably uses plain hard cuts exclusively, but as you start refining your video, consider using these other types of cuts, to help advance the story and make the viewing experience more sophisticated.

TIP

Many beginners in video editing overuse fancy transitions. Modern editing programs are supplied with dozens of different transitions, and spicing up a video with all that eye candy is tempting. But don't forget that most viewers are more impressed by good storytelling than by overused special effects. A good rule of thumb is that 95 percent of your cuts should be plain hard cuts. If you use more than a handful of fades in your video, you're probably overdoing it.

Filling the gaps with B-roll

The term *B-roll* describes supplemental footage that can be used to provide additional context for the viewer or to fill gaps in the main storyline. We talk about how to shoot B-roll in Chapter 7. Having plenty of good B-roll is always a good idea because it makes an editor's life easier.

Use B-roll in your video in these common scenarios:

>> Illustrate what a speaker or an interviewee is saying by showing the subject of the explanation.

>> Add a bit of rhythm and visual polish to an otherwise long and visually boring scene.

>> Separate scenes in a scripted video to give the viewer breathing room. Many TV series use a few pieces of B-roll between scenes — for example, in shots of the city where the story is taking place.

>> Hide cuts in an interview or another continuous scene. If you have only one perspective of an interviewee, shortening the interview is difficult. Cutting directly looks jumpy and indicates that you've omitted material. If you cut instead to a piece of B-roll while the interviewee is still talking, you can easily mask the cut.

>> Disguise small flaws in the footage. Did the camera suddenly shake in the middle of the interview, or did the subject move briefly out of focus? No problem — simply use a bit of B-roll to hide the mistake.

REMEMBER

If you use B-roll only to disguise mistakes, your use of it may become too obvious. Use B-roll frequently to make your video more interesting and varied. But also avoid using B-roll that has nothing to do with the subject and doesn't add true value.

Polishing Your Video

After you refine your rough cut into a well-timed, well-trimmed video, it's time to apply the final layer of polish. A bit of further fine-tuning makes the difference between an acceptable video and one that looks truly professional.

Fine-tuning your edit

Videos can benefit from a number of relatively simple steps you can follow to improve certain aspects that viewers may not even consciously recognize:

1. **Tweak your cut timing.**

   If a cut seems even a little bit off, spend some time fine-tuning it. Even placing a cut a frame or two earlier or later can make a difference.

2. **Add music.** You may have already worked with some temporary music tracks during earlier editing steps, but now is the time to finalize all your audio and background tracks.

3. **Clean up the audio track.** Most audio tracks can use some additional work. Be sure that the levels are correct and consistent throughout the video. Viewers don't like viewing one scene that's too loud followed immediately by one that's barely audible. Some editing programs have the Normalize Audio function, which optimizes audio levels automatically. Also, hard audio cuts rarely sound good. You can add a dissolve transition to the audio track while still applying a hard cut to the picture track.

4. **Use color correction.** Scenes in general should have a consistent look between shots — different video cameras can pick up different color influences. The color correction feature in most editing programs helps fix color inconsistencies between shots and scenes. Color correction also lets you give your video a unique and more interesting feel. For instance, bluer light or colder light is used in many crime scenes, more yellow or warmer light is typically used in more romantic movies.

Adding bells and whistles

You can add a number of elements, as described in this list, to complete your video and make it look more interesting:

>> **Titles:** A video should have a good title sequence, and editing programs offer a variety of different templates. Try a few different styles to see what works best. A general rule for any text onscreen is that viewers should be able to read it quickly twice. Be sure your title sequences aren't too long — viewers on YouTube typically have less patience than viewers in the movie theater.

>> **Sound effects:** A well-placed sound effect can make certain scenes much more interesting. We aren't talking about explosions, alien ray gun sounds, or Wilhelm screams, but rather about basic background tracks or sounds that match the visible content on the screen. Sometimes, your original background sounds for a scene aren't good, and you can use canned sounds to replace

them. Some editing programs come with small libraries of sound effects, and you can find more online.

» **Visual effects:** Most editing programs have effect filters that change the look of your footage completely. Though you should always use these effects sparingly, they may occasionally help make your video look more interesting.

TIP

You can experiment with bells and whistles in the earlier stages of the editing process, though you typically should wait until the end of your editing process before trying to use them fully. They're typically time consuming to apply, and if you change your edit afterward, you may have to do unnecessary work.

Adding Music to Your Video

You may wonder why music is even necessary in a video that isn't destined to sell a pop singer's latest album. Music determines a lot about the perception of your message because viewers make split-second, subconscious judgments about the content of your video depending on the type of music you choose.

In contrast to music videos, the music in your marketing video is meant to complement the message you're trying to convey. Music isn't the focus of a video — it's there simply to add color.

WARNING

You must understand the difference between music you pay royalties to use and royalty-free music. Most of the music you hear on the radio or buy online is copyrighted and can be used in videos only if you pay royalties to its record label — often an expensive strategy because you must pay for every use of a copyrighted music track. Record labels sometimes even charge more, depending on how many views your video attracts. And, "borrowing" music and hoping that you won't get caught is *not* an option. Videos containing copyrighted music can be detected and banned automatically from sites such as YouTube.

The easiest way to save time and expense is to use only royalty-free music tracks — they're sold specifically for use in YouTube videos or presentations. After you pay a fixed price per song, you can usually use it however you want, as long as you stay within the boundaries specified by the music publishing contract. For example, some royalty-free tracks may be available for use in online videos but not in TV commercials. To choose music for your video, follow these steps:

1. **Determine which emotion you want to convey.**

   For example, you may want viewers to feel happy, sad, or uplifted — or neutral.

2. **Watch a rough edit of your video several times.**

Or, if you're still in the planning stage, simply review the video's storyline in your mind. Do you need fast, aggressive cuts? Are your graphics clean and simple or more elaborate and flowery? The music you choose must match the video's storyline, aesthetic value, and editing style.

3. **Choose an appropriate genre.**

You may want to use a rock-and-roll track or a country track, for example, or perhaps electronic music more closely suits your style.

4. **Set the mood.**

The mood of the music you choose has to match the emotion you want to convey. To judge, determine how the music makes *you* feel when you listen to it. If it matches the emotion you chose in Step 1, you're on the right track.

5. **Control the pace of the video by controlling its musical tempo.**

A song's *tempo* refers to its speed or pace. The pace of the video also has to fit the emotion you're trying to convey and the overall storyline. For example, should viewers be relaxed or breathless after watching your video? Choose a tempo between these two extremes that creates the impression you want.

6. **Search for a song.**

After you choose the genre, mood, and tempo of the music in your video, search for a song. (You'll find out more about music to purchase in the following sections. Or, if you're truly talented, compose one yourself.) You'll likely stick with royalty-free music.

7. **Drop in the music.**

After you finish creating the video, you can drop the music into your editing timeline and edit the piece to mirror the pacing of the footage.

Adding built-in music in video editing tools

Most of the video editing software programs we describe in this chapter contain royalty-free song tracks, such as in these two examples:

>> **Apple Final Cut Pro X:** Has over 1,300 royalty-free sound effects and music tracks

>> **Vegas Movie Studio:** Contains 400 royalty-free music soundtracks

Some of the songs you can use from video editing software are so popular and overused (because they're free) that you risk triggering unwanted reactions from your audience. For example, a friend once complained to us that his video reminded him of a late-night TV ad containing questionable content. When we watched it, we found that his video editor had used a free, built-in music track that's often chosen by these low-cost advertisers.

Incorporating stock music libraries

If you have only a small budget and you want to sound different from the standard music libraries that come with many editing programs, you can find a good selection of royalty-free stock music to download online. This list describes some options we recommend:

>> **PremiumBeat** (www.premiumbeat.com): This one has a huge selection of audio tracks and sound effects. These folks, who work closely with composers from around the world, are selective, so it's easier to search the libraries for what you need.

>> **Audiojungle** (https://audiojungle.net): It's less expensive than Shockwave-Sound (www.shockwave-sound.com), the major player in the stock music and sound effects derby, but its selection isn't as large. Songs cost between $10 and $20 apiece.

>> **Audioblocks** (www.audioblocks.com): A subscription-based, royalty free library, Audioblocks has a great selection of sound effects, music, and handy looped tracks for easy editing.

TIP

If you want to use an iconic song such as Nirvana's "Smells Like Teen Spirit" and you have a limited budget or limited time to secure the rights, you can often find inexpensive but similar-sounding songs on stock music sites.

TIP

If you can't find a song that matches the length of your video, don't worry: Viewers don't focus on songs — songs simply enhance the pacing and mood. Therefore, a repetitive song, or looping a song to fit the length of the video, usually works well.

Putting music in your video

After you have selected your music, it's time to insert it in your video.

The mechanical aspect of this task is easy to complete. Follow these steps in your editing software:

1. **Gather all the music you want to use into one folder on your computer.**

   Using one folder helps you find files easily and helps you back them up after editing. If you store your music on a CD, import the necessary tracks to your computer first by using a program such as iTunes.

2. **Import the music files into your video editing software.**

   Most editing programs can process MP3 files and most other commonly used music file formats.

3. **Add an additional audio track to your editing project.**

   Certain simpler programs, such as iMovie, have predetermined tracks for background music.

4. **Drag-and-drop your music piece to the new audio track. Then shift its position until it fits the timing you want.**

5. **Watch the part of the video that now has background music in context.**

   Fine-tune the timing of the music, if necessary.

TIP

If you aren't sure which piece of music will work best with your video, simply import into your editing program multiple music tracks that you're considering. Drop one after the other on the audio timeline, watching the video with every piece of music, to quickly find which track you like best.

Adding emotional impact

The main purpose of your music selection is to enhance the emotional impact of your video. Even the specific way in which you use music in your edit affects the video's emotional impact. Try these simple tricks to give your music more emotional impact:

>> **Work with the volume level.** Music in a video shouldn't always play at the same volume level. It should be softer and drop into the background whenever it supports dialogue or a voiceover narration, and it should be fairly loud when it stands on its own and drives home an emotional point. Most editing programs let you change the volume of a particular track over time. Dramatically increasing the volume of the music track in a key video scene adds quite a powerful effect — Hollywood movies and TV shows do it all the time.

>> **Determine the proper timing.** A music track doesn't have to start at its beginning when you insert it in your video. Match the music to the video's visual content. Most musical selections have *hooks* — particularly remarkable and recognizable parts. For example, the hook of Beethoven's Fifth Symphony is the famous "Ta-ta-ta-daaa." Try to match musical hooks with important moments in the video.

Cutting your video to music

When you have a piece of music that matches well with the emotional purpose of your video, fine-tune your edit to maximize the effect of the music. For example, you can extend a scene slightly to fit the most dramatic moment with a remarkable hook in the music.

Most editing programs let you lock your music tracks to avoid their being affected by other changes in your video. Follow these steps:

1. **Put your musical piece on its own audio track.**

2. **Time the music so that the music begins exactly where you want.**

3. **Lock the music track.**

   Most editing programs use a tiny Padlock icon to indicate locking.

4. **Watch the video and determine how to adapt the timing to best fit the music.**

   For example, cut or extend certain shots slightly.

5. **Make your editing changes.**

6. **Unlock the audio track.**

TIP

Precisely matching cuts in a video with beats in the music can create quite a pleasing effect because the picture and music then seem to move in perfect harmony. Avoid overdoing it, though, because an exact match can quickly bore viewers. The best approach is to match a couple of cuts with the music and then purposely skip the next few cuts before matching again. Alternating makes the final product less predictable and maintains viewer interest.

Cutting your music to video

You may not want to alter an edit just to better fit the music. In this case, cut the music to match your video instead.

Another important reason to cut music is to omit parts that may not fit well with the visual side of your video. For example, the piece of music you selected may have a bridge section that has a slightly different mood from the rest of the track, which can be distracting in a video. Eliminate the unwanted section by cutting precisely at the end of the previous part and at the end of the bridge section.

Almost all video editing programs let you cut audio tracks, which is good enough for completing the basic editing of your music tracks, such as cutting off to the millisecond any unwanted intros or endings.

An alternative is to cut your music tracks in advance by using an audio program such as Garage Band or Pro Tools. They let you edit audio precisely, and they provide a wealth of audio effects to help you enhance your music tracks for video use.

Incorporating Voiceover and Sound Effects

Many videos used for marketing employ *voiceover narration,* using offscreen narrators to tell viewers about the company's products or services. Most video editing programs have a voiceover recording feature, which is useful if you're recording your own voice directly into your computer.

To record your own voiceover, invest in a mid-quality external microphone. You can buy good USB microphones for well below \$100 — a worthy investment because your voiceover tracks will sound much better.

As with voiceover narration, you can also add sound effects. Most noises you hear in a typical Hollywood movie aren't recorded live on the set, but are added later in the process. Recording sounds on location is tricky and often creates mediocre results.

So, sound effects are most often added during the editing process. This list describes the major kinds of sound effects you can use:

>> **Background or ambient:** Continuous background noises that suggest where the video scene is taking place work well to establish location. For example, a busy city scene needs vehicle noises, lots of footsteps, and the occasional siren. A beach scene needs wind and water sounds. These background sounds are easy to apply.

   If you can, record a few minutes of ambient sound on your video set to capture the audio character of the location.

>> **Hard:** This type of sound effect accompanies visible events onscreen, such as slamming doors or passing vehicles. This type is a little more difficult to apply because events must be synced precisely to the picture, though most editing programs let you do it quite easily.

Most advanced video editing programs are supplied with a small library of basic sound effects that you can easily use in your edits. Just add an audio track, drag in the sound recording you want, and shift the track around until it fits the scene.

You can find additional sound effects online from stock sound libraries such as Audioblocks (`www.audioblocks.com`) and Soundsnap (`www.soundsnap.com`). Most of these sounds have specific descriptions, such as "Cars passing by at 25 mph on a somewhat busy street," so you can likely find something suitable.

Exporting the Final Version

When you finally finish editing, you export the video from your editing program so that you can use it later.

Typically, you should export multiple versions of a video because you can use the final product in different ways:

>> **Export an archive master copy with the highest possible quality that your editing program offers.** You can always decrease, but not increase, quality (and therefore file size). That's why you should store a high-quality copy, in case you want to create other versions later.

>> **Keep a copy just for YouTube purposes:** YouTube export settings are always changing, so be sure to double-check the current best practices for settings directly on your YouTube channel upload page. Typically, the settings look like this:

- *Container:* mp4

- *Audio Codec:* AAC-LC

- *Video Codec:* H.264

- *Acceptable and common frame rates:* 24, 25, 30, 48, 50, 60 frames per second

- *Aspect Ratio:* YouTube players are all 16:9; a typical resolution is 1080p: 1920x1080

TIP

Most of the editing programs discussed in this book let you directly upload video to your YouTube channel. Uploading this way is convenient, but if you notice a mistake after uploading the video, you have to remove it, which can be a hassle. Normally, exporting video to your hard drive first is recommended for backing up and testing purposes — watch it one last time, and then upload it manually to gain more control over every step.

IN THIS CHAPTER

» **Preparing your YouTube channel for video uploads**

» **Putting video search engine optimization (video SEO) to work for you**

» **Recognizing what's required to keep your channel in good standing**

» **Setting appropriate defaults for YouTube's uploading options**

» **Posting and removing videos from YouTube**

Chapter **9**

Preparing for Upload Day

I t's hard to believe that, not that long ago, the whole concept of video production and distribution was the domain of specialized professionals. In those bad old days, the entire process was not only difficult but often also extremely expensive. Securing broader distribution rights required lawyers, which added another level of complexity and expense, all in the name of locking out lots of creative folk, as well as many businesses, who were just dying to create great video work.

Fortunately, all that has changed. As computers, cameras, and applications became more powerful — and affordable and a lot less complex — creating a fabulous video could be accomplished relatively easily. So much for the miles of film and the expensive production facilities that used to be standard operating procedure — now you could shoot an outstanding video on your mobile phone and then edit it on your laptop in the local coffee shop. The digital video revolution had begun.

Then along came YouTube, and suddenly you could get your video *immediately* distributed to, and placed in front of, millions of viewers without the aggravation of contracts, lawyers, and distribution partners. Overnight, you could become your own Hollywood studio. YouTube made it powerful and easy by making simplified, video self-publishing a reality. It eliminated nearly all the crazy video file-format issues and removed the complicated conversion issues so that you could simply upload a file and people could watch it nearly everywhere with no special software required.

REMEMBER

Today, video is simpler than ever. But don't be deceived by its simplicity: YouTube gives you powerful tools to do great things with video uploading and distribution. So start off simple and hit the ground running, but be sure to leverage YouTube's additional distribution capabilities as your skills and your channel mature.

Preparing Your Channel for Uploads

Chapters 7 and 8 do a great job of guiding you through the process of capturing and editing great videos for your channel. If you've made your way through those chapters, you may be thinking that you're just a few clicks away from uploading a video, and you'd be absolutely right to think so. That's the great part about YouTube — it makes it easy to get your videos online. However, as Chapter 5 so forcefully puts it, being successful on YouTube requires a bit of planning, so don't rush. The time you invest now in preparing your channel for uploads not only makes your future work easier but also sets up your channel for much better watch time, subscription growth, and audience engagement.

Checking your YouTube account hygiene

YouTube certainly started a revolution in online video by making it amazingly easy to upload and share content. But there's something more: YouTube is also a community that abides by certain guidelines to maintain order and civility. These rules are divided into two categories:

» **Community guidelines:** YouTube is a great place to share your work and do business, but just like your physical community, certain rules govern everyone's behavior — rules that usually have something to do with the type of content you can upload. Just keep in mind that viewers can (and do) use the Watch page to flag what they consider to be community violations. Viewers don't have the last word here — YouTube reviewers review the flag to make sure that the complaint is legitimate — but violations can lead to warnings, known as a *community guidelines strike*, being issued against your YouTube account.

» **Copyright policies:** Individuals and businesses are strongly encouraged to upload content that they own or have legal ownership of. This includes both audio and visual content. Uploading content you have no legal ownership of — or content where the legalities of ownership are murky — can be cause for more strikes against your account. Acquiring three copyright strikes results in account termination. (Copyright issues can be complicated; for a closer look at YouTube's take on copyright issues, check out https://youtube.com/about/copyright. For our take on copyright, check out Chapter 16.)

Copyright violations can be flagged one of two ways:

- *Copyright strike:* A *strike* is a legal request by a copyright holder directing YouTube to take down the video and remove it from your channel.

- *Content ID claim:* YouTube grants some users access to an automated copyright-verification system and database known as Content ID. Claims in Content ID don't result in a strike, because the system gives the copyright owner some control over what to do with violations, such as monetization or blocking.

TIP

Deleting a copyrighted video does not make the claim vanish from your account. You need to wait for the claim to expire in 90 days, get the owner to retract the claim, or dispute it with a counternotification. Be diligent in resolving the issue with YouTube or the claimant.

Your success at following these rules defines your account status in YouTube:

>> **Community guideline strikes:** The repercussions of this type of violation grow more severe with each successive incident. On the first strike, you lose for one week the ability to customize thumbnails; create, add, or remove playlists; and post or upload in any way. A second strike results in the same punishment, but for two weeks rather than one. Your account is terminated if you receive a third strike within 90 days.

>> **Copyright strikes:** This type of violation operates a bit differently. On your first strike, you have to go to Copyright School to complete a brief questionnaire quizzing your understanding of YouTube copyright policies. Your ability to monetize videos and livestream may also be impacted. If you receive three strikes within 90 days, your account is terminated.

Checking your YouTube account status is simple:

1. **In your web browser, go to** www.youtube.com.

2. **Log in to your YouTube account.**

3. **Click your Account icon and then choose Settings from the drop-down menu that appears.**

   The Settings option is the one sporting the small Gear icon on its left.

4. **Select Channel Status and Features.**

   This is the first option listed below your channel in the middle of the page.

TIP

   You can also bypass these steps by going directly to www.youtube.com/features.

5. **Any copyright or community guideline strikes are listed in the Channel Violations box.**

   The top of Figure 9-1 shows an account with no violations.

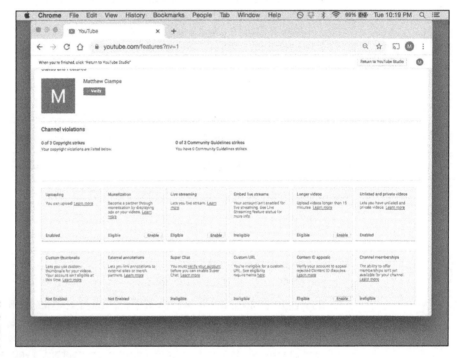

FIGURE 9-1:
Your YouTube
Status and
Features page.

TIP

If your videos have been flagged, for either community guidelines or copyright violations, you probably received an email explaining why. To see more details on the nature of the claim and how it impacts your video, follow these steps:

1. **In your web browser, go to** www.youtube.com.

2. **Log in to your YouTube account.**

3. **Click your Account icon and then choose YouTube Studio from the drop-down menu that appears.**

   This step brings you to the Dashboard for YouTube Studio. If you've received any strikes, a handy Channel Violations widget quickly informs you of any violations.

4. **Click the Videos tab on the YouTube Studio menu.**

5. **Videos with any sort of violation specify the nature of the problem in the Restrictions column.**

   You can limit the list to only those videos with copyright claims by clicking Filter and then choosing Copyright Claims.

6. **Hover the mouse cursor over the restriction and click See Details.**

   You can then see the details of the claim, including how it impacts your channel, the video's visibility, and its monetization. You can also view which components of the video have a claim against them.

7. **To take action toward a claim, click the Select Action drop-down menu.**

   You're given a choice of various actions to take in response to the claim, including trimming the video, swapping the music, and disputing the claim.

Enabling channel features

After your account is copacetic, be sure to check the rest of the fields on your channel's Status and Features page. Checking which YouTube features are enabled is straightforward:

1. **Log in to your YouTube account.**

2. **Click your Account icon and then choose Settings from the drop-down menu that appears.**

   The Settings option has a small Gear icon on its left.

3. **Select Channel Status and Features.**

   Doing so displays your channel violations at the top, as spelled out earlier in this section. Now cast your eye a bit below your account statuses and you see your YouTube features. More specifically, you see three distinct fields for each feature:

   - *The feature itself:* This lists the name of the YouTube feature — one of the many built-in extensions to YouTube channel functionality that allows for greater channel control, monetization, and enhanced viewing features.

   - *The feature status:* Your current ability to use these features. Each feature status is binary: Either you've enabled it or you haven't. You may not be eligible to use all features.

   - *The feature description:* This details what the feature does.

4. **Click to enable the feature you want to add to your channel.**

   For example, if you want ads on your channel, click the Enable button on the Monetization feature.

Tending to Video SEO Matters

In Chapter 5, we introduce the concept of *discoverability* — helping YouTube get your content in front of the right viewers through recommendations and search so that they watch *your* content rather than somebody else's. Though watch time is a critical part of YouTube's recommendation engine, a video's *metadata* — its title, description, and tags — plays an important role in getting the video found in the first place.

Video search engine optimization (*video SEO*, for short) is all about telling YouTube something about your video. For traditional web SEO, search engines such as Google, Bing, and Yahoo! would analyze the content on your site, figure out what was important, and then offer up your content to the most relevant searchers. Over time, these search engines factored in elements such as links, sharing, and clicks to determine how popular particular content ended up being on the web.

YouTube doesn't work like web SEO because it can't (yet) watch your content to determine what your video is about. Instead, it has to rely on your metadata and how the community reacts by way of watch time, social media shares, and embedded links for the video on external sites.

REMEMBER

It's a lot easier to get your video SEO house in order upfront rather than deal with it after you've published all your content.

What exactly do we mean by *optimization* in *search engine optimization? Optimization* is about intelligently and systematically putting together a proper description of your video so that

>> YouTube understands what your content is about in order to better offer your video to the most appropriate searchers

>> Search engines such as Google, Bing, and Yahoo! understand your content and are thus in a position to add your videos to search engine results pages along with web content

>> Viewers are more likely to click on your content versus other search results offered

These are the goals you want to achieve. The next few sections spell out how you can achieve them.

REMEMBER

A bit later in this chapter, you find out where and when to enter information about titles, descriptions, and other important metadata associated with your video. It's important to understand the principles behind all these before you actually upload.

Titles

The video title is the most important piece of metadata that you create. As important as the title is to YouTube and the major search engines, you have to also ensure that it works for people. The trouble is that it can't look as though you're trying too hard to grab folks' attention. Exaggerated, inaccurate titles, such as "You won't believe what happens to the 12 kittens in this video," may generate more clicks, but the search engines won't bite, and they will likely ignore your content. Also avoid "breathless" wording such as "most epic" or "blow your mind."

REMEMBER

Strike a balance between attracting humans and attracting search engines when you create and optimize a title for a video.

Your title appears in many places:

>> On the Watch page under the actual video

>> In a YouTube search

>> In Google, Bing, and Yahoo! searches

>> As part of a playlist

>> Under YouTube recommended videos

Selecting a title isn't complicated, but you must be somewhat methodical.

REMEMBER

Though you can use 100 characters in a video title, only 70 characters show up in search results on a desktop computer, though some mobile devices show only about 40, so you have to make the characters count. Titles on recommended videos are further truncated. You can create a longer title, but it's visible only on the Watch page. The goal of video SEO is to attract viewers to the video in the first place. Limiting the title is no good either because it may impair search algorithm matching.

Use the following approach to pick a title:

1. **Determine the keywords.**

   These are the important words that people search for. Make sure they're part of your video content as well as the other metadata associated with your video, such as the Tag and Description fields. If you work for Acme Electric and you're marketing the new Z500 convection oven, your keywords would include *Acme Electric, Z500,* and *convection oven.*

2. **Add a descriptive phrase to the title.**

   Your keywords alone may not be enough. Determine why your viewers would be searching for your product or your video. They may want installation instructions or product reviews, for example. Terms such as "how to install" and "product review" aid you in both search and views.

3. **Move branding keywords to the end of the title.**

   Viewers will search for your brands, but they need to see the descriptive information first.

4. **If your video is part of a series, include an episode number at the end of the title.**

   Even if your videos are part of a playlist, your viewers may end up searching separately, so make it easy and logical for them to find another episode.

REMEMBER

Include title keywords in the tag and description metadata.

GOING LONG ON SHORTLINKS

Chances are, you've seen some rather interesting web names — like bit.ly, owl.ly, goo.gl, pix.tv, and is.gd — as you've made your way around the web. Often, these web names are combined with what appears to be a random string of characters to produce something that looks like this: http://bit.ly/1xUu7KB. Like any Internet address, this link can be clicked to take you anywhere on the web, including YouTube. You can even click one of these funny-looking strings to get to the Watch page of a specific video.

What is this funky address? It's called a *shortlink,* and it replaces really long web addresses to preserve valuable space on sites such as Twitter and YouTube. How does this work? A shortlink has an associated target link. For example, in our link example, http://bit.ly/1xUu7KB actually points to www.pixability.com. When clicking a shortlink, users end up at the associated target. Shortlinks are formally known as shortened Uniform Resource Locators (URLs). *URL* is a fancy way of referring to a web address.

Many free services are available for link shortening. One of the most popular ones is bit.ly, and you can quickly sign up for it at www.bit.ly. In seconds, you'll be creating shortlinks to your heart's content.

But there's much more to shortlinks than meets the eye. Services such as bit.ly track clicks so that you can see which shortlinks are the most popular. You can actually have different shortlinks point to the same target address so that you can test which tweets work better or which web pages may be most interesting.

The top YouTube channel managers use link shorteners extensively in YouTube descriptions, channel descriptions, and social media.

TIP

Before you even upload anything to YouTube, it's good practice to rename the video file itself to a title that accurately represents its content. YouTube keeps the original reference file title on the video no matter how many times you end up changing the title.

Descriptions

You should make good use of the 5,000-character field that YouTube provides for describing your video. It's a great place to add details about not only your video but also your channel, along with links for other videos, subscriptions, other channels, and websites. In other words, it's a goldmine for both metadata and user guidance. (Figure 9-2 demonstrates what we mean.) The viewers who care about your video will read the description, so make it worth their while.

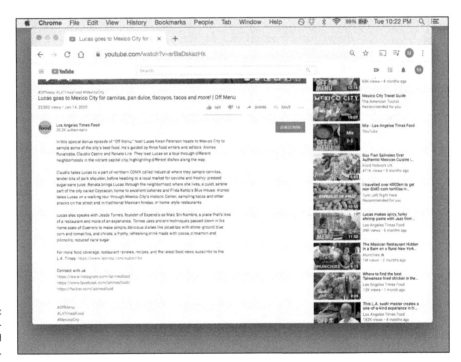

FIGURE 9-2:
A well-constructed Description field.

The video description should

>> **Explain** in greater detail what your video and your channel are about.

>> **Extend** the viewer's experience by providing additional detail around what is shown in the video. For example, if you have a video on cooking, the Description field is a great place to include a copy of the recipe.

>> **Trigger** the viewer to do something. That might include watching another video, making a purchase, supporting your cause, and more.

>> **Entice** people to view. The first couple of lines of the description show up in search results, so you have to write compelling — and relevant — content so that the user somehow takes the next step of clicking and viewing. That's also true on the Watch page, where the first couple of sentences appear under the video, compelling the viewer (you hope!) to watch.

>> **Aid** in discovery. A great description should include hundreds of keywords that help with search. Be sure to use ones that are relevant to the video.

REMEMBER

The Description field isn't the place for a transcript of your video. Be clear and concise, but make it interesting enough that people will want to read it.

Always consider what information is visible in search results by being well aware of which devices your audience is using to search. The first few lines of the description show up on a desktop search, whereas no description data is currently exposed in a mobile device search.

REMEMBER

Two older terms from marketing and advertising are still quite relevant to today's YouTube Description field: *above the fold* and *below the fold.* When people used to receive folded letters or advertisements, they often first looked at the top, which was "above the fold." If the content was compelling, they'd read the rest of it "below the fold." When viewers watch your video, they also see the first part of its description. If the description is compelling, they click the Show More link to see what's below the fold. Make what's above the fold in the video description count.

The Description field should contain enough shortlinks to answer any questions your viewers might have about your video, your channel, and your business. The About page of your channel should contain links that complement your channel. It's okay to repeat some of these links in the video description as well. The short-links in the description field can point to

>> Your channel

>> Other videos

>> Social media sites such as Facebook, Twitter, LinkedIn, Pinterest, or Instagram

>> A website

>> A landing page

TIP

Include only one link in the first paragraph if you want viewers to ultimately end up somewhere else. Include all relevant social links or product page links in the second or lower paragraphs of the description.

TIP

Don't create a fully customized Description field for each video. Put together a consistent framework or template that includes some repeatable information, such as subscription information, social media links, programming schedule, and contact information. Customize only the data in your framework that relates to the video itself. Keep everything else consistent. Your audience will appreciate the consistent layout of your field as well.

WARNING

Everyone hates email *spam* — unsolicited advertisements filled with overdone and repeated buzzwords. If the description sounds at all "spammy," you'll provoke a negative reaction. Instead, try to be informative by using a lot of descriptive words and appropriate shortlinks.

Tags

Tags are special descriptive keywords or short phrases that indicate what your video is about. They are used by search engines to help potential viewers discover your video. Tags also play an important role in helping YouTube make related video recommendations. (Your Description field also has keywords, but tags are used by YouTube to help categorize your video.)

YouTube imposes a limit of 500 characters for the entire Tag field. A tag can contain one or more words, but each individual tag cannot be more than 30 characters long.

TIP

Without wading too deeply into the math, you may end up with room for 10 to 30 tags. Use as many as you can.

What's the best approach to creating tags?

>> **Think broadly.** Everyone searches differently — some use broad terms like *oven*, whereas others use *Acme Electric Z500 convection oven*. Use both.

>> **Choose synonyms.** Though you may use *oven* only in the description and video, it's okay to use the word *stove* in your tags.

>> **Add an action tag.** Sure, people may search for video about the "Acme Electric Z500 convection oven." Think about terms that are relevant, such as *product review, how to install,* and *how to clean.* Pick one around the video content.

>> **Combine and break up keywords.** Language and people are imprecise, so take that into account and use both keywords, as in *cook top* and *cooktop.*

Tags can be modified. Just be sure that they reflect the essence of the content.

Don't use tons of irrelevant keywords to attract viewers and improve your search rankings. This will actually hurt your search rankings as YouTube will think it's spam. Plus viewers may overlook your video if they can't find it.

Thumbnails

Thumbnails are visual snapshots of your video, similar to a poster for a movie. They have a tremendous impact on a video's view rate, so choose a good one. Thumbnails by default are chosen by YouTube — three optional frames from the beginning, middle, and end of your video. You can, however, create a custom thumbnail for each video using Photoshop or any other photo editing program. (See Figure 9-3 for some examples.)

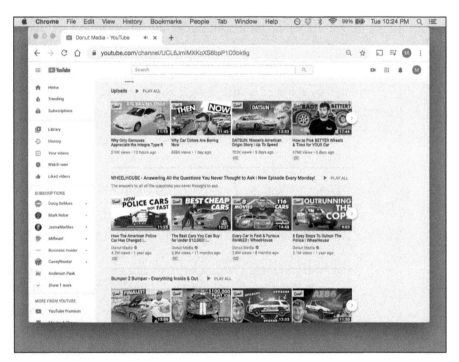

FIGURE 9-3:
Effective video thumbnails.

If you decide to create custom thumbnails, choose a thumbnail that's illustrative of the content in the video. Thumbnails show up in the following areas:

>> Channel page

>> Watch page

>> Playlists

>> Recommended videos

>> Channel guide

>> Subscriber feed

>> YouTube search

>> Web search

>> Mobile display

>> Mobile search

Keep the following key considerations in mind when deciding on a custom thumbnail:

>> **Incorporate boldness:** You're competing for viewers, so you need to stand out among the many other thumbnails across YouTube and the web. Color contrast and image quality and visual layout matter.

>> **Add personification:** Show the close-up view of faces, if possible. Viewers click on faces more than anything else.

>> **Strive for accuracy:** The thumbnail has to relate to the content of the video. Don't use the thumbnail as a way to trick viewers into checking out your video.

>> **Meet the technical specifications:** The image must be 1280x720 pixels and no larger than 2MB.

>> **Add branding:** Viewers may not look at your thumbnail for more than a few seconds; adding branding is a great way to quickly let people know who you are. Plus, consistently branding your videos creates a cohesive look across your channel.

Uploading Your Video

There's always a bit of excitement when you upload one or more videos to YouTube. The feeling is similar to what happens when you see the proverbial light at the end of the tunnel.

REMEMBER

Uploading isn't the final step in getting your videos available for viewing by your growing fan base. You still need to *publish* an uploaded video in order to make it live.

Between uploading and publishing, you have several steps to consider. YouTube rewards you with higher search rankings and supplementary video recommendations based first and foremost on your channel and on individual video watch times. In addition, YouTube looks at characteristics like viewer engagement and video sharing rates. Your job in the planning process is to identify and coordinate each component so that you're in a position to keep your channel active.

Picking the source

Before you upload, your videos have to live somewhere. They might be on your desktop computer, laptop, game console, tablet, or smartphone. What's great about having so many choices for uploading is that you can capture and upload content to your channel anytime and anywhere. It's that easy!

TIP

Sign in using the same YouTube account from all your different computers, consoles, and mobile devices so that all your videos and channel settings stay synchronized.

REMEMBER

The web browser interface to YouTube on your laptop or desktop has the most complete set of YouTube capabilities for uploading, optimizing, annotating, and publishing. For iOS and Android devices, you can run applications such as YouTube and YouTube Studio to upload videos and manage your channel. Though this application is quite powerful and has most of the features of the computer-based versions, we focus here on the browser-based versions.

Going public about YouTube privacy

New YouTube channel managers and creators often ask, "How do I control who can see my videos?" This is controlled by YouTube's privacy settings, which can be found under YouTube Studio — click the Videos section on the far left to display your options in the Visibility column. You need to know and understand the four types of privacy settings in YouTube:

>> **Public:** This is the default setting in YouTube — everyone can view your video. Videos set to Public can also show up in all searches.

REMEMBER

After you make a video public, you've officially *published* it. It shows up in your subscribers' feeds. Though you can readily change the privacy settings on your content, be sensitive to how your audience is using and sharing it, because changing settings may suddenly make your content unavailable to them with no warning.

>> **Private:** This setting, the most restrictive one, prevents anyone but you from watching the video without your explicit permission. Private videos cannot be searched, are invisible on your YouTube channel, and can't be viewed by someone even if they have the video URL. This is ideal if you want to share your video with very specific viewers or even just yourself.

>> **Unlisted:** Unlisted videos don't show up on your channel or YouTube search for viewers. However, anyone with the unlisted video URL can watch the video and share it freely anywhere on the web, including websites like Facebook, Twitter, and other social sites. Unlisted videos can be included in playlists as well.

TIP

Use unlisted content as a way to share special or exclusive content with select fans or as part of a limited-time promotion or sale.

>> **Scheduled:** This special setting automatically sets the video to Private and then changes it to Public on the date and time you specify.

TIP

Use scheduled privacy settings for channel programming consistency to ensure that videos are available at a standard date and time, regardless of whether you have access to your YouTube channel.

Your privacy settings also signal to YouTube to begin its magic. When you publish a video, YouTube starts assessing your video by using its algorithms to determine what your video is about, how good it is, and where it should fall in search results. The best practice is to consistently publish your videos around the same time so your viewers know when to expect it. Publish the video so that it attracts immediate views; this indicates to YouTube that this video is indeed hot stuff and that it may be a good candidate for YouTube search and recommendations.

REMEMBER

Playlists have privacy settings, too. One of your options during the final stages of the upload process is to put your video content into a playlist. Chapter 3 covers playlists and their importance on your channel.

Don't underestimate the power of YouTube playlists. They not only show up in search results but can also be customized to greatly enhance the viewing experience.

Uploading to YouTube

You should have no problem finding the Upload button on YouTube — it's on every page! You'll find it in the top right corner, to the left of the 3-by-3-square YouTube Apps icon in the top right of the window (whether you're logged in or out of your account). It's shaped like a small video camera with a plus sign in the middle. To upload your video content, follow these steps:

1. **Sign in to your YouTube account.**

2. **Click the Upload button.**

   Doing so brings up a drop-down menu with options named Upload Video, Go Live, and — if enabled — Create a Post. Choose Upload Video, which takes you to the Upload window, shown in Figure 9-4.

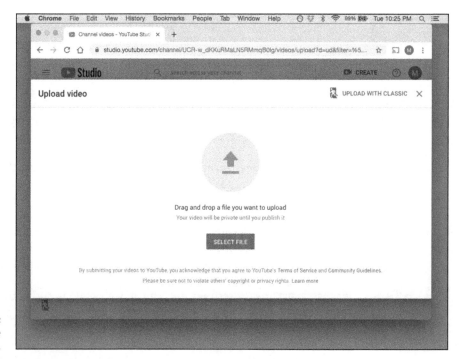

FIGURE 9-4: The YouTube upload window.

3. **Use one of the following two methods to select the video file you want to use:**

   - *Select files to upload:* Click the big, gray up-arrow button or the smaller, blue Select File button. Then use the Look In dialog box to navigate to — and then select — the file you want to upload.

   - *Drag and drop video files:* This one's as simple as it sounds: Just drag a video file to the Upload window and drop it when the drag-and-drop video file's overlay turns green.

4. **If your method requires it, click OK to upload.**

   Your files are on their way to YouTube.

5. **Get ready to enter your metadata.**

   With your videos selected and the upload under way, you're presented with a new Details page (shown in Figure 9-5) that shows important information about the video. (We save adding the metadata stuff to the Details page — title, tags, descriptions, and video thumbnails — for the next section.)

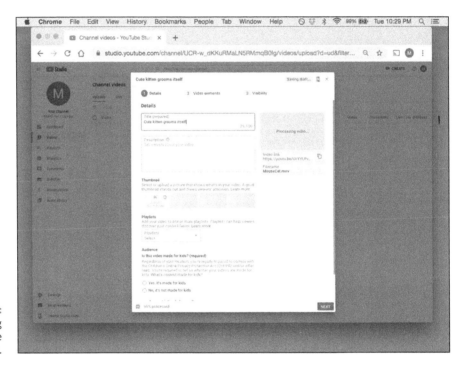

FIGURE 9-5:
Entering metadata via the Details page.

REMEMBER The Details page that you see during the upload process is the same one displayed under the Video Manager of YouTube Studio. This allows you to go back later and modify the video settings, including such tasks as changing the video description, tags, and shortlinks.

TIP YouTube easily handles most video encoding types. If YouTube is having any problems with your file, check out https://support.google.com/youtube for more information.

MANAGING INNOVATIVE CONTENT AND TALENT ON YOUTUBE

Select Management Group (www.select.co) is a Los Angeles-based entertainment company specializing in next-generation talent representation, original premium content, brand, and new venture deals across digital and traditional properties. The company, led by partners Lisa Filipelli, Scott Fisher, Amy Neben, and Adam Wescott, offers full-service talent management across all categories, including endorsements, live events and appearances, film and television, music, publishing, consumer products, and social media.

YouTube is a major digital channel for Select and its talented array of artists, which include pop-culture icons Tyler Oakley (www.youtube.com/user/tyleroakley), Gigi Gorgeous (www.youtube.com/channel/UCzco9CewPf0F-SP1p6LhWrw), LaurDIY (www.youtube.com/user/LaurDIY), MyLifeAsEva (www.youtube.com/user/mylifeaseva), and many others.

Select's success with its artists is helped by its innovation on YouTube, ensuring a continual stream of original content across diverse, contemporary genres, including fashion, beauty, cooking, consumer products, and more. In addition, Select develops and produces original, award-winning film and television series, as well as fosters new business ventures in consumer products and technology under their entertainment holding company, Third Act.

Entering information about your video

It doesn't matter whether your upload is a work in progress or a finished product; you can begin adding the metadata at any time, in a process known as *video optimization.* In the YouTube world, optimization involves dealing with three distinct areas:

>> **Details:** This is the most important information because it contains all the important fields for video SEO, including title, description, and tags.

>> **Monetization:** A creator who has elected to make money from ads being placed against their video can use this section to specify what types of advertising can be shown against the video. Chapter 14 covers this topic in more detail.

>> **Video elements:** You can add engaging or interactive end screens and cards to encourage viewers to watch other videos or visit related sites and links. We cover these in greater detail a bit later in this chapter.

>> **Visibility:** Here you can control who can see your videos. You can choose between four options: public, private, unlisted, and scheduled.

Have at it and edit the details. (Refer to Figure 9-5 to see the layout of the Details page.) Although it isn't rocket science, you still want to make sure to cross your *i*'s and dot your *t*'s. Follow these steps to edit your video's basic info:

1. **Make sure the Details page in the Upload window is selected.**

   The heading of the active section (refer to Figure 9-5) and the number preceding it are highlighted in blue. If Details isn't selected, simply click on the name, and the section fields appear. If you haven't filled out the required fields, you aren't allowed to advance to the next sections.

2. **Using your newly acquired SEO knowledge, come up with an appropriate title for your video and enter it into the Title field.**

3. **Enter an SEO-friendly description of your video into the Description field.**

4. **Upload or choose a thumbnail.**

   Though you *can* choose one of the three autogenerated thumbnails, we highly recommend making a custom thumbnail designed to be as eye-catching as possible.

   The thumbnail, which is your billboard, has a big influence on whether someone watches your video.

REMEMBER

5. **(Optional) Add your uploaded video to one or more playlists.**

   You can also create a new playlist here. Simply click the + Add to Playlist button and select the playlist where you want the video included. (You can select more than one playlist.)

6. **If the video has been made for children, specify that fact.**

   This field is required by YouTube to make sure the video is in compliance with COPPA — the Children's Online Privacy Protection Act. You can find the details about COPPA on the Federal Trade Commission website: www.ftc.gov.

7. **Indicate whether your video contains any sort of paid promotion.**

   If someone else has paid for you to mention their product or service, YouTube asks that you disclose it, to make sure you're in compliance with all advertising and law requirements. You can also add a message to inform your audience of the promotion, if you choose.

8. **Add SEO-appropriate tags in the Tags field.**

REMEMBER

YouTube imposes a limit of 500 characters for the entire Tag field. A tag can contain one or more words, but no individual tag can be more than 30 characters long. Depending on how you divvy up your 500 characters, you can end up with between 10 and 30 tags.

9. **Choose the video language, subtitles, and closed captioning.**

Select a language, caption certification (if it has aired on TV, federal regulations may require closed captions), and maybe add subtitles (which you can upload straight from your computer) in order to make your video more accessible for some viewers.

10. **Add the recording date and location.**

Though not required, this can help your SEO, because viewers can search videos by their location.

11. **Specify the license type and distribution settings.**

You can choose between the default Standard YouTube license (the stipulations of which are laid out in YouTube's terms of service) or Creative Commons, which makes your content available for use by other creators. Here's where you can permit the video to be embedded on other websites and determine whether your subscribers will receive a notification about the video's upload, both of which are on by default.

12. **Indicate which category your video fits in.**

Specifying the category of your video can help viewers find it more easily. For more information on YouTube genres, see Chapter 4.

13. **Finally, you can choose the comment and rating settings.**

By default, all comments are allowed and are sorted by most popular first. You can make it so that some or all comments must be reviewed by you, or you can turn off comments altogether. Generally, viewers like to see comments in real time, and they take note if you require approval. You can also deactivate the viewers' ability to like or dislike the video, though doing so can hide how your audience feels, meaning you won't have access to important information about viewer engagement.

If you're part of the YouTube partner program, the Details page is followed by the Monetization page. (If you're not able to monetize, your next step is the Video Elements page, covered later in this chapter.)

The following steps show how you can set the monetization for your uploaded video:

1. **Click Next in the bottom right corner of the Details page.**

Doing so takes you to the Monetization page, as shown in Figure 9-6.

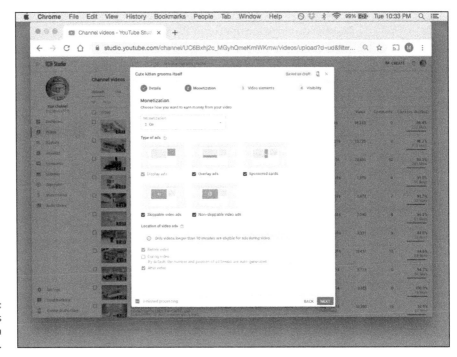

FIGURE 9-6:
YouTube's
monetization
page.

2. **Make sure monetization is set to On.**

If your account is able to monetize, this setting is on by fault. If, for whatever reason, you want to turn it off, choose Off from the drop-down menu.

3. **Specify the types of ads on your video.**

Chapter 14 covers monetization and ad types in greater detail.

4. **Choose the location of the ads.**

If your video is longer than ten minutes, you can choose where in your video the ads occur. By default, they occur at the beginning and end, but you can have them appear during the video. If you select During Video, you can either allow the ad breaks to generate automatically or specify when the break occurs. Though the former is easier, it can cause ads to appear for viewers in the middle of important moments or bits of information. If you choose Place Manually, you can drag or add a break during a preplanned or less important moment (similar to when a commercial break occurs in a TV episode).

You've probably figured out by now that YouTube has lots of bells and whistles. Don't worry: You're halfway there! The next section, Video Elements, allows you to customize your video's cards and end screens, but you can easily skip over it if you're just starting out.

To edit the video elements, do the following:

1. **Click Next in the bottom right corner of the Monetization page.**

Doing so takes you to the Video Elements page, as shown in Figure 9-7.

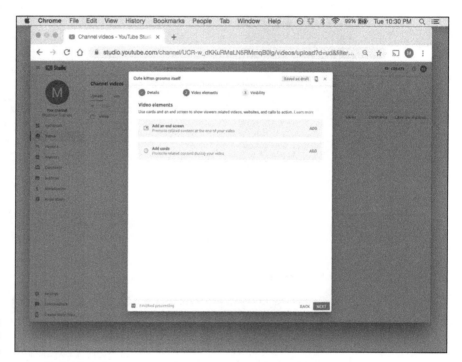

2. **Create an end screen by clicking the associated Add button to the right.**

Doing so opens a new window for creating and editing end screens, as shown in Figure 9-8. End screens can contain any combination (up to four total elements) of the following: videos, playlists, a subscribe card for your channel, links to other channels, or external links. YouTube offers four template card combinations or, by clicking the + Element button, you can customize the layout yourself. A highlighted box over the player shows you where the elements appear and can be adjusted by clicking-and-dragging. You can alter the timing of each element by manually entering new times (shown to the right of the element type) or by clicking-and-dragging the length of the element in the timeline below. To delete an element, click the Trash icon. Once you're happy with the orientation, you can preview it by clicking Play on the player, or you can simply click Save. This takes you back to the Video Elements page.

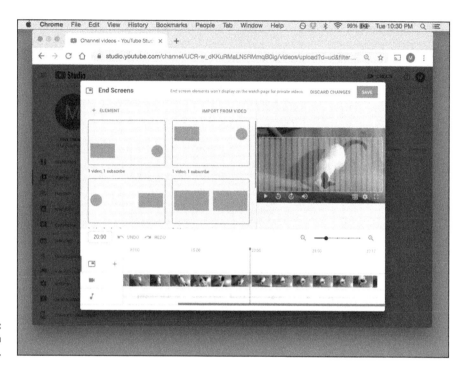

FIGURE 9-8:
The End Screen
editor.

End screens are a great way to boost your viewers' engagement and retention at the end of your videos while also allowing you to direct them to more of your content and brand.

REMEMBER

Videos must be at least 25 seconds long to accommodate end screens, which can be from 5 to 20 seconds long. If your content is marked as being made for children, you cannot add an end screen. End screens appear over the actual video, so if you're using them, it's best practice to edit in a little extra blank space at the end of your video so that important information isn't obscured. When adding end screens to your video, at least one of the elements must be a video or a playlist.

3. **Create cards by clicking the associated Add button to the right**.

You're taken to a page with a big, blue Add Card button on the right, as shown in Figure 9-9. Clicking this button reveals four options: video or playlist, channel, poll, and link. Clicking Create next to any of the options allows you to customize the content of each card. When you're ready, click Create Card.

You can alter the placement of each card within your video by dragging it along the timeline below. To preview, simply hit Play in the player window. If you want to remove a card, click the Pencil icon and then click the Trash icon. When you're finished, click the Return to YouTube Studio button in the top right corner.

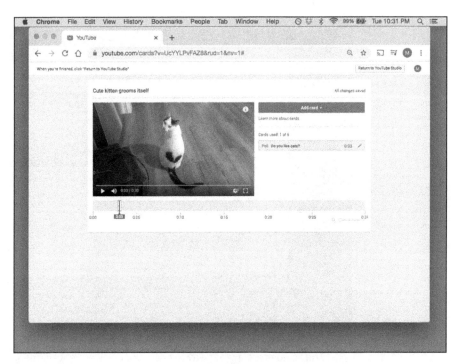

FIGURE 9-9:
The Cards Editor.

Cards help your audience interact with you and your videos and can be a valuable way to direct them to more of your videos or get meaningful feedback.

REMEMBER

Space out the cards in your video; that way, your audience has time to process them and interact. The Card icon disappears after several seconds, allowing your viewers to more easily notice when the next one pops up.

Now that you understand end screens and cards, you're ready for the fourth and final step: publishing your video.

Setting upload defaults

After you hit your groove and are uploading lots of content, you may tire of having to enter the same information over and over again into the various upload screens. Fortunately, YouTube allows you to set default values on the most common Basic Info, Advanced Settings, and Monetization options. Just choose Settings from the YouTube Studio menu on the left side of the screen and choose the Upload Defaults option. Figure 9-10 shows the kinds of things you can set as defaults using this option. These are handy if you format titles and descriptions similarly from video to video

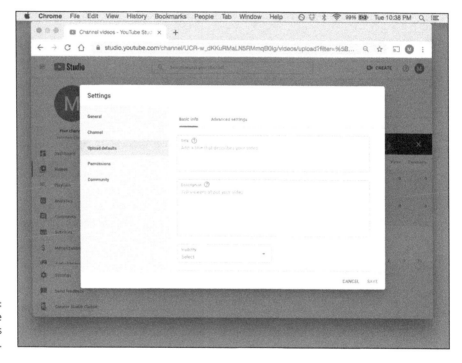

FIGURE 9-10:
The YouTube
Upload Defaults
configuration.

Defaults are simply preconfigured values. You can change values either during the upload process or via Video Manager.

REMEMBER

Publishing and Unpublishing Videos

The fourth and final tab, Visibility, is what stands between your video and your audience. As a YouTube channel manager or content creator, your work may well be done when you've uploaded your videos and set the metadata. Publishing is all about configuring the privacy settings that are most appropriate for your users and clicking Save during the upload process or on the YouTube Studio Video tab. For most channel managers, that means setting the video to Public at a specified time.

The following steps, as shown in Figure 9-11, show you how to — or how not to — publish your video (we cover YouTube's different types of video privacy earlier in this chapter, in the section "Going public about YouTube privacy").

>> **Save or Publish:** This option is selected by default. Depending on how you choose to publicize your video, the blue button in the bottom right corner says Save, Publish, or Schedule. Under Save or Publish, you find these three options:

- *Public:* Post your video right then and there once you click the blue Publish button in the bottom right corner. You can also make it a premiere by ticking the corresponding box below. A *premiere* allows you to watch your video as it is released alongside your viewers, including a live chat where you can interact.

- *Unlisted:* This is the default visibility for your video unless you choose otherwise. YouTube recommends that creators leave this setting alone so that any issues with the video — monetization or otherwise — are caught by YouTube before the video has been sent to your subscribers. Once it passes the filter, you can then publish it for your viewers to see. You can also leave it as unlisted if you only want people with the link to be able to view it. The blue button in the bottom right corner says Save.

- *Private:* Restrict the video's visibility to only you and anyone you choose to share it with.

The blue button in the bottom right corner of the page says Save.

>> **Scheduled:** This option allows you to set an exact date and time for when you want the video to go live, which is handy if you're trying to post with a specific cadence. You can also schedule it to be a *premiere,* which functions as previously mentioned but also includes a public watch page that counts down to when the video goes live. The blue button in the bottom right corner now says Schedule.

REMEMBER

After you've uploaded a video, you can't simply replace it with another one and use the same video URL. If you need to remove a video from general viewing, you have two choices:

>> **Unpublish it.** Set it to Private.

>> **Delete the video.** Remove it from YouTube permanently.

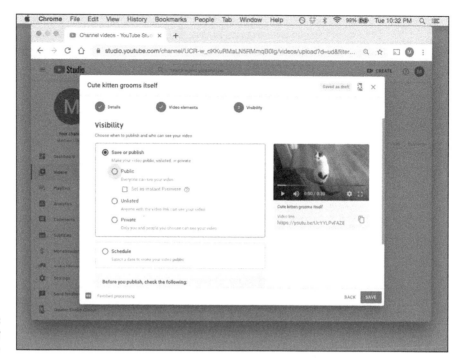

FIGURE 9-11:
The Visibility
page.

You can delete only videos that you own. To delete a video, follow these steps:

1. **Log in to your YouTube account.**

2. **On your YouTube page, click your Channel icon and then choose YouTube Studio from the menu that appears.**

3. **Click the Video tab in YouTube Studio.**

   You can also bypass these steps by going to www.youtube.com/my_videos.

TIP

4. **To delete one video, click the box to the left of the thumbnail of the video and choose Delete Forever from the More Actions drop-down menu that appears.**

   You're presented with a confirmation dialog box.

5. **Select I Understand and then click Delete Forever if you want to delete, or click Cancel if you've made a mistake or changed your mind.**

6. **To delete multiple videos, select one or more check boxes to the left of the thumbnails of the videos you want to remove, and then click Delete Forever beneath the More Actions drop-down menu that appears.**

   You're presented (again) with a confirmation dialog box.

7. **Check I Understand and then click Delete Forever if you want to delete, or click Cancel if you've made a mistake or changed your mind.**

   Figure 9-12 shows multiple videos selected for deletion.

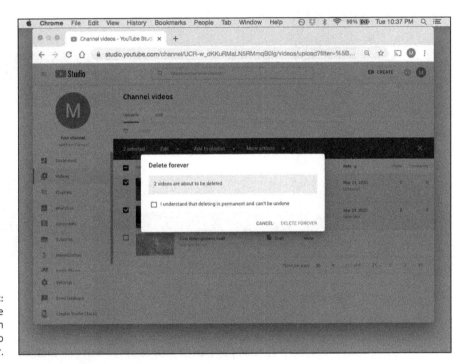

FIGURE 9-12:
Deleting multiple
videos from
YouTube video
manager.

3

Growing and Knowing Your Audience

Get the word out about your channel.

See what it takes to expand your audience.

Work with analytics tools to get a better sense of your audience.

Chapter **10**

Building Your Audience

There's obviously more to being an excellent channel manager than simply uploading a few videos and arranging a playlist or two. To truly excel as a channel manager, you have to realize that the core of your YouTube channel activities centers on your audience and on recognizing and responding to their needs. Your audience, whether it consists of 1,000 people or 10 million people, is coming to your channel and watching your videos for a reason, whether it's education, entertainment, product information, or what-have-you. Building an audience is about catering to the requirements of your viewers.

In the "good old days" of television, content was broadcast to a mass of viewers who were, for the most part, anonymous. It was never truly clear how many people were watching, so companies such as Nielsen provided estimates. The only feedback the audience delivered was either watching or not watching. As important as it was to retain regular viewers, the television networks knew they had to grow the addressable audience as well. They did this by putting together good shows and advertising lots of products. There wasn't much else for the audience to do than show up and watch shows when the networks aired them.

Fast-forward to Generation YouTube, where a completely different set of audience expectations affect not just viewing patterns but also how viewers expect to interact with the stars of the show. In this sense, the YouTube world is a two-way street, where the audience expects a back-and-forth exchange with the content providers. Audiences want an experience on their terms.

As a YouTube channel manager, you need to keep that engagement going. If you manage a YouTube celebrity, consider yourself the agent. Got a brand or a business channel? You need to put on your social-media-and-press-relations hat. Either way, you need to treat your audience with the same care and attention as you do your own content.

Developing a Community

Your audience consists of the people who watch your videos. As you acquire bigger audiences, YouTube ranks your channel and content higher, greatly aiding *discoverability* — the process whereby potential viewers are led to view your content. It's that simple, and it's why audience development is vital to your channel strategy. You want that newly acquired audience to visit your channel and experience more of your great content. It's a good pattern to establish.

Deciphering audience evolution

Unless you're already a celebrity, you probably won't acquire an audience overnight. That's okay. You need to understand that it may take years to build the right audience. Also remember that your channel may be evolving as well. Where you start on YouTube may not be where you end up. Nonetheless, consider the evolution of your audience and how they engage with your content. That process should (you hope) play out with these characteristics:

>> **Interest:** Viewers are interested in something, whether it's Bruno Mars, monster trucks, Indian cooking, radiant floor heating installation, or so much more. They search and come to YouTube to find out more about the topics they're interested in.

>> **Curiosity:** Impressed by watching one of your videos, your viewers then visit your channel to look for more of your content. A nicely designed channel and well-organized playlist enhance their experience.

>> **Connection:** Liking their experience with you and your channel, they now want to stay current and be informed of updates. They choose to subscribe.

>> **Engagement:** Your audience wants even more, so they begin to click that handy Like button on some of your videos and start offering comments. They may engage with each other using the Comments section of your channel.

>> **Promotion:** They then share your content via Facebook, Twitter, and other social media channels with others who share similar interests — others who (hopefully) also become part of your audience.

>> **Collaboration:** In addition to giving you feedback, your most passionate fans may even work with you on content.

Determining what you want your audience to do

Though your final goal may be to become a YouTube celebrity and have your audience request autographed pictures of you, you have some other homework to do before the audience is eating out of your hand. Your audience requirements come down to two simple things you want them to do:

>> **Watch:** You know the importance of watch time on discoverability. Your audience needs to view your content regularly — and you need to feed them good content regularly.

>> **Engage:** Having viewers watching content is great, but having them actually do something is the frosting on the cake. Engagement is a broad topic that you can read about at length in this chapter. It includes actions such as liking, commenting, messaging, sharing, and clicking.

REMEMBER

Engagement is a two-way street. You need to engage back as well. Lilly Singh (www.youtube.com/user/IISuperwomanII) didn't get where she is today without listening to her fans; the proof is that she has gone out of her way to create different channels for her different types of content. With more than 14.9 million subscribers on her main channel, she's doing it right. She even has her own late-night TV show because of her amazing content and loyal fans on YouTube. Despite all that success, Lilly still asks her fans to comment at specific parts of the video so that she knows what they love, as shown in Figure 10-1.

REMEMBER

As you gain viewers, your watch time and engagement level increase. That's why building an audience for your channel can't be left to chance. You need to comment even when you have millions of subscribers.

Appreciating the importance of community

Communities have developed around common interests for thousands of years. From medieval guilds to book groups to political movements, people have banded together into communities. As the Internet grew in both reach and popularity, virtual communities began to spring up. Suddenly, people could be part of large, diverse communities spread over continents and time zones.

FIGURE 10-1:
Audience
engagement
through channel
owner
comments.

By bringing the video component to the Internet picture, YouTube made these communities more engaged — and more real. You could actually see your peers. As a result, YouTube communities quickly showed that they could be extremely important resource for creators as well as companies.

REMEMBER

Your community could do much to drive the audience growth of your YouTube channel, but for that to happen you need to be a genuine and active member of the community.

Over time, many members of your community will take that extra step and subscribe to your channel. Subscribers are worth their weight in gold because they watch more and engage more. Clearly that's a good thing, but there's something else: The YouTube Partner Program (YPP) offers additional features to channels that have higher subscriber counts. As you acquire more subscribers, YouTube gives you more perks.

In the YouTube world, you also hear a lot about fans. Aren't all subscribers fans? Not exactly. Your fans are that subset of your subscribers who exhibit considerably higher levels of engagement. Take care of your subscribers, and take special care of your fans.

Determining your subscription source

If your channel has a large number of subscribers, YouTube provides interesting options for analyzing them in order to learn a bit more about them and (hopefully) communicate with them more effectively. These features are found in the Analytics section on the Audience tab within YouTube Studio.

TIP

Your subscribers might all be watching a specific type of content from your channel, so be sure to *listen* to what your audience wants to watch, by reading and responding to their comments, and then *analyze* the content they're spending their time watching.

Here's how you can access some of the more helpful dashboards for subscriber analysis from YouTube Studio:

1. **From YouTube Studio's main page, choose Analytics from the menu on the left.**

2. **Click the Audience tab at the top of the new screen that appears.**

3. **Click the blue See More link in the bottom left corner of the main view of the Audience Report overview.**

   A whole set of new dashboards appears for your viewing pleasure.

This view of the channel reporting is crucial to understanding how your community is consuming your videos — where they find the content, who they are, how old the viewer is, what gender, where the viewer originates, and so much more. It is important to look at all of your viewer statistics and not just those of your loyal subscribers. There may be many untapped opportunities for you once you really know who your viewers are and where they are coming from.

It's important to achieve a good balance between creating content for subscribers and non-subscribers. Be sure to review your loyal subscribers when analyzing your channel statistics. Figure 10-2 shows the many ways in which you can slice and dice the subscriber data.

REMEMBER

Be sure to choose the date range you want to analyze. If this is your first time looking at this report, it might help to view the lifetime of your channel and then work your way up to the present month.

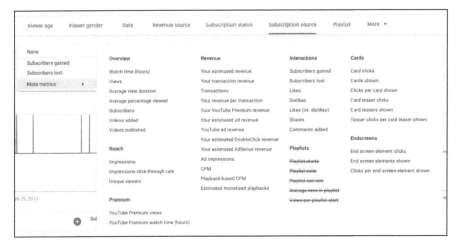

FIGURE 10-2:
The metrics you can use to analyze your channel subscribers.

Understanding Subscribers and Their Value

YouTube allows viewers to connect more deeply with the channels they like, by allowing them to become subscribers. To subscribe to a channel, all a viewer needs to do is go to a channel's home page and click either the red Subscribe button or a link to the Subscribe button. Viewers can also subscribe from a watch page or a subscriptions channel list. Understand that your subscribers have both YouTube value — in the sense that a higher number of subscribers lets YouTube know that your channel and content are important — and in some cases monetary value. If you make money from YouTube or are planning to, you look at the audience data and revenue source to determine what your subscribers are worth. You can read more about these topics in Chapters 11 and 14.

REMEMBER

Viewers must be logged in to subscribe to a channel. If they happen to click the Subscribe button when logged out, YouTube simply asks them to log in with their Google credentials.

If a viewer is logged in and visits a channel page that they have subscribed to or if they visit a video watch page that's part of one of their subscribed channels, they see the gray Subscribed button, as shown in Figure 10-3 — not the Subscribe button, in other words. Note that each Subscribed button has the bell-shaped Notifications icon next to it: click that icon and a menu appears, listing options that allow subscribers to control how they receive channel notifications.

Subscribed

FIGURE 10-3:
The Subscribed
button, for
existing
subscribers.

Persuading viewers to subscribe

Channel managers have several options when it comes to providing viewers with the tools necessary to subscribe:

» **Buttons below the channel art:** On every page that has channel art (such as the home page, the about page, the watch page, and the various channel pages) you'll find the Subscribe button under the right side of the channel art. (Channel art is described in Chapter 3.)

» **Buttons on the watch page:** Users can subscribe to a channel by viewing a video on the *watch page* — the page where viewers watch a video. The Subscribe button is underneath the right side of the video — below the channel name and next to the Channel icon. Chapter 2 describes the characteristics of the Watch page.

» **Custom links:** Channel managers can create subscription custom links that appear on the channel's About page and in the channel art. Start with the following line of code, and add the name of your channel to *yourchannelname*:

```
http://www.youtube.com/subscription_center?add_user=
    yourchannelname
```

>> **Links in the channel description:** Subscriber links can be useful in the descriptions uploaded as part of your video metadata. Just use the subscription link code shown in the preceding paragraph. Chapter 9 describes how to modify and optimize (for video SEO) a video description.

WARNING

Subscription links can grow long and unsightly. Don't be afraid to substitute a shortlink instead. You also get additional tracking to see which subscription links generate the most clicks. Chapter 9 introduces shortlinks and the software needed to track them.

>> **Links on end screens:** End screens are a helpful way to add a subscription link to a video. YouTube provides all the tools necessary to handle the task without requiring you to do any video editing.

>> **Buttons tied to recommendations:** Subscription buttons also show up under the Recommended Channels section of a channel page. The channel manager can hand-select, to display on the channel page, specific channels that may be of interest to the viewer. (Note that, unlike other Subscribe buttons, which are red, these buttons are gray.)

>> **Web URLs:** It's easy to get people to subscribe from places not on YouTube: Just include a Subscription link, like the one shown earlier. Clicking the link brings them to a YouTube channel, so determine whether you want the link to open in another tab or window if you don't want the subscriber to exit your site.

TIP

Many channel managers put a link to the channel page as the target of the Subscribe link. If you want to bring people to your channel, please let them know that — otherwise, make the Subscribe button trigger a subscription request.

>> **The old-fashioned way:** Have your video personality look straight into the camera and ask them to subscribe. There's no harm in asking!

REMEMBER

You can ask viewers to subscribe in many ways — don't feel that you have to use only one method. YouTube allows a good deal of flexibility in generating subscription requests, so go ahead and experiment to see what works best for your audience.

Specifying how subscribers get updates

Being a subscriber to a channel is a lot like being a supporter of a local museum: You get notified first about events, and you get to see things before anyone else. Yes, being a subscriber has its benefits. Subscribers have the option to be notified when you

>> Upload a video

>> Add a video to a public playlist

>> Like a video or save a playlist

>> Subscribe to a channel

>> Create a community post (available only for channels with 1,000 subscribers or more)

Subscribers can choose between being notified of all your events, no updates, and personalized updates. (They make their choice by clicking the Bell icon, next to the gray Subscribed button, and making their choice from the options that appear.)

WARNING

Your subscribers are your gold, so keeping them happy with your channel and the frequency of your notifications is important. If they receive too many from you, they may unsubscribe; too few and they may forget about you. Moderation is important.

You should understand how your subscribers actually receive your channel updates:

>> Email

>> Mobile device notification

>> Accounts connected to social media

In addition, subscribers can receive updates from several areas of the YouTube platform:

>> **Home:** When viewers log in to YouTube, click the YouTube button in the top left corner of their browsers, or start the YouTube app on their mobile devices, they land on the home page.

REMEMBER

This page is customized for each user because YouTube makes video suggestions based on a viewer's subscriptions and recommendations derived from their viewing history.

>> **Subscriptions:** When viewers are logged in, they find their subscriptions on their home page or at www.youtube.com/feed/channels.

Controlling channel settings and privacy levels

You can control what your subscribers see and also set the privacy of your likes and subscriptions using your channel's account settings.

To do so, follow these steps:

1. **Log in to your YouTube account.**

2. **Click the Channel icon in the top right corner of the YouTube home page, and choose YouTube Studio from the menu that appears.**

3. **On the Account Settings page that appears, select Privacy on the navigation bar running down the left side of the page.**

4. **Select the check box for the information you want to make private.**

   Here are your privacy options, as shown in Figure 10-4:

   - *Keep all my subscriptions private*

   - *Keep all my saved lists private*

5. **Click Save.**

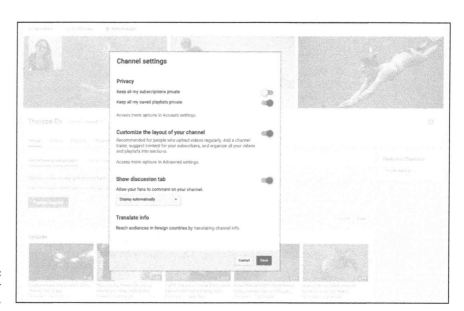

FIGURE 10-4:
Privacy on your
channel settings.

TIP

You can also go directly to your privacy settings by using yet another method: Visit www.youtube.com/account_privacy.

REMEMBER

Your public channel uploads are automatically part of your feed and can't be hidden or omitted by using the feed settings or privacy settings. Only the subscribers can specify whether they want to be notified about your new public videos.

Treating subscribers and nonsubscribers differently

To provide a more customized experience for viewers, YouTube allows you to treat subscribers and nonsubscribers differently when they visit your channel. (Subscribers don't necessarily want to see the same video when they show up at your channel, because they've likely already seen it, so it makes sense to treat them differently from nonsubscribers.)

Working with a channel trailer

The *channel trailer* is a prominent video that's shown whenever viewers first arrive at your channel. It's your chance to convert nonsubscribers, inform them about what they can expect from your channel, get them excited about you and your content, and give them the details of your programming schedule.

REMEMBER

You don't need to change out your channel trailer frequently, because a viewer who subscribes isn't shown this trailer again. Subscribers are greeted by a What to Watch Next page instead of a channel trailer.

Several factors affect what shows up on the What to Watch Next page. If you're livestreaming, that livestream shows up first. When you're running a TrueView YouTube advertising campaign (see Chapter 13), you can choose where your ads will show — on the watch page or channel page.

Customizing your channel

To show a channel trailer for new visitors, do the following:

1. **Log in to your YouTube account.**

2. **Click the Channel icon in the top right corner of the YouTube home page and choose Your Channel from the menu that appears.**

   The My Channel screen appears.

3. **Click the blue Customize Channel button on the right side, under your channel art.**

   Doing so brings up your channel in an editable state where you can modify your channel's home page.

4. **When you're viewing the channel as "yourself," which is the default, click the second link, For New Visitors. (See Figure 10-5.)**

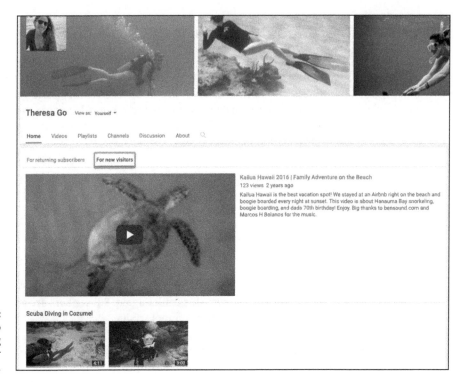

FIGURE 10-5:
YouTube Studio
setup for adding
a channel trailer
for new visitors.

5. **In the pop-up dialog box that appears, choose the desired channel trailer videos from your uploads or enter the YouTube video URLs.**

6. **Update the title and description of your chosen video, because this metadata is what new visitors see on your channel.**

You will need to edit the metadata on the video in YouTube Studio under the Videos tab.

7. **Click Save.**

TIP

Managing Comments

Many people tend to forget that YouTube is also a social media platform. That's a bit odd because it's one of the most heavily trafficked websites on the planet. In fact, one reason YouTube is so effective for creators and companies is precisely that its platform provides a powerful connection not just between a viewer and your brand but also *among* your audience.

Seeing why comments matter

Your interaction with your viewers and channel visitors is an important signal to not just your current subscribers but also your potential subscribers. It tells them that your brand and your channel and content are worth their time. Encouraging comments is a great way to grow an audience and feed your community.

Make a concerted effort to add your own follow-ups to comments posted when you upload a video. Channel programming is about regularly scheduling uploads. Channel *manager* programming is about always responding to comments in a timely manner.

Your options for managing any particular comment are listed here:

>> Allow the comment.

>> Allow and respond to the comment.

>> Remove the comment.

>> Report spam or abuse.

>> Ban the commenter from the channel.

You typically allow and respond to comments. You can learn the details of managing comments in the following sections.

Similarly to likes and dislikes on video, viewers can like and dislike comments. Pay attention to comments that receive large numbers of both likes and dislikes.

Viewers generally appreciate being recognized by creators and channel managers. You can add the name of a viewer in a comment by typing a plus sign (+) and then their name. YouTube helps by autocompleting the name, so you're assured that the person will be notified of your outreach.

You can respond to comments in one of two ways:

>> **On the watch page:** Both viewers and channel managers can add comments just below the channel description. (Refer to Figure 10-1.) The Comment field is in the All Comments section; just type right where it says Add a public reply.

Commenters must be logged in to make a comment. If they aren't logged in, YouTube asks them to do so.

>> **The Channel Comments section in YouTube Studio:** Only channel managers can comment here or reply to a comment. You can also add a thumb's up or thumb's down or "heart" a comment.

Setting up your channel for comments

You may hear some people say not to allow comments on your channel. We're convinced that you give up much of the effectiveness of YouTube by following that advice. Much of the concern that folks have about comments stems from the fact that some channel managers have done a less-than-stellar job around content moderation, which means that some channels' Comments sections turn into toxic cesspools. That's a sign of a channel manager falling down on the job, not proof that comments can't work in a YouTube context. In the next section, you can find tips and techniques you'll need in order to keep yourself from falling down on the job.

First, you need to decide what level of channel comments you're comfortable with. Here's how to set it up channel-wide:

1. **Log in to your YouTube account.**

2. **Click the Channel icon in the top right corner of the YouTube home page, and choose YouTube Studio from the menu that appears.**

3. **Select Settings in the navigation bar running down the left side of the page.**

   Doing so opens a dialog box.

4. **Under Upload Defaults, choose an option:**

   - Allow all comments.

   - Hold potentially inappropriate comments for review. Google automatically flags comments it deems suspicious or inappropriate. You, the channel owner, can be the final judge if a comment should or should not be posted.

   - Hold all comments for review.

   - Disable comments.

5. **Click Save after you have chosen the correct settings for your preferences.**

TIP

Though we feel that it's important to choose what's best for you as a channel manager, our recommendation is the second one: Hold potentially inappropriate comments for review. The algorithms Google uses to flag comments are quite sophisticated, so they do a good job. You can always come back and change the setting if you feel differently.

With your channel enabled for discussion, your videos can now receive comments. You can also control comments on a video-by-video basis. You have three ways to enable comments on individual videos:

>> **Default:** YouTube allows all video comments by default.

>> **Upload defaults:** In YouTube Studio, under Settings; refer to the preceding Steps list).

>> **Advanced settings:** In the YouTube Studio Video section, set the comments controls for an individual video by hovering the mouse cursor over the video title in order to display the Comments Edit icon.

Moderating comments

As your audience engages more and more with your videos and as your channel becomes increasingly successful, comment moderation on a video-by-video basis can become rather tedious. Fortunately, YouTube allows you to moderate comments all in one place — in the Comments section of YouTube Studio. To start moderating, follow these steps:

1. **Log in to your YouTube account.**

2. **Click the Channel icon in the top right corner of the YouTube home page and choose YouTube Studio from the menu that appears.**

3. **Select Comments from the navigation bar on the left side of the screen.**

   Note the following three tabs, as shown in Figure 10-6:

   ● *Published:* These are the comments currently posted on your channel. You can do all the standard things with these comments — allow the comment, allow and respond to the comment, remove the comment, report the comment as spam or abusive, or ban the commenter from the channel.

REMEMBER

   Whether you're on the watch page or in the Comments section, the icons and pull-down menus to the right allow you to remove a comment, block a commenter, or report spam. (You'll probably make much use of the Trash icon, which quickly vaporizes an inappropriate comment.)

   ● *Held for Review:* Comments are held here when you don't allow automatic posting or when comments are caught by the Hold for Review filters you set in the community guidelines. If the comment is acceptable, click the Check button; otherwise, click its associated Trash icon to remove it. Review your held comments regularly so that the appropriate ones get posted on your channel.

- *Likely Spam:* YouTube, in its efforts to root out spam, places comments here that it regards as likely spam. Ultimately, however, you are the judge of what's spam and what's not. Make sure that YouTube hasn't jumped the gun and mischaracterized a comment as spam. If it's not spam, just click the Check button to accept; otherwise, click the Trash icon to remove it.

FIGURE 10-6:
Channel
Comments
section.

Anything you can do to a single comment on the Comments page — accept, respond to, delete — can be done to multiple comments in one fell swoop. Simply check one or more of the comments you're moderating and take bulk action.

TIP

Reacting to inappropriate comments

As a channel manager, you need to draw the line on what comments are appropriate to be shown on your channel. Just because someone disagrees with you doesn't mean you have to call out the military. Some channel managers and creators like a debate, but in certain situations, comments are abusive and inappropriate and provide no benefit to you, your viewers, or your community.

With comments, you have the following options:

» **Remove:** This option simply deletes the comment.

» **Report Spam or Abuse:** Comments and those who comment are subject to the same community guidelines. (For more on community guidelines, see Chapter 9.)

The Report Spam or Abuse flag is there to report a guideline violation, not a channel or video comment disagreement. See the next option if community guidelines are adhered to yet you still need to address a situation.

>> **Hide User from Channel:** Sometimes you just need to divorce yourself from certain viewers. This setting prevents them from posting comments. If circumstances change and you want them back, you can remove them from the Hidden User list in your Community settings. (For more on Community settings, see the next section.)

>> **Always Approve Comments from This User:** Save yourself time by always approving comments if you know and trust a user.

>> **Add This User as a Comment Moderator.** Use good judgment and take advantage of a little help from your friends for comment moderation.

Configuring Community Settings

You've probably noticed some similarities between comments and the Discussion tab on your channel. Both of these involve the management of users. YouTube makes it easy to manage users from a central location known as Community settings. To access Community settings, do the following:

1. **Log in to your YouTube account.**

2. **Click the Channel icon in the top right corner of the YouTube home page and choose YouTube Studio from the menu that appears.**

3. **Select Settings in the navigation bar running down the left side of the page.**

4. **Choose Community from the Settings navigation menu on the left side of the screen, as shown in Figure 10-7.**

Community settings consist of two sections:

>> **Automated filters:** Some viewers are constructive, and some viewers aren't. That's just the nature of YouTube. This is where you manage

- *Moderators:* Enables these users to remove comments, which then appear on your Held for Review page; these folks can also moderate your live chat messages.

- *Approved users:* Enables the automated posting of comments and messages from identified users; it even allows them to post comments that include blocked words, links, or inappropriate content.

FIGURE 10-7:
YouTube
Community
settings.

- *Hidden users:* Comments and live chat messages from these users don't show up on your channel. After you hide them, it may take a couple of days for their comments to disappear completely.

REMEMBER

  Both approved and banned users can be managed using their YouTube channel URLs.

- *Blocked words:* Comments and live chats that match phrases or words in this list are held for review.

- *Block links:* New comments with hashtags or URLs are held for review. Live chat messages with URLs are blocked for the safety of all users.

WARNING

Think hard before disabling comments. It's tough to develop a community when you've taken away a key engagement component of YouTube.

Getting Viewers to Engage

After you have a solid channel and an active audience commenting, messaging, and sharing your content, you have to ask whether they're doing everything you expected. In Chapter 5, we talk about establishing the goals for your channel.

Some of those goals may be YouTube-related, such as attracting more views and subscribers, or they might be more commerce-oriented, such as influencing a brand decision and driving a product purchase from a website. Either way, you need to entice your audience to click on the video and take the next action. End screens and comprehensive video descriptions are some of the best tools at your disposal for drawing post-view clicks.

Audiences engage with your channel, but they also come to recognize your *brand* — those unique elements that tell the world that your content is *yours* rather than someone else's. YouTube recognizes that branding is a big deal in our content-saturated world. That's why it goes out of its way to provide some additional capabilities to apply branding without forcing you to invest the additional time and effort that always come with an additional video edit.

Branding was previously known by its more confusing name: *InVideo programming.*

When it comes to branding, YouTube allows channel managers to add a brand watermark to the bottom right corner of the video player. To set up such branding for your channel, follow these steps:

1. **Log in to your YouTube account.**

2. **Click the Channel icon in the top right corner of the YouTube home page and choose YouTube Studio from the menu that appears.**

3. **Select Settings in the navigation bar running down the left side of the page.**

4. **On the new page that appears, select Channel in the navigation bar running down the page's left side.**

5. **On the new page that appears, click to select the third tab, Branding. (See Figure 10-8.)**

   You can upload an image that's in PNG or GIF format, 150 x 150 pixels, 1MB or less. This watermark should be simple and transparent, if possible — something eye-catching and easy to read or understand, because viewers will see it on mobile phone screens, which are relatively small.

You can always remove the watermark later, if you don't like it or if you change your branding.

FIGURE 10-8:
The YouTube
Channel Branding
preview and
upload page.

Capturing the Captioning Opportunity

You don't have to let language and sound be barriers to connecting with your audience. YouTube provides tools for subtitles and closed captions, which allow viewers who are hearing impaired or who don't speak your language to watch and understand your videos. Adding subtitles and closed captions can even have a positive impact on your video's YouTube Search results.

By the way, don't let the thought of dealing with closed captions and subtitles scare you. Working with these elements is similar to working with any other video element on your channel — in this, as in all matters, YouTube Studio is your friend. Use the following steps to create subtitles and closed captions:

1. Log in to your YouTube account.

2. Click the Channel icon in the top right corner of the YouTube home page and choose YouTube Studio from the menu that appears.

3. Select Subtitles in the navigation bar running down the left side of the page.

4. **On the new page that appears, click the drop-down arrow from any video to add subtitles.**

TIP

By clicking the Gear symbol in the right-hand corner, you can turn on the option to let the community add video translations to your uploads.

5. **Click the Add button to the right of the video and choose the method you want to use to add subtitles or closed captions.**

Doing so opens the new tab shown in Figure 10-9.

REMEMBER

You may need to choose your language or search for it in the search box first. After your language is selected, you're prompted to choose how to add your subtitles or closed captions.

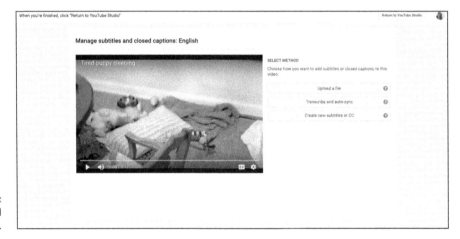

FIGURE 10-9:
Subtitles and captions.

6. **Select a captioning/subtitle method:**

● *Upload a File:* Add a text transcript or timed subtitles in the form of an uploadable file.

● *Transcribe and Auto-Sync:* Type or paste a transcript into the video transcript box that comes up to the right of the video. YouTube autoconfigures the timing.

● *Create New Subtitles or CC:* Add captions as you watch the video by either uploading a transcript file or entering the text directly into a transcript box. You can pause and play while doing this.

Producing Live Events

Putting together live events on YouTube is a great way to build an audience and drive engagement. You have several options for managing live content on YouTube:

» **YouTube live events:** Livestreaming with active management of the comments. You can live stream from your house, on set, or anywhere with good connectivity.

» **Off-platform events:** Consider live streaming in real life at an event. Grab the opportunity to meet with your fans in real life, outside of your usual shooting locations. Many YouTube creators use physical community events, such as VidCon (www.vidcon.com), to meet with their fans — and shoot some live content with them.

TIP

Repurpose your live event content for your channel. Your audience will love the attention.

Chapter **11**

Knowing Your Audience

I magine driving along in your car and suddenly your dashboard goes out: no lights, no gauges, no navigation. You can either pull over to the side of the road and call a tow truck or just keep driving. Whatever the decision, you'll have a tougher time making it to your destination. As a YouTube channel manager driving down the video highway, you need a dashboard, too: That dashboard is YouTube Analytics.

YouTube Analytics is designed to help you uncover meaningful information about your audience, viewership, and engagement. If you're working with YouTube creators and other online video personalities, chances are good that you'll be prompted to provide some interesting reports about all the wonderful things happening with the YouTube channel. In some cases, though, you may have to deliver some not-so-good news: Maybe your audience and fan base just aren't liking the new videos that are being uploaded to the channel. YouTube Analytics is there to help you figure out what may have gone wrong — and a whole lot more.

YouTube Analytics is where you find the details about your audience: where they're finding you, what they like, where they're watching, and so on. After a while, YouTube Analytics will likely be your first YouTube stop every day. Spend time mastering the analytics process and extracting the key insights it contains, because it will help you craft a more robust channel — and significantly better video content. If you're making money from your channel, YouTube Analytics can help you earn even more.

REMEMBER

YouTube Analytics isn't just for new channels. If you already have a channel and it's not performing to your satisfaction, YouTube Analytics is a valuable resource for diagnosing and subsequently fixing problems.

Getting Started with YouTube Analytics

It's tough to talk about analytics with YouTubers without hearing supporting terms like *metrics* and *insights.* Don't be put off by all the geeky terms. In Chapter 5, you can find out all about setting goals for your channel. This chapter, however, is all about determining whether you're meeting your goals; to be able to do that, you need to work with metrics and insights.

Here's the skinny: Metrics are *quantitative* measurements, such as the number of views and the click-through rates on your channel. Metrics gauge your goal attainment against your plan. Insights are *qualitative* and *actionable* things you learn and do from analyzing metrics — determining whether your content is working for you, for example, or figuring out whether your interactive cards are well placed in your video.

YouTube Analytics shows you how you're tracking against your goals and also where you may need to make adjustments. Understanding metrics and insights is relatively straightforward, but you need to know where to look in YouTube Analytics to get the data you need.

REMEMBER

As a channel manager, always think in terms of metrics and insights. You must *act* on those insights, though. For example, if the view count and number of likes (metrics) for your new video are only 25 percent of your target, your video may not be resonating with your audience or maybe you released it at the wrong time (insights). Take the time to fix what may be immediately wrong (such as poor metadata), or change future content or programming. You should monitor the video metrics again over time.

As you become more sophisticated in your use of YouTube Analytics, you realize that certain metrics may depend on other metrics. For example, your earnings metrics may be impacted by view metrics, which may be impacted by engagement metrics. Don't sweat the details — the relationship among all metrics comes together quickly.

Reading YouTube Analytics reports

Your go-to place for all aspects of YouTube Analytics is the Analytics section of YouTube Studio. To make your way there, do the following:

1. **In your web browser, go to** www.youtube.com.

2. **Log on to your YouTube account.**

   If you see a blue Sign In button in the top right corner of the YouTube home page, enter your email address and password.

3. **Click the Logged-In icon and choose YouTube Studio from the menu that appears.**

   The YouTube Studio navigation menu should appear on the left side of your browser.

4. **Choose Analytics from the navigation menu.**

   By default, you should go directly to the Overview tab, as shown in Figure 11-1.

TIP

You can also bypass these report-reading steps by going to www.youtube.com/analytics.

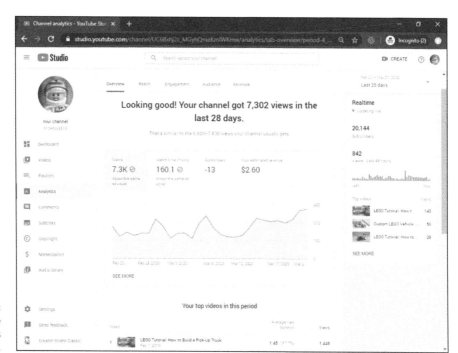

FIGURE 11-1: YouTube Analytics overview.

YouTube Analytics is divided into five subsections, indicated by the five tabs running across the top of the screen. They're described, from left to right, in this list:

>> **Overview:** Presents a high-level view of your channel's overall performance. It includes the following summary reports:

- *Main graph:* Data on views, watch time, and subscribers over a specified period. If your channel is monetized, you also see estimated revenue data in this graph.

- *Top videos:* A list of your top videos for the selected period, ranked by watch time.

- *Realtime:* Displays your video views and top viewed videos over the past 48 hours.

- *Latest Videos:* Shows an embedded video of the latest videos you have uploaded, as well as its views, average view duration, and watch time.

>> **Reach:** Displays the overall *reach* — how many people watched the content on your channel categorized by your different traffic sources, in other words. This section is composed of several summary reports:

- *Main graph:* Displays the number of impressions, click-throughs, views, and unique viewers your videos have generated over a selected period.

- *Impressions and how they led to watch time:* A funnel chart displaying how your video impressions led to views and, ultimately, watch time. This report also shows how often, on average, YouTube has recommended your videos to users.

- *Traffic source types:* Provides a breakdown of where and how often users found your videos on YouTube, such as YouTube Search, suggested videos, channel pages, and more.

- *Traffic source: External:* Displays a list of websites and apps outside of YouTube that link to or have embedded your video, as well as the percentage of times these sources led to views.

- *Traffic source: Playlists:* Shows the total percentage of views you accumulated from playlists containing your video and the names of those playlists that led to the most views.

- *Traffic source: Suggested videos:* Shows the total percentage of views you accumulated from other videos suggesting your content and the names of the videos that led to the most views.

- *Traffic source: YouTube Search:* Shows the total percentage of views you accumulated from the YouTube Search results and the keywords that led to the most views.

» **Engagement:** Presents a summary of what your audience is watching on your channel. It includes these summary reports:

- *Main graph:* Displays the total watch time and average view duration of videos on your channel over a specified period

- *Top videos:* Displays a list of your top videos ordered by their watch time in hours

- *Top videos by end screen:* Shows a list of your top videos, ordered by the number of end screen element clicks

- *Top playlists:* Provides a breakdown of your playlists ordered by the percentage of watch time attributed to each one

- *Top end screen element types:* Shows a list of clicks per each type of end screen element type you use

- *Top cards:* Shows a list of end screen cards, ordered by the highest number of clicks

» **Audience:** Describes who is watching your channel. It contains these summary reports:

- *Main graph:* Displays the number of unique viewers, average number of views per viewers, and subscriber growth over a specified period.

- *When your viewers are on YouTube:* Shows the times of day and days of the week your viewers watch YouTube so that you can determine when to publish your videos or launch a live stream.

- *Age and gender:* Provides a breakdown of your audience by gender and age bracket based on a percentage of views.

- *Subscriber bell notifications:* Shows the percentage of your audience that has turned on all notifications for your channel. Also displays a typical channel benchmark range for this action on other YouTube channels.

- *Top countries:* Shows what countries your audience is located in, based on a percentage of views.

- *Top subtitle/CC languages:* Displays your audience's usage of subtitles as well as which languages are most frequently being used based on a percentage of views.

REMEMBER

YouTube reports demographics data for users who are signed in to Google. Because of this, the data you see may not completely reflect all traffic visiting your channel.

>> **Revenue:** Displays a summary of earnings from your channel. It includes these summary reports:

- *Main graph*: Shows your estimated revenue, estimated monetized playbacks, and playback-based CPM (cost-per thousand impression) for a specified period.

- *Monthly estimated revenue*: Displays your estimated revenue for the past six months.

- *Top earning videos*: Shows you which of your videos are generating the most money and how much money they have earned.

- *Revenue sources*: Provides a breakdown of where your channel revenue is coming from, from sources like advertisements and YouTube Premium.

- *Ad types*: Shows the types of ads (such as skippable ads, nonskippable ads, bumper ads, and display ads) that are running on your videos, ordered by the percentage of revenue they provide. (For more on ad types, check out Chapter 13.)

REMEMBER

The Revenue tab is accessible only to YouTube creators who have been accepted into the YouTube Partner Program. (Chapter 14 has more on monetization opportunities.)

If you want to see deeper analytics on any summary report described in the preceding list, you can click the See More link at the bottom of the report to open Advanced Mode, which provides access to additional metrics. Similarly, you can launch Advanced Mode by clicking the Advanced Mode link above the Date dropdown menu in the upper right corner of the page at any time to see more granular reporting details. We discuss in the next section how to use features within the Advanced Mode window.

TIP

To learn more about the main reporting tabs of YouTube Analytics as well as the summary reports just described, visit `https://support.google.com/youtube/answer/9002587`.

Breaking down the report components

Beyond the summary reports available within the main pages of YouTube Analytics, YouTube provides a richer set of reporting options within Advanced Mode that may seem overwhelming at first. You quickly discover, however, that navigating this comprehensive reporting module is quite easy because it consists of these four distinct sections:

>> **Filters:** Over time, you do a lot of different things with your channel, including adding video content, constructing playlists, engaging subscribers, and so much more. You'll definitely want to set up dynamic filters that are meant to show you only the information associated with each of these aspects of your channel. The Advanced Mode filter section, shown in Figure 11-2, lets you do that.

>> **Reports:** Advanced Mode reports provide greater detail than the summary reports that are available on the main pages of YouTube Analytics. You can also access some additional reports that aren't available on the main YouTube Analytics pages and add additional metrics to all reports. You can access this feature from the menu beneath the filters and above the chart within Advanced Mode, or by clicking the See More link at the bottom of any summary report.

>> **Chart:** After you've determined which report you want to analyze, you can get lots of information with some fairly flexible graphical representations (charts, in other words) to guide your understanding. This helps you assess the performance of your channel, your content, and your community. (You can see an example in Figure 11-3 of a YouTube Analytics chart showing views over several weeks.)

>> **Table:** Shows itemized details that correspond to the particular YouTube Analytics report. For example, in the Videos report, you can create a detailed, organized list of your top 50 videos, including name, views, percentage growth in view, estimated minutes watched, and average view duration. Figure 11-4 shows what the table of a YouTube Analytics report might look like.

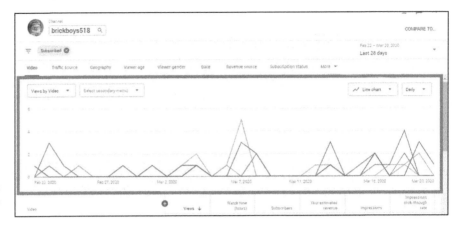

FIGURE 11-3:
An analytics chart.

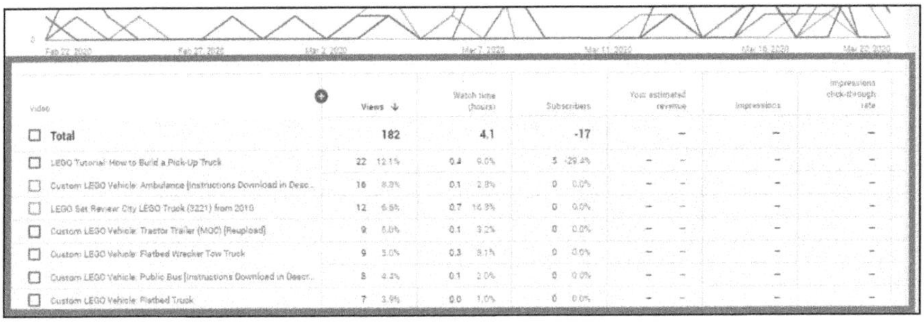

FIGURE 11-4:
An analytics table.

Grouping information

To simplify some of your channel analysis, you can create custom groups of videos or playlists. For instance, if you manage a baking channel, you may want to create one group for all your bread videos and playlists and another for your cake baking videos and playlists. To create a group, simply follow these instructions:

1. **With the Advanced Mode window open, click on your channel name within the top left search input field.**

2. **Choose Groups from the pop-up menu that appears.**

3. **Then choose the Create a New Group option from the bottom of the Groups menu.**

   Doing so opens a new window from which you can select videos to add to your group.

4. **Give the group a name, select the videos you want in the group, and then click Save.**

REMEMBER

A group is used for your analysis work; it lets you aggregate related content. It's different from a playlist, which is meant for audience viewing.

Comparing data

In the earlier (hypothetical) example of a baking channel, wouldn't it be great if you could compare how your bread-baking videos are performing against your cake-baking videos? Well, with YouTube Analytics, you can do precisely that. (You can even make comparisons by country and date.) To compare videos or groups, click the Compare To link at the top right of the Advanced Mode window and enter the names of the items you want to compare. YouTube Analytics pulls the data together for you and presents it side by side.

TIP

If you're running a YouTube advertising campaign (see Chapter 13), groups and comparisons are effective ways to determine which channel videos may be the best ones to advertise.

Setting up report filters

Creating truly informational reports is easy: Just figure out which data you want to include and which data you don't. The filter section not only makes this task possible but also lets you see the results of what you're doing *immediately*, which lets you fine-tune the filter so that the data is exactly what you want.

By using the following text fields and drop-down menus found in the filter section, you can ensure that you're looking at only the data you need:

TIP

» **Search for Content field:** Located at the top left of the Advanced Mode window, next to your Channel icon, this field allows you to select only a specific video, playlist, or group for analysis.

If you want to include more than one video, group the videos first. This feature doesn't let you filter for multiple individual videos unless they're part of a group or playlist.

» **Selectable drop-down filters:** Located beneath the Search for Content field is an upside down triangle next to the word "Filter". Clicking the upside down triangle launches a drop down menu of selectable filters, including:

- *Device type:* Isolate video data that is gathered by computer, TV, game console, mobile phone, or tablet devices to determine what types of electronic devices your audience likes to use.

- *Geography:* Select specific countries to analyze the behaviors of your audience around the world.

- *Live/on demand:* If you livestream on your channel, use this filter to see what percentage of your content is consumed during your broadcasts compared to content that's accessed on demand.

- *Operating system:* Identify which operating system your audience uses most commonly when watching your content.

- *Subscription status:* Your analytics reporting looks at the behavior of your entire audience. For certain reports, such as Demographics and Traffic sources, you can look at behavior by only your subscribers.

- *Traffic source:* Filter your data down to a specific traffic source to take a closer look at how different sources perform.

- *Translation use:* Select video data by whether your audience translated it or watched it in the original language.

- *YouTube product:* Separate your video data by YouTube, YouTube Kids, and YouTube Gaming products.

REMEMBER

Not all filters work for all data sets. For example, when looking at age range data, you cannot filter by device type. Many of these filters can be used simultaneously, however, which can help you analyze very specific segments of your audience and gain a better understanding of how to reach your goals.

>> **Date drop-down menu:** The default value is Last 28 Days. Click the drop-down menu beneath the Compare To link to choose common date criteria, such as this year, last year, or this month. If a preconfigured date doesn't work, you can pick a more suitable range by choosing the Custom option at the bottom of the menu.

>> **Compare To:** Clicking the Compare To link divides the Advanced Mode window into two and brings up a second filter section immediately across from the first. (YouTube allows only two comparisons.) When you're finished with the analysis, merely click the Cancel Comparison button that appears near the top right of the window.

REMEMBER

You need to set up a filter only once in the Analytics section of YouTube Studio. You can move among all report types, and your filters will remain in place.

Selecting a report

Beneath the filters section and above the chart section, you find a variety of pre-configured Advanced Mode reports that you can select to gain valuable insights about your channel. Many of these reports should look familiar to you from the summary reports available on the main reporting tabs of YouTube Analytics (which we describe in detail in the earlier section "Reading YouTube Analytics reports").

Figure 11-5 shows the Reports menu within Advanced Mode. If you haven't already selected a report to analyze, choose one from the menu to gain a greater understanding of your audience and how they're interacting with your channel. We help you take a deeper dive into how to utilize some of the most meaningful reports a little later on in this chapter.

FIGURE 11-5:
The report menu within Advanced Mode.

Understanding visual charts

Moving from report to report, you're sure to see both the graphs and the data changing in the chart section below the report menu and filters. Though many reports appear similar, each may have specific metrics based on the report type. For example, you'll find likes and dislikes in a Videos report, but such items would make no sense in a Traffic Source report.

REMEMBER

YouTube Analytics always presents data relevant to the particular report type.

In the chart section, you generally see the following elements:

>> **Primary and secondary metrics:** A drop-down menu on the left side of the screen (right below the Reports menu, shown in Figure 11-5) indicates the commonly associated metrics for a particular report. Clicking on one of these metrics immediately graphs it on the chart. You can also select a secondary metric if you want to compare two different metrics at the same time. Charting different metrics against one another can provide insight into what channel actions influence another. For example, on a Videos report, you may find that charting views and CPM show similar and aligned graphs. You can use this information to formulate the actions needed to drive views and accelerate earnings.

TIP

To add additional metrics to a chart, choose More Metrics from the drop-down menu. A complete list of available metrics is shown in Figure 11-6.

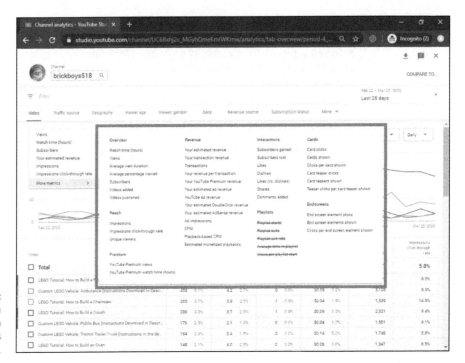

FIGURE 11-6:
Metrics you can
show on a
YouTube analytics
report.

>> **Chart type:** Near the top right corner of the chart, you find the Chart Selection drop-down menu. YouTube Analytics supports two chart types to analyze all preconfigured reports:

- *Line:* Shows the primary metric and a secondary metric over a period that you select. This is effective for showing trends or viewing patterns over time. For a Video report, it may show total view counts for your channel over time. (Figure 11-7 shows a sample line chart.)

- *Bar:* Illustrates relative proportions of a selected metric as horizontal bars, as shown in Figure 11-8. This type of chart is good for comparing things in aggregate, such as video views by age and gender.

>> **Graphing controls:** You can find additional graphing controls on the drop-down menu to the right of the chart selector. You can graph using daily, weekly, monthly, or even yearly spans. Additionally, you can change what data is graphed by selecting the check boxes in the table beneath the chart section. By default, up to five results are graphed, depending on the report you have selected. You may choose up to 12 items to graph at the same time from the table.

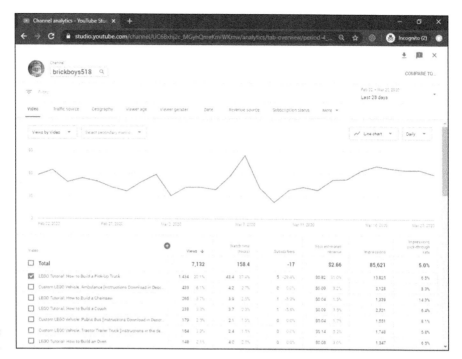

FIGURE 11-7:
Sample line chart.

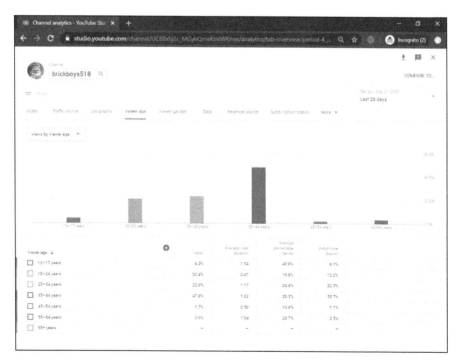

FIGURE 11-8:
Bar chart.

Understanding the table

Sometimes, it's easiest to digest data by looking at a grid of results. The table section of Advanced Mode, located beneath the chart, provides corresponding details and metrics to help you better understand how your channel is performing. For each report, the table dynamically changes to display whatever information is the most relevant to help you with your analysis. For example, in the Video report, the table displays your top 50 videos along with metrics such as impressions, views, and watch time. Moving over to the Geography report presents a different set of data, such as the countries where your audience is located and average view duration.

Similarly to the chart, you can customize the table for a given report using additional metrics by clicking the big blue Plus (+) button located between the first and second columns. Remember, however, that not all reports support every metric.

TIP

Sometimes, you want to customize your own charts or combine details of your YouTube Analytics data with other information. You can either export your data directly into Google Sheets or export it first as a comma-separated values (CSV) file that you can then import into Microsoft Excel or another common spreadsheet program. To do so, just click the Export Current View button, represented by an arrow pointed toward the ground, in the top right corner of the Advanced Mode window.

Learning about Video Views

YouTube Analytics provides plenty of insights, but you still have to come up with the final answers. To be effective, put on your proverbial Sherlock Holmes hat, and pick up a magnifying glass as you sift through all the YouTube metrics clues. To see how that might work, let's look more closely at a specific report type: the Video report.

Seeing which content is the most popular

Like most YouTube channel managers, you want to know which videos are attracting the most views. Getting that info is simple:

1. **In your web browser, go to** www.youtube.com.

2. **Log on to your YouTube account.**

   If you see a blue Sign In button in the top right corner of the YouTube home page, enter your email address and password.

3. **Click the Logged-In icon and choose YouTube Studio from the menu that appears.**

   The YouTube Studio navigation menu should appear on the left side of the browser.

4. **Choose Analytics from the navigation menu.**

   By default, you should go directly to the Overview tab. (Refer to Figure 11-1.)

5. **Click the See More link at the bottom of the main graph in the Overview tab.**

   Doing so launches Advanced Mode and brings up a line chart that shows your channel views by video over the past 28 days. (**Note:** You can change the analysis period by changing the time from the filter section that sits above the chart.)

6. **Examine the lines in the chart.**

   Are they moving up and to the right? Do you see peaks during certain days? Look for patterns and look for spikes, both high and low.

TIP

   If you see consistent peaks, that means your audience is viewing your content regularly. Think about the programming tips from Chapter 5, and align your schedule with your audience's viewing patterns.

REMEMBER

You won't break anything by looking at a different chart type or changing the analysis timeframe. You should become comfortable navigating and modifying your analysis.

Determining whether viewers are watching or leaving

One of the truly great aspects of YouTube is the detail it can provide about how much of your videos your audiences actually watch. If you're thinking about the view duration, that's partially correct: If you have a 4-minute video and viewers watch only about half of it, it has a 2-minute (or 50 percent) view duration.

View duration, though important, tells only part of the story. A channel manager needs to know more, including the answers to these questions:

>> Where is my audience dropping off?

>> How does the audience attraction compare with similar videos?

Audience *retention* — determining the steps you need to take to hold on to your audience — should be a critical part of the analytics process because it increases your overall watch time (another *key* metric we discuss later on, in the "Making

Sure Your Audience Is Engaged" section). Audience retention is a video-specific analytics report that allows channel managers to see these two factors:

>> **Absolute audience retention:** You're greeted by a timeline that displays what percentage of your audience views your video. If you have a 3-minute video, you see a retention graph for the entire three minutes aligned with the player for the entire video. You can see exactly where an audience watches and where they drop off.

REMEMBER

Don't become upset when you discover that your audience isn't watching 100 percent of your videos for their entire duration. Drop-offs are perfectly normal — think about your own viewing patterns on YouTube.

>> **Relative audience retention:** After you realize that you won't have 100 percent audience retention, you need to determine how your retention rates compare with similar content from other channels. You can use the relative retention rates displayed in the Audience Retention report to show how your video compares over time with other videos and to display whether parts are average, above average, or below average.

So, does an audience retention report sound intriguing? Here's how to carry one out:

1. **In your web browser, go to** www.youtube.com.

2. **Log on to your YouTube account.**

   If you see the blue Sign In button in the top right corner of the YouTube home page, enter your email address and password.

3. **Click the Logged-In icon and choose YouTube Studio from the menu that appears.**

   The YouTube Studio navigation menu should appear on the left side of your browser.

4. **Choose Analytics from the navigation menu.**

5. **In the overview section, scroll down to the summary report for your top videos in this period.**

   You see a list of the top ten videos for your selected period, with the option to view more from the Advanced Mode window.

6. **Click on the name of a particular video you want to analyze.**

   Doing so directs you to a video-specific YouTube Analytics page. The audience retention graph for this video is located underneath the main graph in the Overview tab. (See Figure 11-9.)

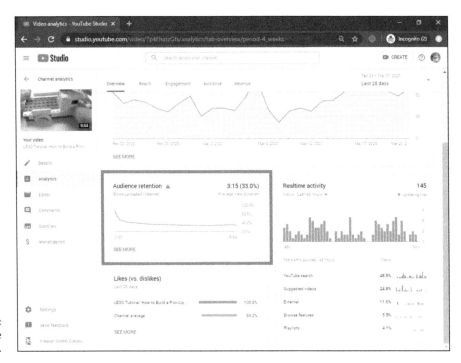

FIGURE 11-9:
An audience
retention graph.

FIGURE 11-9:
An audience
retention graph.

TIP

If you don't see the video you want to analyze for retention within that top ten list on the Overview page, click on the Videos tab from the left-side navigation menu, and search for it within the Channel Videos page. When you find the video you're looking for, hover the mouse cursor over the description and click the Analytics icon that appears in order to open the video-specific analytics page.

7. **Click the See More link in the audience retention graph to open Advanced Mode view.**

   This allows you to more easily compare the audience retention graph in relation to your video. If you click on any particular point in the graph, you automatically link to that point in the video above the graph.

8. **Search for peaks and valleys in the graph.**

   You may be scratching your head and trying to figure out why a peak is showing up on a viewing graph. Your audience may be choosing to *rewatch* a segment, signaling vital content. The valley represents viewer loss, so look at what's happening at that point in the video above the graph. The cause might be boring or overly long content, which is something that you should consider when editing upcoming content.

9. **Change the graph type to Relative Audience Retention by choosing that option in the drop-down menu just above the graph.**

   You should determine how your content is performing against comparable videos. If it's consistently below average, look at other content to understand in what ways it's different and why it may be more interesting to the audience than yours.

REMEMBER

The watch time plays a crucial role in increasing your video's dicoverability in YouTube Search results (as we talk about in Chapter 5). Audience retention provides you with insight you need in order to keep viewers watching and increase your watch time.

REMEMBER

A retention drop always occurs at the beginning of a video because that's when viewers decide whether they've chosen the right video to watch. However, if the drop seems rather precipitous at the beginning, it may be a sign that the title, metadata, or thumbnail is out of sync with what viewers expected when they found the video. Never mislead viewers, and fix any concerns based on what your retention reports indicate.

Understanding Your Audience

Video reports and audience retention graphs are designed to help you understand how well your viewers are responding to your channel content. To find out who's watching your videos, you have to try a different tack: audience reports.

Diving into demographics

It helps to know who's watching your content so that you can make important content-planning decisions. The Audience tab of YouTube Analytics is a fascinating way to analyze your channel demographics, because you can get concrete information about your audience members' gender, age, and country of residence.

REMEMBER

Certain audience reports allow you to filter to see results explicitly from your subscriber base. Sometimes, it's interesting to see whether your subscriber demographics mirror your general audience demographics.

To access audience reports, follow these steps:

1. **In your web browser, go to** www.youtube.com.

2. **Log on to your YouTube account.**

If you see the blue Sign In button in the top right corner of the YouTube home page, enter your email address and password.

3. **Click the Logged-In icon and choose YouTube Studio from the menu that appears.**

The YouTube Studio navigation menu should appear on the left side of your browser.

4. **Choose Analytics from the navigation menu.**

5. **Click to open the Audience tab on the Reports menu.**

Here you find summary reports of age and gender, as shown in Figure 11-10.

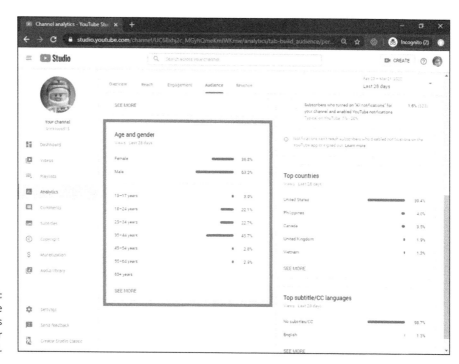

FIGURE 11-10:
YouTube
Analytics
age-and-gender
report.

6. **Click the See More link at the bottom of the Age and Gender summary report, and examine the charts and their accompanying details.**

It's terrific if your audience is exactly what you thought it would be. If it isn't, revisit your assumptions. You may find that your content is having wider interest, which may be a good thing. Conversely, if you're not seeing enough traction, perhaps you're not engaging enough with key creators and fans in your core demographic to help you get the word out.

7. **Refine the report to show only subscribed viewers by choosing Subscription Status from the filter drop-down menu.**

   Look closely at how the graphs change. If you see a big difference, determine whether subscription requests are working more broadly than expected, because your content certainly is appealing to others.

TIP

Make it a habit to compare your demographic information over time to detect any shifts in your audience.

Diving into subscribers

Knowing your subscribers' patterns and where they're doing their subscribing is an important part of your channel management responsibilities. YouTube is well aware of that, which is why it offers a subscription source report as part of YouTube Analytics. Here's how to access it:

1. **In your web browser, go to** www.youtube.com.

2. Log on to your YouTube account.

   If you see the blue Sign In button in the top right corner of the YouTube home page, enter your email address and password.

3. **Click the Logged-In icon and choose YouTube Studio from the menu that appears.**

   The YouTube Studio navigation menu should appear on the left side of your browser.

4. Bring up the Analytics section of YouTube Studio.

5. Click on Advanced Mode from the top right of the screen.

6. Within the Advanced Mode window, click on More from the Reports menu and find the Subscription Source option.

7. Look at the report's table section to see where on YouTube your audience subscribes to your channel.

   In addition to subscriber gains, you see the number of subscribers lost, too, which is a normal part of channel activity. Figure 11-11 shows a typical subscription source report.

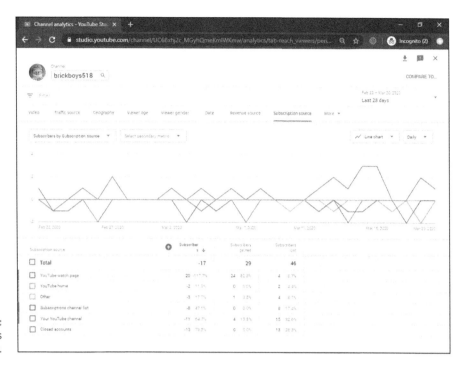

FIGURE 11-11:
Subscribers
report.

Optimizing Discoverability

YouTube is a huge place, and it's growing every day. In Chapter 5, you find out about the importance of discoverability and its importance for helping YouTube put your content in front of the right viewers. Ideally, you want your content offered up first, but that takes some time. (Rome wasn't built in a day, you know.) As a channel manager, you use analytics to figure out whether your quest for discoverability is moving in the right direction.

Seeing where viewers find your content

As your content becomes more popular and relevant for specific viewers, YouTube offers up your videos as Recommended videos and as part of its search results. These are important ingredients in your overall channel performance. So too is community engagement, which helps your content show up on playlists, on websites, in social media, and more. YouTube Analytics can help you determine where your audience is discovering your content.

The Traffic Sources report from YouTube Analytics is designed to show you how viewers discover your content. It includes not only sources within YouTube but also external sites and social media. To see how your viewers find you, do the following:

1. **In your web browser, go to** www.youtube.com.

2. **Log on to your YouTube account.**

   If you see the blue Sign In button in the top right corner of the YouTube home page, enter your email address and password.

3. **Click on the Logged-In icon to and choose YouTube Studio from the menu that appears.**

   The YouTube Studio navigation menu should appear on the left side of your browser.

4. **Bring up the Analytics section of YouTube Studio.**

5. **Click on the Reach tab from the Reports menu.**

6. **Beneath the main graph, find the summary report for traffic source types.**

   This step displays your top YouTube channel traffic sources. (Figure 11-12 gives you an idea of what such a view looks like.)

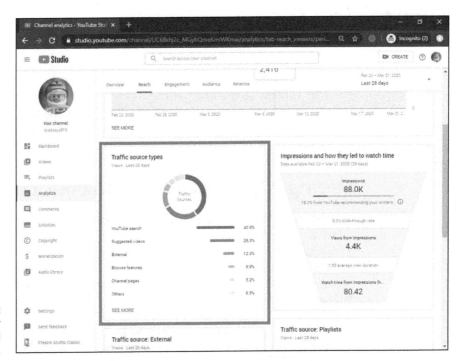

FIGURE 11-12:
Viewing your YouTube channel traffic sources.

7. **Click See More at the bottom of the Traffic Source Type summary report to take a closer look in Advanced Mode.**

Doing so reveals a detailed list of all your traffic sources in the table beneath the chart in the Advanced Mode window.

8. **Review your traffic sources.**

Sources here might include

- YouTube advertising
- Channel pages
- Browse features
- YouTube partner promotion
- Playlists
- Playlist pages
- Google Search
- YouTube Search
- Suggested videos
- Video cards and annotations
- Unknown — direct (mobile apps and external website)
- Unknown — embedded player (views from external websites)
- External app
- External (website)
- End screens
- Notifications
- Other YouTube features (analytics, editing screen, and other random stuff)

9. **Click on a traffic source in the table section.**

Doing so brings up additional information about that traffic source category. For example, if you click Playlists, you see a detailed list of all playlists — yours and others — that include your videos. Or, if you click YouTube Search, you will see the top keywords that drive people to your channel. Consider working these keywords into your video descriptions and tags to optimize your discoverability.

Finding out where (and how) viewers watch your content

Channel managers also need to know where their video content was watched and on what kind of devices, including computers and mobile devices. You can get that information with the help of two specific reports:

>> **Playback location:** Shows whether the video was viewed from YouTube or an external website or device

>> **Device type:** Specifies the device format and the operating system used to view video content

REMEMBER

Don't underestimate the importance of how your audience consumes your content. If mobile devices dominate, be sure that your videos don't require a 55-inch, 4K display to get your point across.

To determine where your audience is viewing, follow these steps:

1. **In your web browser, go to** www.youtube.com.

2. **Log on to your YouTube account.**

   If you see the blue Sign In button in the top right corner of the YouTube home page, enter your email address and password.

3. **Click on the Logged-In icon and choose YouTube Studio from the menu that appears.**

   The YouTube Studio navigation menu should appear on the left side of your browser.

4. **Bring up the Analytics section of YouTube Studio.**

5. **Click the Advanced Mode link at the top right of the screen.**

6. **Within the Advanced Mode window, click on More from the Reports menu and find the Playback Location option.**

7. **Click the Embedded in External Websites and Apps link in the table section.**

   The report highlighting embedded players appears, as shown in Figure 11-13.

   YouTube allows websites to embed your video, which is one of the highest forms of engagement.

REMEMBER

You always get full view credit for embedded videos. If you have a website, feel free to embed videos from your YouTube community and your subscribers as well. It's good practice because it highlights how you interact with your subscribers.

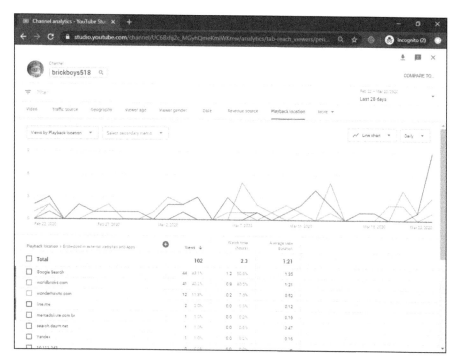

FIGURE 11-13:
Reporting your
embedded-player
locations.

8. **To probe a bit deeper, go back and click on the Device Type report.**

Under the graph, you can toggle between the device type and the operating system. Here are some popular devices:

- Computer

- Game console

- Mobile phone

- Tablet

- TV

Understanding which devices your audience watches your content on can help you to develop better content for your audience's viewing experience. For example, if you see that a majority of your audience watches your videos on mobile phones, you shouldn't use small text.

Making Sure Your Audience Is Engaged

Engagement is all about your viewers going beyond just watching a video. You want them to comment, share, and interact with you. Here are some key metrics that can be added to a Video report in Advanced Mode to help you monitor your channel engagement:

>> **Subscribers gained and lost:** This metric displays information on subscriber gains and losses relative to specific videos. If you find that one specific video has caused a departure of several subscribers, consider removing that video from your channel and avoiding that type of content in the future.

>> **Likes (versus dislikes):** This metric captures the percentage of likes out of the total number of likes and dislikes to help you identify the content your audience likes best.

>> **Comments:** This metric highlights those videos that receive viewer comments. Don't forget the date dimension here to find out when most of the comments are posted.

TIP

If comments are made in the first few hours after you post a video, you may want to make sure you're always available after posting, for immediate engagement. This can be managed from the Comments section of the YouTube Analytics left-side navigation menu.

>> **Sharing:** This metric itemizes which videos are shared the most. You can also take a look at a separate report called Sharing Service, which shows you which social media service your videos were shared on. (You might use this latter bit of information to find out whether your community prefers a particular service, such as Twitter or Facebook.)

>> **End screen element clicks and card clicks:** These metrics help you analyze the performance of your end screen elements and cards, showing which ones generate the most clicks.

In addition to these interactions, one key engagement metric that you should pri-oritize is achieving high watch time on your YouTube channel. Watch time is the cumulative amount of time that your audience watches your videos. Having a high watch time is an indication that your channel and its content are genuinely interesting (and are often associated with driving the highest revenue if your channel is monetized).

The Engagement tab offered by YouTube Analytics lets you look at several types of engagement reports to help you assess this key metric. Here's how it's done:

1. **In your web browser, go to** www.youtube.com.

2. Log on to your YouTube account.

   If you see the blue Sign In button in the top right corner of the YouTube home page, enter your email address and password.

3. Click the Logged-In icon and choose YouTube Studio from the menu that appears.

   The YouTube Studio navigation menu should appear on the left side of your browser.

4. **Bring up the Analytics section of YouTube Studio.**

5. **Click to open the Engagement tab on the Reports menu.**

   For the purposes of this example, say that you want to see which videos drove the highest watch time across your channel.

6. **Beneath the main graph, find the Top Videos summary report.**

   You're presented with the top five videos, sorted by watch time over the period you have specified.

7. **Click the See More link to take a closer look at more videos on your channel.**

   Doing so brings up a Video report sorted by the watch time metric.

8. **Select specific videos from the table to compare them in the chart.**

   Select a few of your top videos to see how watch time varies for each one over time. Try to identify patterns that maximize watch time. For instance, maybe videos about dogs bring in higher watch times than videos about cats. Consider adding this type of analysis to your overall content strategy. It will not only increase the likelihood of your audience engaging with your content but also may result in higher ad revenue.

REMEMBER

After you have a general idea how to analyze watch time for your top videos, check out the other Engagement reports, such as top playlists, top cards, and top end screen cards. Drill down into the details of these reports to understand exactly what content your audience prefers.

Imagining the Future of YouTube Analytics

As you undoubtedly know by now, YouTube Analytics is a powerful tool to help you optimize your channel and improve your performance. In early 2019, YouTube launched the YouTube Studio beta to replace Creator Studio, which was described in the first edition of this book. As the YouTube Studio beta continues to evolve, some reports and metrics described in this chapter may change slightly. We also expect even more features to be released to help creators enhance their channels, which is *exciting.*

4

YouTube Channels Are Serious Business

Chapter **12**

How and Why Businesses Use YouTube

rban legend has it that when asked why he robbed banks, the famed criminal Willie Sutton responded, "Because that's where the money is." You won't learn much about bank robbery in this chapter, but you will find out why doing business on YouTube is a big deal: *because that's where your customers are.* In fact, that's where nearly everyone who's doing business today is.

YouTube now reports that it receives over 2 billion logged-in users *per month* who watch over a billion hours of video. They're watching from desktops, laptops, tablets, smart TVs, game consoles — and 70 percent of YouTube views come from mobile devices. They're watching around the world from over 91 countries. Wherever a YouTube video is played lies a potential opportunity to help your business.

If you're serious about taking your business to the next level, YouTube can provide you with some rich capabilities designed to help you reach that goal. In later chapters, you find out how to work as an *advertiser* (someone who buys ad space) or as a *creator* (someone who sells ad space). Fortunately for you, Google and YouTube take care of most of the messy work for you while helping you integrate YouTube into your paid marketing initiatives.

Today, many social media platforms try to lure in creators to generate video content; none, however, has as robust a platform for creators as YouTube. In 2019, the number of YouTube creators earning a 6-figure income has grown more than 40 percent year over year.

Understanding Video and Business

Before you think about YouTube for business, you may want to think about video for business. It doesn't matter whether you're part of a Fortune 500 multinational corporation or running a community nonprofit on your own: Your business will benefit greatly by bringing video into your marketing efforts. YouTube helps you make that happen easily while also giving you the tools to help you reach your business goals.

If you're a business, the audience you're trying to reach also includes those viewers who can help you sell more. They're your prospective — or existing — customers, other businesses that can help you sell, or potential advocates who may become your brand champions. Your challenge is to draw their attention, which is especially difficult these days because they're being bombarded by digital media from so many different sides. That's why video is vital: It helps you cut through all your audience's distractions and deliver your value proposition fast and effectively. It's all about video marketing

Because the focus of this book is on YouTube, you've probably already embraced the broader concept of video marketing and advertising. If not, check out the book we reference in Chapter 5, *Video Marketing for Dummies*, by Kevin Daum, Bettina Hein, Matt Scott, and Andreas Goeldi (Wiley). It deals with the broader concept of video as an effective medium for helping your business. In this chapter and the following one, you'll see how YouTube fits into the business equation.

BRAND DECISIONS ARE MADE ON YouTube

YouTube is now where consumers frequently turn to make decisions about what products to buy. Because of the rich engagement capabilities that YouTube provides, the site is far more than just a place you visit when you want to watch a few videos — it has become a gathering place, a true community, a powerful social platform. By combining the social aspect with video (both branded video and video that's independently produced), YouTube now hosts its fair share of trusted advisors who act as product experts and influencers who are in a position to guide consumers on their journey to making a decision about a product or service.

Viewers don't even need to leave YouTube to shop for products — creators can now sell merchandise with YouTube's Merch Shelf feature. Creators and brands have historically linked to products within the video description for products mentioned in the video, so if you're a brand marketer, you'll be happy to know that the watch time for shopping-related video content grew over 500 percent in the US between 2016 and 2018, according to Google data.

The sidebar figure shows consumer search patterns around smart TVs in the consumer electronics industry. What's most striking is the amount of ongoing YouTube Search traffic that's shown. Compare that with the corresponding Google Search graph, which shows only seasonal search spikes — a sure sign that consumers are looking for the big sales after having already selected their products. The implications of the figure are profound, especially for business: Brand and product decisions are being made on YouTube, and purchase decisions are being made on Google.

Being on YouTube is no longer just an advantage — it's a necessity for business. If you've doubted where YouTube fits into your business cycle, think again. YouTube now represents the first few steps in your marketing or sales funnel. YouTube is effectively flattening the once cone-shaped marketing funnel that traditional marketers have been focused on for decades into a virtuous loop. You can reach a new customer and easily convert the lead into a sale, all within a single video.

As a brand advertiser, you must ensure that your ads are placed in a suitable environment on YouTube. If you're a beauty brand, for example, you may not want your ads shown before a video about animal testing. Even if your brand doesn't partake in such practices, it's best not to associate your brand with these themes. The TV advertising industry calls these x *DNR* lists, or *do-not-run* lists. You can exclude content you don't find suitable for your brand by choosing the Limited option as your advertiser acceptable inventory category on YouTube when building your video campaigns, or you can create extensive negative URL lists. (For more on these topics and other YouTube advertising best practices, check out Chapter 13.)

(continued)

(continued)

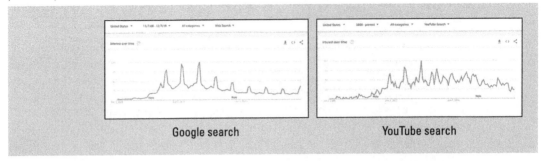

Google search   YouTube search

REMEMBER

Using video for marketing and advertising is nothing new, especially for larger companies that have spent fortunes on television advertising and paid infomercials. Lots of cutting-edge organizations alternatively jumped on the online video bandwagon, but many became frustrated because it was difficult to gauge whether video advertising actually helped their businesses. Many businesses today employ agencies or social media experts to help manage their YouTube channels and Google Ads accounts. You *must* understand your audience, what they like, and how they're consuming your video content. This can be a full-time job, depending on the size of your business and YouTube channel.

WARNING

Betting your business on viral video is like betting your retirement on lottery tickets: It's just not a sound strategy. You'd end up investing all your money and time in something that has little or no chance of succeeding. A much better strategy is to make great content regularly and add a dash of paid advertising to build your business the right way.

Most folks are well aware that a revolution has occurred in video capture, production, and editing over the past decade. We're at the point where someone using the smartphone in their pocket can shoot, edit, and upload a high-quality video, all within minutes. The thing is, the revolution didn't stop there. It happened in distribution and social media, too. With YouTube, you can also reach viewers in over 91 countries. Keep that point in mind as you make your way through this chapter.

Understanding Your YouTube Business Components

If you have a business, more likely than not you also have a *business model* — a plan that sets down how you intend to make money, not to put too fine a point on it. This chapter is designed to help you find a place for YouTube in your business model. (You may want to read this chapter in combination with Chapter 5, where we talk a bit more about how you can ensure that your YouTube channel objectives and video content align with your business goals.)

Don't be rigid about your YouTube business model. Ultimately, your audience is the judge. Relevant content, engagement, and collaboration may all be important factors to consider. YouTube Analytics — and your sales performance — are your guides, so be sure to scrutinize your channel's numbers. (See Chapter 11 for more on YouTube Analytics.)

Content matters

No ifs, ands, or buts — content is critical to business on YouTube. If you come from the TV world, your first instinct may be to drop the standard 15- or 30-second commercial on YouTube. Your first instinct would be wrong. YouTube viewers don't want commercials; they want authenticity. They don't want glitz; they want reality.

If you have a product to sell, picture your viewer's journey with you and with your brand as a series of steps that viewers must take. Each step represents a stage where your viewer, who may now be a bona fide business prospect, is looking for more — yet different and increasingly detailed — information. These steps are shown as the classic Sales Funnel in Figure 12-1.

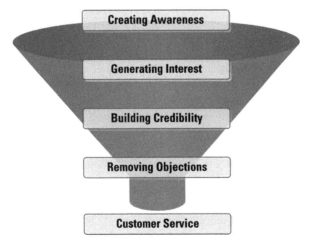

FIGURE 12-1: Using your YouTube channel to channel sales.

You may believe that these steps look and sound a lot like the proverbial sales funnel. You'd be right to think so. Viewers frequently complete a series of distinct phases before they make a product decision. The reason it's called a *funnel* is that it's wider at that top than at the bottom because not everyone who looks at your products (or terrific videos) will buy something. Your business goal is to use YouTube to help them pick you when they make a purchase decision.

With these steps in mind, your YouTube content should align with the stages of your customer's journey. Here are some phases to consider as you try to help viewers make a decision:

>> **Create awareness.** Initially, viewers likely have no idea who you are or what you offer as a product or service. You want to elevate their knowledge of you in the fastest way possible. Consider creating a channel trailer that targets nonsubscribed viewers *and* explains your business mission and vision. This trailer may also be a good video to reuse for YouTube advertising. (See Chapter 13 for more on advertising strategy.)

REMEMBER

Don't make viewers think too hard! Make it ridiculously easy for them to find more information about what is shown in the video. Use all the tools in your toolbox — descriptive thumbnails, the merch shelf, and metadata, for example — to keep them engaged. (For more on the tools you can use to keep viewers engaged, see Chapter 11.)

>> **Generate interest.** Think of endorsements or partnerships. If you're big enough — or rich enough — you're talking about *celebrity* endorsements or working with top YouTube influencers.

REMEMBER

Aside from being expensive, celebrity or influencer endorsements often come with severe licensing restrictions. If you end up attracting a million views — and lots of business — from a celebrity endorsement, that's great, until you're forced to pull the video after licensing rights expire. Be sure to create licensing contracts that don't require you to remove the video from your YouTube channel. Or, negotiate a contract that allows you to post a version of the influencer's video on your channel, not just a cut posted to the influencer's channel. After you delete a video or list it as private on your channel, your channel can't show those particular video views as contributions to your YouTube Partner status for additional monetization features or as views on your About page. In addition, your channel won't be rewarded for them in YouTube Search.

>> **Build credibility.** Building credibility usually necessitates adding tutorials and longer videos that take the time to describe product details. Don't be surprised to see a 15-minute, long-form video at this stage perform as well as short-form content at an earlier stage.

REMEMBER

Content curation — playlisting videos you haven't produced, in other words — is often as important as content creation. If your raving fans are making awesome videos about your products, don't hesitate to include them in your playlists. There's probably no better way to establish credibility with sales prospects than to show the enthusiasm of your fans. Don't forget that including your community on your channel is a great community high-five as well.

>> **Remove blocks to purchasing your products.** Having collaborators produce tutorials is helpful for not only building trustworthiness but also removing potential obstacles to a sale. Sometimes, though, you need something different from a tutorial — perhaps videos that describe how your product or service benefited the customer. This is where you make the sale happen, so make sure it counts.

>> **Provide a service.** After your prospective channel viewer has turned into a paying customer, you may think that your YouTube work is done. Not exactly. Remember that if customers love their experience with you and your business, they'll likely buy from you again, and again, and again. One way to ensure this level of loyalty is to make the experience they have with you and your brand *after the sale* a rewarding one. We're talking about customer support and service. This is where YouTube can truly shine. Your customer will no doubt have questions about your product, application scenarios, maintenance, and so much more. That's okay and perfectly normal, so help them out. For example, the auto manufacturer Audi does a great job with customer service on YouTube, as shown in Figure 12-2. As car electronics became more advanced and sophisticated, Audi stepped up as one of the first companies to offer tutorial videos. Check them out at www.youtube.com/audiusa.

When your customers visit your YouTube channel for product support, they also see your new product offerings — which is an excellent upsell or referral opportunity.

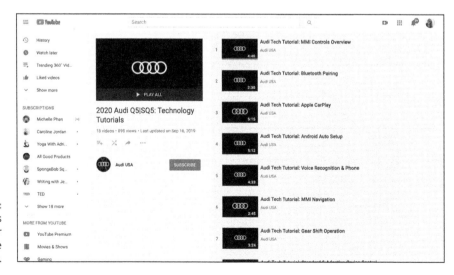

FIGURE 12-2: Audi uses YouTube for customer service and support.

Rob and Theresa spend much of their time working with brands and agencies in order to help them tweak their YouTube business models. One of the top challenges they face is inspiring companies to move beyond producing content for only the top of the funnel. (Refer to Figure 12-1.) Creating awareness, which is a necessary marketing function, has for many years served well the brand advertisers targeting television audiences. The digital world, however, expects something more from the content on your YouTube channel. Give them an authentic video experience, in addition to your 15-second ad. Moving beyond dumping repurposed one-off TV commercials on YouTube to a more holistic approach is the most important way to help your business.

Effective content doesn't have to be all about products, either. American Express (www.youtube.com/AmericanExpress) does an outstanding job of producing channel content that provides important advice for small businesses, as shown in Figure 12-3. Doing so isn't the core business of a credit card company such as American Express, but it's obviously quite important to its target audience. Always remember that your best content aligns with your audience's needs.

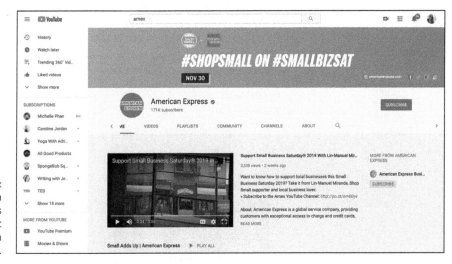

FIGURE 12-3: American Express delivers audience-centric content on YouTube.

REMEMBER

Video optimization and effective channel management are essential to effective business on YouTube. For more on these topics, check out Chapter 9, where you can find out all about the importance of video thumbnails, metadata, playlists, and more.

Community and content creators

If you have an interesting product or service that people are passionate about, you can likely find a conversation about it on YouTube. Chances are good that you can find *many* conversations and that they'll happen whether or not you're involved. This situation often comes across as quite strange to companies that are accustomed to controlling the business conversation around their brands and products. Though YouTube shatters that notion of control, don't be afraid of having others talk about you: They may be your army of brand champions — and the best salespeople you've ever had.

One of the most interesting business segments found on YouTube is the beauty industry. Now, before you roll your eyes and close this book because your business has nothing to do with mascara and eyeliner, take a moment to reconsider the implications. The dynamics of the beauty industry show where the future of YouTube is for business: independent creators producing fantastic content for a passionate and purchase-motivated fan base. These creators, or beauty influencers, also know the importance of subscribers. Figure 12-4 shows the number of subscribers for the top beauty brands versus the top independent beauty influencers. It's not even close: The audience often prefers authentic, independent voices.

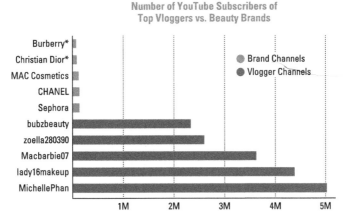

FIGURE 12-4: Number of YouTube subscribers of top YouTube influencers versus top beauty brands.

In many industries, you'll find a strong, independent, and creative force where YouTube creators are crafting content in your topic space. Don't fear that force. In fact, you can embrace the representatives of that force if you

>> **Include their content in your playlists.** This is the ultimate tip of the hat to independent creators.

>> **Comment on their channels.** Add to their conversation in a meaningful way.

BRANDS VERSUS INFLUENCERS

Recently, Pixability conducted a comprehensive study of the quick-serve restaurant industry, which is an active industry on YouTube. The report, titled *Order Up: Unwrapping How Audiences Devour Quick-Service Restaurant Video Content*, identified and analyzed how major quick-serve restaurant brands and YouTube influencers and top creator personalities manage, produce, and socialize video. (See the blurb about the report in the sidebar figure.) The report highlights striking differences in impact between brand-owned video content and influencer-produced content. Some of the findings are listed here:

- **Brands own a surprisingly small share of YouTube's audience.**

    Influencers drive 85 percent of the views on YouTube videos focused on quick-serve restaurants, and only 8 percent of views come from brand-owned videos.

- **Brands need to consistently create a wider variety of YouTube content — and more of it.**

    Reviews and *challenge videos* (videos that portray the proverbial hot dog eating contest, for example) drive most of the engagements on YouTube, but brands are publishing mostly ads on their channels.

- **Breakfast wars heat up on YouTube, with a 78 percent rise in breakfast content since 2016.**

- **Over 80 percent of influencer video views are driven by videos longer than 5 minutes. Brands still have a majority of short-form videos on their channels.**

>> **Respect their independence.** They may show your products and your competitors' *in the same video.* Don't ask them to do otherwise. Creators do what is best for their audience.

>> **Consider sponsorship or another type of promotion.** Whether you are the creator or the brand, enter only into partnerships that support your channel objectives and provide your audience with an experience that will keep them coming back for more.

REMEMBER

If you're an independent creator in your own right, brands and larger companies may not be in a position to work like you do, because they have neither the content production flexibility nor the means to engage with subscribers at the same level of intimacy you may have.

REMEMBER

Brands steer clear of creators who want something — whether it's product bling or cold, hard cash — in exchange for a favorable review. It's best to work with creators who genuinely like your products. You may not attract the audience engagement if the creator isn't really into your product or services, because the audience can tell when it isn't authentic content.

Advertising

Discoverability — the ease with which potential viewers can find your content — is crucial on YouTube. Your content needs to be easy to find if you want to capture the most engaged target audience. You can let discoverability grow *organically* over time on its own by way of community engagement, increased watch time, and more. Sometimes, though, the business world doesn't work at that organic speed, so you may need to add a bit of "fertilizer" to help the process move a little faster. That's what YouTube advertising is all about: Apply some cash to help get your content in front of viewers who may turn into customers or avid viewers. YouTube can be a pay-to-play platform if you're a brand fighting for views in a market niche where influencers play a huge role. You may need to use advertising to get your videos in front of the right viewers.

As a YouTube channel manager, you need to decide whether advertising will work for you and figure out which side of the business ad equation you're on:

>> **Publisher:** You're a content creator or an influencer looking to monetize your YouTube channel.

>> **Advertiser:** You want people to become aware of your channel and consume more of your content — and perhaps even subscribe. Maybe you have a product and you want viewers to buy something — at a store, online, or via a business partner.

Chapters 13 and 14 have lots more detail about YouTube advertising from both sides, but for now just remember that there are no hard-and-fast rules or thick walls between publishers and advertisers. You may find that your business is okay doing a little of both.

REMEMBER

Effective advertising is all about measurement, so you'll use YouTube Analytics extensively to make sure you're getting the most out of your ad dollars or maximizing your monetization potential. (For more on YouTube Analytics, check out Chapter 11.)

Don't view YouTube advertising as an isolated activity. Done correctly, an outstanding ad campaign not only moves the sales meter in the right direction but also generates important, free, follow-on channel activities, like additional playlist views and subscriptions from engaged viewers, which are critical to increasing discoverability. Unlike other paid media, YouTube TrueView advertising helps organic growth since each view can count towards your channel's total view count and watch time.

PAID, OWNED, EARNED

If you hang out around marketers long enough, you hear them talk about paid, owned, and earned media. Each of these three categories plays an important but related role in your business strategy, so this is as good a time as any to figure out exactly what the terms mean. They're easier to understand if you change the order a bit, though:

- **Owned** consists of the web properties and resources you control, which includes your website and your YouTube channel.

- **Earned** is what your customers are saying about you and how they engage with your channel. From the YouTube perspective, this one includes videos about your products that are produced by independent creators.

- *Paid* **here means paid advertising.** The good part about the paid category is that you can experiment and discover audiences that may not find your channel and content organically. Paid works well on YouTube because it can drive up view counts for your channel, help add subscribers, and increase sales.

All three types of media — paid, owned, and earned — feed off one another, so your YouTube strategy and your business strategy should always take all of them into account.

REMEMBER

Not all paid advertising on YouTube counts toward your video views. Some ad units, like those 6-second bumper ads, don't count toward your video view count.

WARNING

If you're a creator who's working with a brand or another type of sponsor, you're required to be transparent about it in order to remain in the Partner Program. Your success on YouTube is closely tied to your authenticity and openness. Nailing down a sponsorship deal and placing products in your videos is fine, as long as your audience knows what's going on. You'll find your YouTube audience extremely loyal — but unforgiving (and unsubscribing) if they feel misled in any way. If you're a brand or sponsor, your brand reputation on YouTube should be treated with the same care you'd expend anywhere else. Be conscious of your YouTube partners.

Integrating YouTube with Other Campaigns

Broadcast television, cable, newspapers, magazines, and direct mail may not have the same impact they once did, but they're not going away any time soon, either. And don't forget your email and display campaigns: They're probably an important part of your business strategy, so you should nurture them. If you're holding special events and conferences, keep them coming, too. The point is that YouTube is a great way to not only integrate all your diverse business campaigns but also make them more effective and memorable.

Cross-media integration

To see what an effective integrated business campaign might look like on YouTube, look no further than the campaign put together by the NBA (www.youtube.com/nba), one of the better sports leagues on YouTube. The NBA does many things well for its business, including

>> **Content generation:** The NBA updates its YouTube content quite frequently, often releasing custom highlights just for its YouTube audience. It's a useful example of how to repurpose TV content for a YouTube audience.

>> **Promotion integration:** The NBA's YouTube channel sections are always up-to-date with the newest content, *tentpole* events (seasonal or timely content releases around an event, such as the playoffs), and more. If the NBA is doing something on the court or off, it's guaranteed to be on YouTube.

>> **Video optimization:** Well-chosen, accurate, custom thumbnails entice viewers to click and watch. Many of the NBA's videos also have other interactive elements such as end screens.

>> **Channel monetization:** The NBA knows how to make money, and it has taken that formula to YouTube. You'll see extensive use of pre-roll ads against its channel content. (The idea behind *pre-roll* video ads is that they play before the actual NBA video, and the channel then earns money from each view of an ad.)

Figure 12-5 shows the highly engaging NBA YouTube channel.

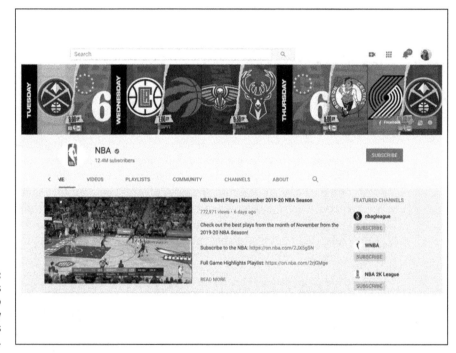

FIGURE 12-5: The NBA uses YouTube to integrate many of its highlights and activities.

YouTube is TV now

Business professionals who treat their YouTube channels as dumping grounds for old TV commercials are the ones who complain most loudly about the lack of organic performance. The truth is that most television commercials just don't perform well in terms of both views and engagement on YouTube from an organic perspective. Rather than do what the NBA has been doing — repurposing excellent content specifically for its fan base on YouTube — many brands simply plop down their TV ads on YouTube and expect miracles to happen. It just doesn't work that way. If you're coming from the world of television advertising and programming, look through the YouTube lens, not the TV camera.

REMEMBER

YouTube TV is YouTube's version of a cable subscription package, or a skinny bundle. It's Internet-supported, live nationwide TV with local network coverage. Though it won't have *your* YouTube channel in the app, it will have your local news and sports TV networks based on your zip code. It has advertisements, just like regular TV. If you're a brand, and you want your ads running on YouTube TV, you need to work with your Google Rep to buy the ad space; it cannot be purchased currently via Google Ads. (One final distinction: YouTube TV is *not* YouTube Premium. YouTube Premium is a paid streaming subscription that allows its viewers to watch all YouTube-hosted videos without advertising.)

According to Nielsen, one of the major media-measurement companies, YouTube reaches more 18-to-34-year-olds than any cable network. This shows something important: Younger audiences aren't consuming traditional media in the same old way. Many people, affectionately known as *cord cutters or cord-nevers,* no longer even subscribe to cable or have ever held a subscription. They are, however, watching a good deal of video by way of YouTube, Hulu, Amazon FireTV, Roku, Facebook, and other online video providers.

But don't assume that people outside this age bracket aren't consuming online video. Remember to use demographics as a guide, not as a rule. If your content is relevant and your target audience is online, you'll get the business results you want.

Keep in mind as well, when migrating from television advertising to YouTube, that many of the traditional metrics associated with performance, especially those around viewership of the ads, differ radically between the two platforms. TV tends to focus on impressions, which measures how many people may have been exposed to a program or an ad. The dominant metrics on YouTube are how many people actually watched your content and your ads.

WARNING

YouTube videos are viewed over 250 million hours per day on TV screens, and these viewing statistics will only continue to grow. Cord cutters and cord-nevers are turning to the YouTube app on their connected TVs, streaming from their mobile devices and consuming YouTube on the biggest screen in the house. Don't forget to make content that scales well from mobile phones to TVs; your videos need to be optimized for every viewing experience. If your video has only extreme-close-up shots, that might be okay for a mobile viewing experience, but could be truly scary on a TV screen.

You don't measure distances with your bathroom scale, so don't measure your media the wrong way, either. Use the proper measurement in the digital world. Use television advertising metrics for TV, and YouTube metrics for your channel. For more on YouTube metrics, see Chapter 11.

YouTube isn't Google, either

It's a fact: How a viewer searches on YouTube is different from how a viewer searches on Google. (Don't believe us? Take another look at the figure in the earlier sidebar "Brand decisions are made on YouTube.") Google is indeed the number-one search engine, and YouTube is the number-two, but it's *how* viewers search that makes them so vastly different.

It's worth repeating: Brand and product decisions are being made on YouTube, and purchase decisions are being made on Google

From an advertising perspective, YouTube advertising — specifically, TrueView by way of Google Ads — behaves much differently from traditional Google Search ads. (For all the details on the nature of these differences, see Chapter 13.) It's important to note, though, that effective business management requires understanding the difference between traditional search and display for business, compared with YouTube search, display, engagement, subscriptions, and views.

IN THIS CHAPTER

» **Using advertising to reach a broader audience on YouTube**

» **Setting up and running a YouTube ad campaign**

» **Picking the right type of ad campaign**

» **Understanding the importance of earned metrics**

» **Adjusting ad campaigns to increase performance**

Chapter **13**

Expanding Your Audience with Google Ads

M any YouTube channel managers believe that after their channels are set up, their view counts are increasing, their subscriptions are growing, and engagement is up, they can then sit back and focus on making some content. Well, that's not exactly the case. You have another powerful resource in your tool chest that can potentially take your channel to the next level: It's *advertising.* Yes, this chapter is all about how to place ads on YouTube to promote yourself and grow your channel — not how to get advertisers to place ads on your channel (that's called *monetization* and it's covered in Chapter 14).

Now, before you close this book with a sigh, sure as sure can be that advertising is nothing more than a fancy way of throwing away money and annoying people, you'd better think again. YouTube advertising is highly effective because it allows you to reach a large part of your target audience who may not have discovered your channel and your content *organically* — without the help of advertising, in other words.

Unlike many other types of advertising, well-run YouTube ad campaigns end up delivering not only views but also increased watch time and additional subscriber growth, both of which are great for your channel in the eyes of YouTube. Why? Because effective YouTube advertising can help with discoverability, creating a virtuous cycle for your channel. A well-targeted ad campaign lets the right kind of viewers discover your channel — those you really want to reach. Once they subscribe and watch other videos on your channel after seeing your ads, your channel's search ranking will improve, which in turn will let other viewers with similar interests discover your content.

YouTube advertising is accessible to consumers by way of the Google Ads product — one of the world's most popular advertising platforms. As you can probably imagine, you can buy many ad types via Google Ads to advertise on YouTube. Chances are good that you've seen the video masthead ad on YouTube's home page or the ad overlays that appear over the lower center area of YouTube videos. This chapter focuses on a specific ad type you configure via Google Ads. It's the YouTube *TrueView* ad.

A YouTube TrueView ad is different from many other types of ads because you, as the advertiser, pay only if the viewer does something concrete, such as watch your video ad or click on a link to visit your website. A TrueView ad includes both video and display ad formats. In other words, some ads use videos, and others use regular display ads, with just a static image and some text. A *pre-roll* ad is a video ad shown immediately before displaying the video that the viewer clicked to see. If you've been on YouTube, you've seen them. They're the ones that let you skip off after 5 seconds. Concerned that tons of people are sure to skip off after the first 5 seconds? Don't be. The good part about TrueView ads is that you pay only for the viewers who choose to watch rather than those who skip off. In other words, you pay only for viewers who have a strong interest in the ad you've put in front of them.

GOOGLE DISPLAY NETWORK

You're not restricted to YouTube for your TrueView ads. Google also has the Google Display Network (GDN), a massive, worldwide collection of more than 2 million websites that allow display and video advertising. The GDN can support all screen types, including desktop computers, laptops, tablets, smartphones, game consoles, and connected TV screens. A majority of the world's most heavily trafficked websites and apps are part of the GDN, but that doesn't ensure that you'll be able to run ad placements on only the best sites.

During the YouTube ad campaign setup, you have the option to include the GDN for placement of your ads. When setting up targeting groups for your ads, you can also itemize specific placements within YouTube and within the GDN.

Most channel managers should have no problem setting up an ad campaign for YouTube. Google has worked hard to make Google Ads a user-friendly experience. Though you have to complete quite a few steps to set up an ad, most of the time you can simply use the default settings. Over time, you can tweak the settings to produce even better results, but for your first campaign, we recommend sticking with the defaults.

Understanding YouTube Advertising

To understand YouTube advertising, you need to know a little bit about Google advertising. You may believe that Google is simply a big search engine company, but it's really a big *advertising* company — that's where it makes its money. The same logic holds true for YouTube: People think of it as an amazing video site, but at its core, it's a major advertising platform.

A fortune is being spent and made on YouTube. You know all those YouTube stars, like Ryan Kaji, Rhett and Link, and Dude Perfect? They're earning the lion's share of their money from advertising. Granted, they're also now signing other types of lucrative endorsement deals, but their YouTube fame led to their first fortune — and that came from advertising. (If you're interested in learning more about monetization, be sure to check out Chapter 14.)

There are two sides to the advertising equation:

>> **Advertiser:** The person or organization paying for and placing the ads

>> **Publisher:** The person or organization whose property has the ad placed on it and who receives a cut of revenue from the ad

On YouTube, you can be an advertiser or a publisher, or both. In this chapter, you can read about the advertiser side. Chapter 14 tells you all about the publisher side.

Google and YouTube help on both sides of the advertising equation and have product offerings for both. On the advertiser side, you use Google Ads, which we cover later in this chapter. On the publisher side, you use Google AdSense to manage how your YouTube channel receives ads. (For more on Google AdSense in a YouTube context, again, check out Chapter 14.) Don't assume that you have to connect with publishers directly. Google acts as an intermediary — for a share of your profits, of course. (It's more proof that nothing in this life is ever free.)

Recognizing the importance of ad policy

If you're new to YouTube advertising, take a few minutes to understand its ad policy, which basically states that advertising should conform to certain behavioral standards. (Go to `https://support.google.com/adspolicy` for details.) Better yet, check out Chapter 9, which talks in some detail about the YouTube community guidelines — rules for everything from obscene material to copyright infringement and privacy controls. Google does its utmost to ensure that appropriate and relevant ads are placed, but both advertisers and publishers have further control as well.

REMEMBER

Community guidelines are upheld nonstop, all day and all year. Not only do violations jeopardize your ability to advertise, but you also risk having your channel taken down.

In addition to being in line with the YouTube community guidelines, ads must conform to technical guidelines and specifications. This helps ensure both consistency and fairness across the YouTube platform; it also lowers the likelihood that you'll annoy viewers. Ad format details can be found at `http://support.google.com/displayspecs`.

Looking at YouTube ad types

This chapter concentrates on YouTube TrueView ads. These formats work well for many advertisers because charges occur only when a viewer watches an ad to a certain length, interacts with an ad, or clicks on a video ad thumbnail. These actions are a signal of a higher degree of audience interest, making those viewers much better targets for your ads.

YouTube TrueView ads come in two flavors: in-stream and video discovery. *In-stream* ads work a bit like TV commercials: Before users can see the video they want to watch on YouTube, they have to watch your video ad first. (This is known also as a *pre-roll* ad.) YouTube lets users skip an in-stream ad after 5 seconds. Advertisers are charged if a user watches an in-stream ad to completion or to 30 seconds (whichever comes first) or interacts with the ad by clicking on the display URL, call-to-action overlay, or companion banner.

As for the video discovery ads, they appear on search results pages and on YouTube Watch pages and are marked with a gold AD icon. (Figure 13-1 shows a typical example of a video discovery ad above the organic search results.) Advertisers are charged as soon as a user clicks on the video thumbnail of a video discovery ad.

TIP

Since YouTube prioritizes videos with longer viewer-session watch times and high engagement rates in its search results, highly engaged viewers from paid ads can support your SEO efforts.

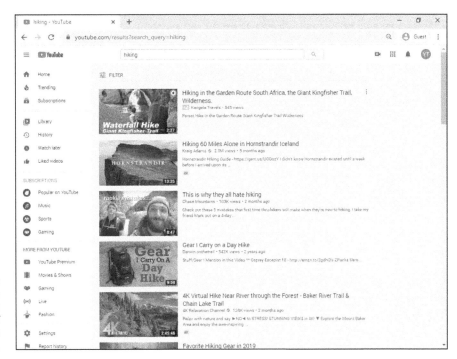

OTHER YouTube AD FORMATS AND PRICING MODELS

TrueView in-stream and video discovery aren't the only ad types available on YouTube, but they're highly effective for many advertisers because Google charges for them only when a viewer decides to watch the whole ad or — for longer ads — at least the first 30 seconds. They're also the ad types most recommended by Google to grow consideration and interest from a target audience, which makes them a perfect way to bolster your YouTube channel. You can investigate other types of YouTube ads, however, such as bumper and nonskippable ads (short pre-roll ads that viewers cannot skip off of), a *masthead* (the big ad that shows up on the YouTube home page), or an *in-video overlay* (an ad that appears in the lower center of a video and acts like an annotation). For more on these (and other) ad types, go to www.youtube.com/ads/running-a-video-ad.

The TrueView ad's claim to fame is that it uses cost per view (CPV) pricing. Other ad types may have different pricing methods, including cost per thousand impressions, also known as CPM ("M" in this acronym represents the word "mille", which is Latin for "thousands"). As you advertise more, it's worth your time to explore all ad types available via Google for YouTube.

Planning for Advertising

Advertising on YouTube requires some familiarity with Google Ads. (Luckily for you, you can achieve the necessary level of familiarity by simply reading this chapter.) First and foremost, you need a Google Ads account, which you can easily access via your regular Google account. Note, however, that you need to explicitly tie your Google Ads account to your YouTube account. (Don't worry: We show you how to do it.)

REMEMBER

You don't need to learn all about Google Ads to work your YouTube advertising magic. However, if you have a commerce website and need to drive more traffic, consider learning a lot more about topics such as conversions, which we don't touch on in this chapter.

Creating a Google Ads account

Creating a Google Ads account used to be pretty involved, but that was long ago. Fortunately, Google has greatly simplified the process of opening a new Google Ads account:

1. **Point your web browser to** `https://ads.google.com`.

2. **Click the Sign In link at the top right and log in with your Google account.**

   We recommend using the same Google account you'd use to manage your YouTube channel.

TIP

If you already have a Google account for Gmail, YouTube, or another Google service, you can use it for your Google Ads account. If you're a Gmail junkie, for example, connect the accounts so that you don't sign yourself out of Google Ads every time you check your mail. If you already have a Google Analytics account (a free service that measures what visitors do on your website), the email address of your Google Ads account must be the same as your Analytics admin user email.

3. **On the new screen that appears, click the New Google Ads Account link to create an account.**

   Doing so brings up the New Campaign page.

4. **Click the Switch to Expert Mode link near the bottom of the New Campaign page.**

   You want to do this so that you can bypass the initial questions that Google asks to get an understanding of your advertising goals. That setup process is designed for search advertising, not video ads, so you don't need to do it.

5. **On the new screen that appears, click the Create an Account Without a Campaign link beneath the campaign goal selection boxes.**

   This step allows you to get your account set up for success before jumping straight into campaign creation.

6. **On the new screen that appears, select your billing country, time zone, and currency from the dropdown lists and then click the Submit button. (See Figure 13-2.)**

REMEMBER

   Google might change the sign-up process and its billing practices at any time, so take the preceding instructions with a grain of salt. They may be accurate for years — or they may be out of date one week after this book shows up in the bookstore.

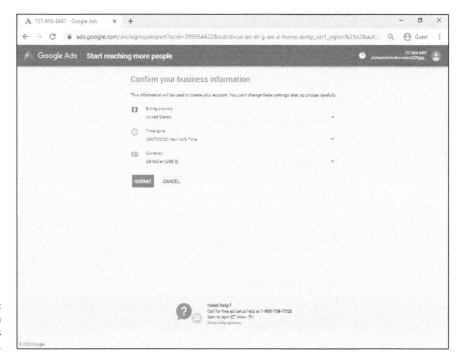

FIGURE 13-2: Setting up a Google Ads account.

Linking your Google Ads account and YouTube channel

For your YouTube advertising project, you should link your Google Ads account with your YouTube channel to access deeper ad analytics and to set up YouTube remarketing lists. A well-run YouTube ad campaign produces lots of views, subscriptions, engagements, and clicks. By linking your accounts, you have access to much deeper statistics.

To link your accounts, follow these steps:

1. **Log in to your Google Ads account, or, if you're continuing from the steps in the preceding section, click the Explore Your Account link.**

2. **Copy your customer ID.**

   Your Google Ads customer ID is a 3-part number that uniquely identifies your Google Ads account. You'll find it in the top right of your Google Ads page, right above your email address and to the left of the account icon.

3. **Log in to your YouTube account.**

4. **On the YouTube home page, click your account icon in the top right, and then choose YouTube Studio from the menu that appears.**

   Doing so brings up the YouTube Studio dashboard.

5. **In the navigation menu on the left, click the Settings link.**

   A window labeled Settings opens in the middle of the screen.

6. **Select Channel from the navigation menu on the left side of the Settings window.**

7. **Click the Advanced Settings link in the Channel section, located in the main part of the window.**

8. **Next to the Google Ads account linking subheading, click the hyperlink labeled Link Account.**

   Doing so opens a small dialog box, as shown in Figure 13-3.

9. **In the Link Name field, enter a descriptive name for the Google Ads account you're linking.**

10. **In the Google Ads Customer ID field, paste the Google Ads customer ID that you copied in Step 2.**

11. **Using the check boxes below the text fields, select the account permissions you want for your Google Ads account.**

    Linking your Google Ads and YouTube accounts gives you access to additional capabilities. These include

    - *View counts,* which provide you with more detailed information about video views

    - *Remarketing,* which enables you to show your ad to viewers who previously visited your channel

    - *Engagement,* which shows you what viewers do after seeing your ad

    We recommend selecting all options as part of your initial campaign, to maximize the benefit of connecting your accounts.

TIP

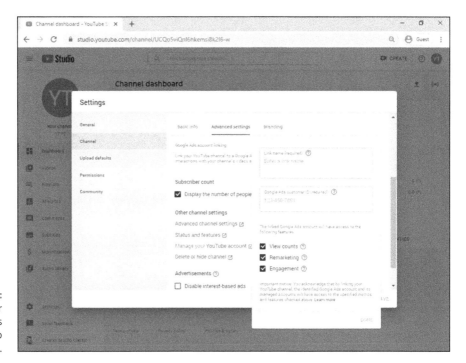

FIGURE 13-3:
Moving your
Google Ads
customer ID into
YouTube.

12. In the same dialog box, click Done.

13. Back in the Settings window, click Save.

14. Log back in to your Google Ads account, and then navigate to the main screen of your customer account.

15. From the menu across the top of the page, click the Tools & Settings link and then choose Linked Accounts under the Settings heading.

16. Find YouTube in the list of accounts and then click its associated Details link.

17. Within the Link Requests table, find your YouTube channel and then click the View Request link under the Action heading.

A window appears, as shown in Figure 13-4.

18. Click Approve to link your YouTube and Google Ads accounts.

Your Google Ads account is now linked with your YouTube channel, and your settings are saved.

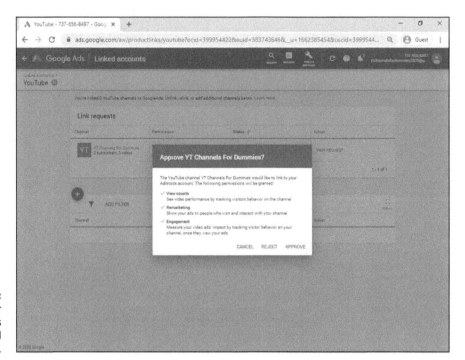

FIGURE 13-4:
Linking your Google Ads account and YouTube channel.

REMEMBER

You can unlink the Google Ads account that you associated with your YouTube channel at any point, if you feel so inclined. Just remember that by unlinking your accounts, you lose access to earned metrics, which measure the impact your advertising has had on important channel metrics, such as views and subscriptions. You can find out more about earned metrics later in this chapter, in the section "Getting earned metrics."

Determining Your Ad Targets

Before starting your campaign, you have to determine where you want your ads placed. This is known as *ad targeting*. Google Ads provides extremely rich and powerful targeting options. Each set of options can be broken out into separate *ad groups*, and you can use multiple, simultaneous ad groups in the same campaign.

REMEMBER

Running a YouTube ad campaign isn't like placing an ad in a magazine or a commercial on television, where the ad is placed and you're done. Effective digital marketing — marketing that relies on YouTube and on display and search advertising — allows advertisers to constantly optimize, or tune, ad performance by making adjustments throughout the campaign, which may include changing the targets.

TIP

You can set up multiple ad groups throughout a campaign, so don't try to be exhaustive out of the chute. You can always update your targeting after your campaign launches, too.

To get started with YouTube TrueView advertising, you need to get a handle on the basics of ad targeting. The default Google Ads setup lets you target using the following criteria:

>> **People:** Who you want to reach

>> **Content:** Where you want your ads to show on YouTube

People targeting

When it comes to targeting people, Google Ads gives you a few options to choose from:

>> **Demographics:** This option lets you select your audience characteristics by age, gender, parental status, and household income, as shown in Figure 13-5. Always choose the age and gender of your target audience, if you know it. (Household income isn't available in all countries.)

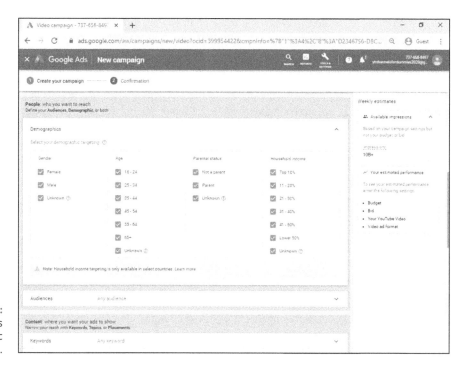

FIGURE 13-5:
Your Google Ads demographic targeting options.

YouTube doesn't let you target viewers under the age of 18. In fact, if you are promoting content made for kids (anyone under the age of 13), you need to comply with the Children's Online Privacy Protection Act, also known as COPPA, which may restrict your advertising opportunities. For more information on COPPA compliance on YouTube, visit Chapter 14.

>> **Audiences:** This option lets you identify specific viewer characteristics and interests that you want targeted. Audience targeting groups allow you to reach viewers who are interested in a certain content category even when they're interacting with unrelated content. Google determines viewers' interests by analyzing the type of videos they're watching and by the types of websites they're visiting.

For YouTube campaigns specifically, Google Ads allows you to utilize the following types of audience targeting to reach people:

>> **Detailed demographics:** People who share common traits, such as parents of teens, college students, or homeowners or renters

>> **Affinity and custom affinity:** People based on their lifestyles, buying habits, or longer-term interests

>> **Intent, custom intent, and life events:** People actively researching products or shifting purchasing behavior and preferences during life milestones, like a job change, moving, or getting married

>> **Remarketing:** People who previously interacted with your video content or website

REMEMBER

Remarketing is one of the most powerful types of targeting you can leverage on YouTube because it helps keep your brand relevant to your audience, increasing the likelihood that they will engage with your content again. With remarketing, you can target viewers who have previously interacted with your channel, videos, or website. That means they have done one of the following:

- Viewed your content

- Watched your ads

- Engaged with or shared your videos

- Visited your channel

- Subscribed (or unsubscribed) from your channel

By linking your Google Ads and YouTube accounts, you can remarket to these viewers or visitors. You target with remarketing by creating a remarketing list, which you can find out about later in this chapter. You can use several different remarketing lists in the same advertising campaign.

REMEMBER

Remarketing is just a fancy term for targeting users who have already interacted with you. Google and YouTube privacy rules prevent you from knowing who they specifically are, but that shouldn't prevent you from giving those remarketed viewers a more customized ad experience. For example, if viewers have watched a particular video, you can serve them a different video ad next, rather than the same one. You can even exclude a remarketing list from your campaign if you want to ensure that you show ads only to people who have never seen your content.

You can also remarket to viewers who have watched videos similar to the ones on your channel. This strategy significantly increases the reach of your ads. We cover the process of implementing a remarketing list later in this chapter in a section called "Setting up remarketing lists."

Content targeting

For content targeting, Google Ads gives you a couple different options as well:

>> **Keywords:** This option lets you target videos that are relevant to the keywords you itemize. For example, if you have a video ad for your pottery product, *pottery* would then be a good keyword to add to your campaign.

REMEMBER

Start off with broad keywords; you can always add in more niche terms after testing to narrow your reach. It's also a good idea to group similar keywords together so that you can separate them into distinct ad groups. This makes it much easier to optimize your performance later on. If you're having difficulty coming up with keywords, consider using the Google Ads Get Keyword Ideas feature (accessible within the campaign targeting set-up workflow for keywords) to generate a broad list of keywords based on your business.

TIP

Adding a minus sign (–) in front a keyword ensures that your ad doesn't show against content that matches this keyword. If you don't want your audience to be reminded of the fact that pottery might break, you might enter –glue as a keyword to filter out any videos dealing with glue. You can actually exclude any of the types of targeting we talk about in this main section. For an example of how to exclude audiences from your ad campaign, visit `https://support.google.com/google-ads/answer/2549058`. The process is similar for demographics, topics, and placements.

>> **Topics:** You can target specific content on either YouTube or the Google Display Network (GDN) corresponding to a selected topic. When configuring topic-based targeting, you can go broadly, such as Home & Garden, or be more specific in the category, by selecting Rugs & Carpets under the Home Furnishings subcategory. (Note that you can select different topics in the same group.)

>> **Placements:** You can create a list of YouTube channels, specific videos, exact websites, or itemized pages in the GDN where you want your ad served. This is an excellent way to ensure that your content is appearing in the right places, next to videos about specific topics. (Placements apply only to YouTube videos and to the GDN, not to YouTube Search.)

REMEMBER

We're giving you the lay of the land right now when it comes to preparing for your YouTube ad campaign. As for the nuts-and-bolts of setting up a YouTube ad campaign, we cover that topic a bit later in this chapter (in the section that just happens to be entitled "Setting Up a YouTube Ad Campaign"). For more information on all the targeting types available on YouTube, visit https://support. google.com/google-ads/answer/2497941.

Navigating Google Ads

Google Ads has a powerful interface that lets you set up and check the status of your campaigns. Using this single interface, you can look at the performance of your entire account (see Figure 13-6) or dive into a particular campaign.

The landing page for a customer account in Google Ads consists of these five main components:

>> **Navigation menu:** This collapsible, dark gray menu, located on the left side of the screen, shows you all the campaigns within your Google Ads account. (Not visible in Figure 13-6, unfortunately.) The top portion of the Navigation menu allows for quick filtering by campaign type and status. Beneath the filter division line, you can see a relational tree of your campaigns and their ad sets. Clicking on a campaign or ad group within this menu immediately directs you to that specific campaign or ad group's page within the main reporting interface. (If you don't see this menu right away, try moving the mouse all the way over to the left side of the screen. That should bring the menu into view.)

>> **Page menu:** This light gray menu, located to the right of the Navigation menu, allows you to view different settings and reporting pages within your Google Ads account. (Refer to Figure 13-6.) From this menu, you can access anything — from a high-level account overview to the most granular device targeting reporting from your campaigns. We cover more of this powerful menu later in this chapter, in the section "Looking at Your campaign details".

>> **Subpage menu:** Located beneath the Top bar menu, the Subpage menu provides information about the page being actively viewed and allows for some customization, such as date range adjustments.

Page menu   Top bar menu

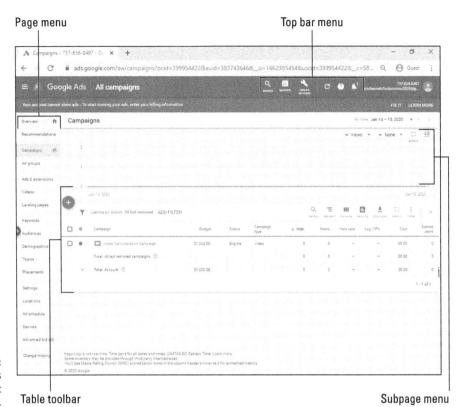

FIGURE 13-6:
The Google Ads
customer account
interface.

Table toolbar   Subpage menu

>> **Top bar menu:** This one provides quick access to your customer account
settings, alerts, help guides, and more from the top of the Google Ads
interface.

>> **Table toolbar:** You can create new campaigns, filter tables, segment table
data, change metric columns, view preconfigured reports, export data, pause,
enable, or delete current campaigns, and much more. This is located between
the Subpage menu and the reporting grid.

TIP

If you're familiar with the YouTube Analytics interface, you may see some similarities. For example, you can filter your results using the Date pull-down menu
in the top right, just as you would with YouTube Analytics. For a quick reference
map of the Google Ads interface and the menus we just described, visit https://
support.google.com/google-ads/answer/7635053.

Setting Up a YouTube Ad Campaign

So you've informed yourself about the costs and benefits of YouTube advertising and decided to give it a shot. We can only say, "Smart move." Now it's time to get your hands dirty and set up your first YouTube ad campaign.

Going with a general campaign

Unfortunately, no one has yet invented a robot that sets up YouTube video ads for you. The process might sound a bit complicated at first because Google Ads is quite powerful, but it's fairly easy to start your first campaign. To set up a new YouTube ad, follow these steps:

1. **Log in to** https://ads.google.com.

   If you haven't created a Google Ads account yet, do so by following the instructions in the "Creating a Google Ads account" section, earlier in this chapter. If you haven't yet created any campaigns in your account, you may be prompted to create an ad with help from Google. You should navigate away from that prompt in order to create a YouTube campaign. To continue, click on the Google Ads logo in the top left of your screen to navigate to the landing page of your Google Ads account.

2. **After you're within the regular interface of your Google Ads account, you should click the Campaigns tab from the Page menu.**

   TIP

   If you want your account to open to the Campaign tab whenever you log in to Google Ads, click the Home icon on the Campaign tab. Doing so ensures that the Campaign tab opens by default whenever you log in. (The standard setting is to have the Overview tab open by default.)

3. **Click the big blue Plus Sign (+) button in the top left of the Table toolbar, and select + New Campaign from the menu that appears.**

4. **(Optional) Click the Load Campaign Settings option if you have an earlier campaign and you want to reuse some of its configuration data.**

   As you become more proficient in running campaigns, you can save time and automatically populate new campaign fields by reusing older content. You can also change the settings for the campaign even after you've autoloaded it.

5. **On the next screen, choose the Product and Brand Consideration campaign goal you want.**

   Google Ads offers a variety of campaign goals to help guide you through the process of setting up a campaign, though not every goal supports setting up a YouTube campaign. If you want to learn about each of the campaign goals that

Google Ads offers, simply hover your mouse cursor over the goal to see a definition and the supported campaign types. You also have the option to create a campaign with no guidance, if you prefer. We recommend starting with the Product and Brand Consideration option because it's designed to help you set up YouTube TrueView skippable in-stream ads and video discovery ads. As long as the videos you are advertising are at least 12 seconds long, these two ad types can help add to the public video view count on your channel, whereas other ad types that are impression based do not.

6. **In the new box that appears, select Video as your campaign type.**

7. **In the new box that appears beneath the previous step, select Influence Consideration as your campaign subtype and click Continue.**

8. **On the new page that appears, enter a name for your campaign in the Campaign Name field.**

   Choose a relevant and informative name, such as Acme Electric Z500 Product Launch, as opposed to Campaign #1. If you plan to segment your targeting into separate campaigns, add words such as *mobile* or *desktop* to the campaign name. This strategy makes it easier later to identify and manage these particular campaigns in the list of all your campaigns.

TIP

Don't rush through the naming process; be as descriptive as possible. Trust us: You're sure to forget important campaign details even if you have only a few campaigns. If you need to make your campaign names more descriptive after publishing, however, you can always edit them from within the Campaigns tab of Google Ads.

9. **Then, select your budget type and enter a budget.**

   Google Ads allows you to select one of two budget types: a campaign total budget or a daily budget. A *campaign total budget* specifies the total amount of money you want to spend for the duration of your campaign. This method is useful when you're running a single YouTube campaign. Google optimizes your campaign spending for you and aims to spend your total budget by the campaign end date. Alternatively, a *daily budget* specifies the average amount you want to spend *each day* over the course of a month. This method requires a bit more precision because Google can spend up to twice as much as your daily campaign budget for you on days when a lot of people are browsing YouTube. However, if you're interested in manually optimizing your budget across multiple campaigns, a daily budget is the way to go.

   You can increase or decrease a budget at any time, so enter an amount that you feel comfortable experimenting with to begin. Start with a small amount, such as $50, and increase it gradually as you start seeing the results you want.

10. **Pick your ad delivery method.**

You set the rate at which your ads are served over the course of a day. Choose the Standard option if you want them spread evenly over your ad day. Choose the Accelerated option to deliver your ads rapidly.

REMEMBER

If you run an accelerated campaign and max out your daily budget, your ads stop for the day and start up again during the next day you're serving ads.

11. **Select your networks.**

As a YouTube advertiser, you have three choices for where your ads are shown:

- *YouTube Search:* You get to post your TrueView ads in the YouTube search results. The only allowed ad type is video discovery.

- *YouTube Videos:* You can run either in-stream video ads against YouTube videos or video discovery ads on the YouTube Watch page.

- *Google Display Network:* For this network, you also have to select the YouTube Videos network option. The GDN supports both in-stream and video discovery ad formats.

12. **Choose the language of the viewers who will see your ads.**

This step ensures that your ad appears only in places where the language of the ad matches the language of the targeted audience — an important consideration when you're dealing with GDN targeting.

13. **Pick your locations.**

Don't let the simple interface fool you. You have the option to pick worldwide, United States, or Canada, but when you click the Enter Another Location link and then select Advanced Search, you're accessing a powerful interface that lets you do precision location targeting of your ads, down to the city or area level. (To see how specific geolocation targeting can get, check out Figure 13-7.) You can mix and match locations, but you also have the option to exclude certain areas.

REMEMBER

You can run ad campaigns in a specific region or put together simultaneous campaigns with region-specific offers.

14. **Select your inventory type.**

YouTube has *a lot* of content, and some of it's unsavory. In recent years, you may have heard news stories about famous brands running their ads on politically sensitive or controversial content by accident. The Inventory Type setting was developed to help advertisers opt out of categories of sensitive content on YouTube that don't align with their brand.

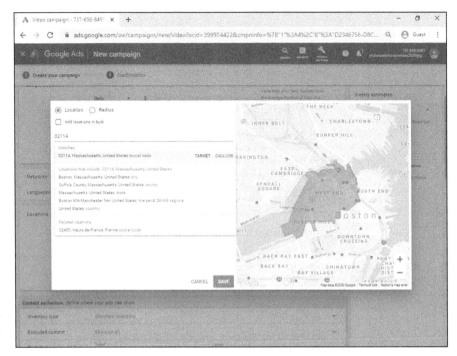

You can choose from three inventory-type settings for your campaign:

- *Expanded:* This is the broadest inventory setting that allows ad placement on what some would consider "sensitive" content. This setting excludes content that contains excessive profanity, graphic sexual content and nudity, and graphic violence and serious injury.

- *Standard:* This setting is the most recommended inventory option because it has mostly brand-appropriate content. It excludes the same content as the expanded inventory setting as well as repeated strong profanity, strong sexual content and discussions of sex, and violence either real or dramatized.

- *Limited:* The most limited inventory setting, it excludes most sensitive content categories. Using this setting can severely limit your ad's reach. This setting excludes the same content as expanded and standard as well as moderate profanity and moderate sexually suggestive content.

15. **(Optional) Exclude content types and labels.**

In addition to opting out of sensitive content categories by selecting an inventory type, you can elect to exclude additional content types and content labels. These options allow you some finer control over exactly what types of videos your ads show up on. For content types, you may exclude embedded videos and livestreaming videos, if you choose. For *content labels* — they act a lot like movie ratings — you can exclude content that hasn't been labeled or content labeled for specific age groups (such as mature audiences, teens, PG, or even G).

16. **Using the Additional Settings drop-down menu in the new page that appears, select the devices on which the ad can appear.**

    Your target audience may prefer one type of device or carrier over another. Google Ads therefore lets you specify desktops, smartphones, tablets, or TV screens as targets and choose to place ads only on specific mobile providers by country, such as AT&T, Verizon, or others in the United States. If you're just starting out, we recommend targeting all eligible devices, but if you want to edit your device targeting, click the Set Specific Targeting for Devices link to explore your options.

17. **(Optional) Set a frequency cap for your ads.**

    This feature sets the average number of times a unique user will view your ad over a given period, such as a day, week, or month. For video campaigns, you can set a frequency cap on impressions or views, or a combination of the two.

18. **Schedule when your ad runs.**

    You get to pick when your ad campaign starts and ends, along with the days and times you want it to run. You can leave this option empty and manually start and pause campaigns as needed.

REMEMBER

Ad scheduling is helpful if you know when your viewers are watching and will likely see your ads. For example, if you're in the beauty or fashion business and you want to target women getting ready to leave home for the workplace, you'd likely schedule your ads for weekday mornings. This strategy is especially helpful if you accelerate your ads — you don't want to burn up all your budget before your core target audience is even awake.

Creating an ad group and setting up targeting

After your general settings are in place, you need to determine who will see the ad. To ensure that your targeting isn't too narrow, we recommend building out one specific ad group per targeting type. We describe the process of adding another ad group to your campaign later in this chapter, in the "Creating a YouTube Ad" section. To specify the audience targeting for your first ad group, follow these steps:

1. **Continuing from the last step in the previous section, enter a name for your ad group in the Ad Group Name field. (See Figure 13-8.)**

    Similar to choosing your campaign name, consider naming your ad group something meaningful by calling out the type of targeting it will contain. This makes it easier to understand your campaign performance later on.

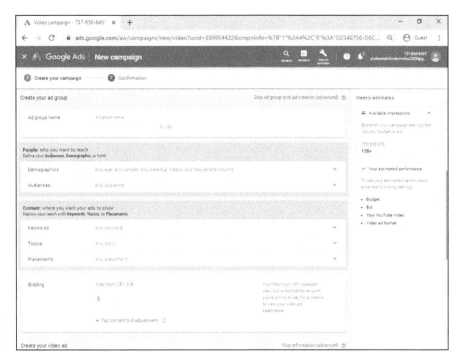

FIGURE 13-8:
Adding a
new ad group.

2. **Select your demographics targeting. (Refer to Figure 13-5.)**

   You can select any combination of age, gender, parental status, or household income by selecting or deselecting the respective categories. Remember that household income isn't yet available in all countries.

3. **(Optional) Add in audience targeting.**

   Search for specific terms, phrases, or website URLs to find relevant audience targets to add to your campaign. You can also click the Browse option from the Audience Targeting submenu to see a full list of all available audience types, if you prefer. We describe all available options in detail earlier in this chapter, in the "People targeting" section. After you have selected a few targets, you can explore the Ideas submenu tab to see even more relevant targeting ideas based on your settings.

4. **(Optional) Add in keywords, topics, or placements targeting.**

   We explain the purpose of these targeting types earlier in this chapter, in the "Content targeting" section. Each of these targeting types specifies the types of content you want your ads to run on. (Figure 13-9 shows some of your choices for the Autos & Vehicles topic.) When you're happy with your selections, move on to the next section.

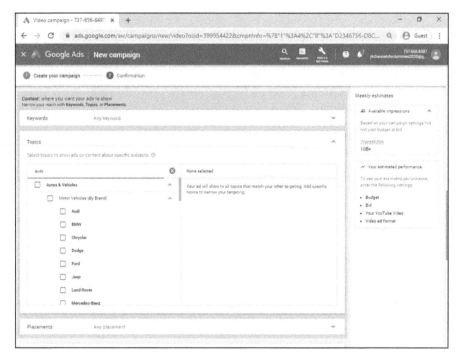

FIGURE 13-9:
Choosing specific topics to target for YouTube TrueView ads.

Creating a YouTube Ad

With the campaign and ad group targeting settings completed, you must now associate one or more ads with your campaign. Here's how to get that scintillating ad of yours in front of your viewers:

1. **Continuing from the last step in the previous section, enter a maximum cost per view (CPV) bid for your campaign in the field labeled "Maximum CPV bid."**

   This is the maximum amount you're willing to pay each time a viewer watches your video to completion or 30 seconds (whichever comes first), interacts with your ad's clickable elements, or clicks on your video discovery ad. A good amount to start with is 5 cents. You can increase or decrease the amount later, after your campaign starts running.

   REMEMBER

   TrueView ads are sold on an auction basis. You're competing with other advertisers who want to reach a similar target audience and are willing to bid a certain amount per view. If your bid is too low, you won't win at the auction very often. Your ad won't get many views and you'll need to adjust your bid. If you leave a campaign running year-round, take seasonality into account and understand that you may need to raise your maximum bid to win enough views during high-volume ad buying seasons, like the beginning of December.

For video discovery ads, you pay only if people click on an ad, not for the ad just showing up. In the case of in-stream ads, you're charged only when the viewer watches at least 30 seconds of your video ad. This *pay per view* method makes YouTube ads highly cost effective.

2. **(Optional) Enter a top content bid adjustment.**

   Top content consists of the most popular content on YouTube and the GDN as determined by audience engagement. By entering a top content bid adjustment, you're more likely to have your ad placed in the top content inventory. Bid adjustments can range from 0 percent to 500 percent of your initial bid, which means that you can end up paying a lot more to run in the top content.

   Top content is available only in select markets for YouTube, so check the help tips in Google Ads before testing it out.

3. **In the next section of the campaign creation workflow, paste the YouTube video URL of your ad into the Your YouTube Video field.**

   The video you use has to be uploaded to your YouTube channel before you do this. Videos that are to be used as ads need to be either public or unlisted. Check Chapter 9 for details on how to upload a video.

   As soon as you paste a correct video URL, you see your video with its thumbnail picture, and several additional options appear, as shown in Figure 13-10.

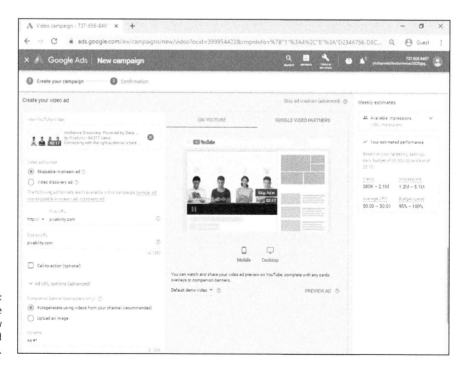

FIGURE 13-10: YouTube TrueView in-stream ad configuration.

Your YouTube ad might be the first thing people see about your company, so use a video that is short, catchy, and to the point.

4. **Select the video ad format you want to use.**

   Select either skippable in-stream or video discovery ad formats, depending on which one you want to use for this ad. If you want to use the same video in different formats, create separate video ads for each one.

5. **If you've chosen an in-stream ad, configure your ad by filling in the new fields that appear.**

   Again, Figure 13-10 shows you the in-stream configuration options of the Create Your Video Ad page. (Note that you have an input panel and a preview pane that shows what your ad will look like for both types of TrueView ads — in-stream and video discovery.)

   Here's a rundown of the in-stream fields you need to fill in:

   - *Final URL:* This is the actual web location where viewers end up after they click.

   - *Display URL:* This is the website link that is shown on your video ad.

     Do not indulge in bait-and-switch tactics. Always send viewers to a web page that clearly has something to do with the ad. If you try to trick your viewers, you'll only end up wasting your ad budget and alienating viewers who may be interested in your channel, product, or services.

   - *(Optional) Call-to-action:* This optional feature gives you another opportunity to convince a viewer to engage with your ad. With a call-to-action overlay, you have 15 characters to create a compelling headline and 10 additional characters to entice users to take an action, such as click on your link. It appears as soon as your video starts playing in the lower left of the advertisement. This feature is recommended when website clicks are your primary campaign goal.

   - *Companion banner:* This is a 300 x 60-pixel image that appears next to your video ad. The companion banner should have a strong call to action so that viewers are more likely to click on it. Note that the companion banner is the only element that remains up after your video ad has finished playing or has been skipped by the user. We generally recommend using the YouTube default banner, known as a *video wall,* if you have several videos on your channel or if you're looking to gain subscribers with your ad.

6. **If you've chosen a video discovery ad, follow these steps to configure your ad:**

    a. Choose the thumbnail picture you want to use. YouTube gives you only four predefined options. See the thumbnails discussion in Chapter 9 for tips on how to select an effective thumbnail.

    b. Write the ad text. This short bit of text appears next to the video thumbnail in your ads. (See Figure 13-11.) You get one headline with a maximum length of 100 characters and two lines of descriptive text with 35 characters apiece.

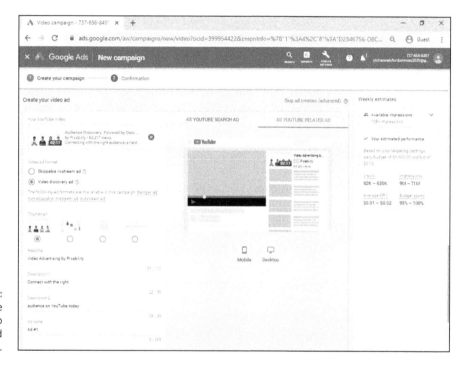

FIGURE 13-11:
YouTube
TrueView video
discovery ad
configuration.

TIP

Attach a catchy headline, and be sure to tell people why they should watch this video. You can test ad copy by creating multiple versions of the video discovery ad. Try to limit your headline to 25 characters or fewer, to ensure that the characters aren't cut off on devices with smaller screens.

7. **Enter the name of your ad in the field provided.**

Use a descriptive name that makes it easy for you to identify the ad later.

8. **Click the Create Campaign button at the bottom of the screen.**

9. **On the new page that appears, review the campaign summary and click the Continue to Campaign button.**

This step places you within the campaign you just created on the Ad Groups tab.

10. **If you want to create another ad group to add targeting to your campaign, click the big blue Plus Sign (+) button to launch the ad group creation process.**

You can set up multiple targeting groups for your ads to optimize the results. Simply follow the steps in the earlier sections "Creating an ad group and setting up targeting" and "Creating a YouTube Ad." If you want to add remarketing targeting but haven't yet created a YouTube remarketing list, we cover those steps a little later in this chapter, in the section "Setting up remarketing lists."

11. **If this is the first time you've bought ads on Google or YouTube, you need to enter your billing information before your campaign can start. Use the Billing settings under Tools & Settings on the Top bar menu to begin this process.**

Follow the simple process on the screen to provide your credit card information.

You're billed for your Google Ads account only after you start your ad campaign.

12. **Verify the status of your ad.**

If your billing is set up correctly, you should see your new ad on the Ads & Extensions tab of the Page menu. Looking at the Status column in the reporting grid, you should see the text *Under review*. That's a good sign. It's proof that your ad is complete — you just need to wait on final approval from Google. Usually, that takes no more than 24 hours. If it's taking any longer, call Google Ads support at 1-844-756-8495 for help with troubleshooting.

Be sure to check out how your ads are performing after your ads are approved by Google. (You can find out more in the next section on how you can actually do that.) Monitor your campaigns regularly to find the most effective videos, targeting groups, and ads, and make small optimizations to improve your performance.

If you need to modify an ad name or ad copy after the ad has been saved, you lose all the performance data associated with that ad and have to wait for the ad to be approved by Google again. Click the little arrow next to the title of the ad to make any edits. (If you want to keep your performance data, we recommend duplicating the ad and then making changes to the new version of the ad.)

REMEMBER

You can always pause an ad campaign from the Campaigns tab by highlighting the check box next to the campaign name, clicking the Edit dropdown menu that appears, and then selecting Pause. We recommend that you never remove an ad, because you can't get it back in case you change your mind.

Now that the campaign, targeting, and ad have been set up, it's time to learn how to launch your campaign and interpret the results. You can find out how to do that in later sections, but first we take care of one last side issue — your remarketing lists.

Setting up remarketing lists

Remarketing is all about targeting viewers who have already interacted with your channel, videos, or website by either viewing your content, seeing your ads, visiting your channel, or subscribing to your channel. If you want to set up remarketing lists, follow these steps:

1. **Log in to** https://ads.google.com.

    The home page for Google Ads appears.

2. **On the Top bar menu along the top of the interface, click to open the Tools & Settings menu, and choose Audience Manager under the Shared Library heading.**

    This step brings up the Remarketing page.

3. **Click the big blue Plus Sign (+) button in the top left of the Table toolbar, and select + YouTube Users from the menu that appears.**

    You see the New Audience: YouTube Users page.

4. **In the field provided, provide a name for the audience you are creating.**

5. **Choose the list members.**

    You can choose users who have interacted with your content in a variety of ways when creating a YouTube remarketing list, as shown in Figure 13-12. A good place to start is by creating an audience of people who have seen any video on your channel. You can even prefill this list with people who have interacted with your content in the past 30 days. These people are likely to positively engage with your ad campaign. One thing to keep in mind, however, is that in accordance with the Children's Online Privacy Protection Act (COPPA), you cannot create remarketing lists from any video content you upload that is directed at children.

6. **Set a membership duration for your remarketing list.**

   YouTube allows you to keep users in your remarketing lists for as long as 540 days (1 & 1/2 years). To ensure that your list is staying fresh as your channel grows, however, consider using a smaller membership duration, such as 30 to 90 days.

7. **Click the Create button.**

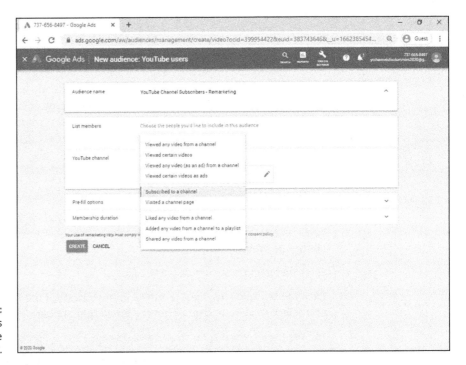

TIP

You can also remarket to viewers who have watched content similar to yours. Google automatically creates Similar To lists after you create your YouTube remarketing lists. You can find these lists on the Remarketing page and in the targeting options for audience targeting. (Note that YouTube decides what content is similar — you have to take its choice or leave it.)

You can find more in-depth details about remarketing with YouTube by making your way to https://support.google.com/youtube.

Looking at Your campaign details

After you have created a video campaign, you should see some (or all) of the following tabs appear on the Google Ads Page menu (if you don't, try refreshing the page):

» **Overview:** Shows relevant highlights, insights, and metrics about your campaigns to help you quickly digest how your campaigns are performing

» **Recommendations:** Generates suggestions that can improve your campaign's performance based on your account's history, campaign settings, and trends across Google

» **Campaigns:** Shows an overview of the performance of all your campaigns and is also used to set up a new campaign

» **Ad groups:** Shows an overview of the performance of all your ad groups

» **Ads and extensions:** Displays your actual ads (because you can have multiple ads running in a campaign)

» **Videos:** Lists the videos that are used as your ads

» **Landing pages:** Shows the performance of the landing pages of your ads

» **Keywords:** Shows the performance of the keywords in your ad groups and lets you add or edit your keywords

» **Audiences:** Displays the performance metrics of the audiences you're targeting and lets you add or edit your audiences

» **Demographics:** Shows performance metrics broken out by the age, gender, parental status, and household income of your ad groups

» **Topics:** Shows the performance of the topics in your ad groups and lets you add or edit your topics

» **Placements:** Displays the performance of the YouTube videos, YouTube channels, or specific websites you're targeting and lets you add or edit your placements

» **Settings:** Shows a grid of all your campaigns and their basic settings and lets you access account level settings

(Clicking on a specific campaign from the navigation menu reveals additional campaign-level settings for that campaign within this tab.)

» **Locations:** Shows the performance of your targeted geographical locations

» **Ad Schedule:** Allows you to configure specific times of the day and week when you want your ads to show (configured, by default, to show all the time)

>> **Devices:** Provides a breakdown of campaign performance between desktops, mobile devices, tablets, and TV screens

>> **Change history:** Shows a list of changes you have made to your campaigns and ad account over time

Measuring Clicks and Results

Regularly tracking the performance of your campaign is essential for success. If you don't pay attention, you may be spending ad dollars for ineffective views, or you might miss out on interesting opportunities to reach your audience. Fortunately, the YouTube ad management tool gives you all the important numbers you need in order to manage your campaign.

When you analyze your campaign results, it's important to understand the following distinction:

>> **Paid metrics:** Represent the direct results of your ads, such as ad views and the average cost per view

>> **Earned metrics:** Can be thought of as the follow-on activities that occur as a result of your ads, including new subscribers and additional channel views

Both sets of metrics are important to advertisers and YouTube channel managers because they tell them whether their ad money is being spent effectively.

You're charged for paid metrics, not for earned metrics. If your video ad results in a viewer visiting your channel and watching ten more videos, you paid for 1 view and received 10 for free. In other words, that's 11 views for the price of 1.

Looking at campaign information

Google Ads is your friend. To gain the full benefit of this friendship, you need to visit (you guessed it!) `https://ads.google.com` and click the Campaigns tab within the Page menu to see the most important performance numbers. You can also see the details for every video campaign.

These are your *paid metrics*. This list of common metrics describes what the numbers mean:

- **Impressions:** These figures represent how many times your ad was shown to a user (irrespective of whether the user clicked on it or watched it for any certain length of time).

- **Views:** This number shows how many views your videos got by way of paid ads. For video discovery ads, a view is counted when a viewer clicks on an ad and starts watching the video. For in-stream ads, a view means that the user watched at least 30 seconds of the ad (or the whole ad if it's shorter) or clicked on one of the ad's interactive elements.

- **View rate:** This rate represents the percentage of people who saw your ad and either clicked on it (for video discovery) or chose not to skip it (for in-stream). Don't be disappointed if this number seems low. Typical rates are well under 1 percent for video discovery and around 25 to 30 percent for in-stream ads. The higher the number, the more effective your ad.

- **Watch time:** This is the total amount of time that people watched your video ads, in seconds.

- **Average watch time / impression:** This one measures the average number of seconds someone watched your ad per impression of the ad.

- **Average CPV (cost per view):** This figure tells you how much you spent for one person to watch your video. This value can differ depending on the topic and the amount of competition you face, but ranges between 1 cent and 20 cents are typical.

- **Cost:** This is the total amount you spent on all your YouTube ads.

Successful campaigns have a high view rate and a low CPV. But what the numbers should be depends strongly on your industry. Some industries, such as financial services, are highly competitive in their online marketing efforts, so expect a high CPV amount. In other industries, you may be able to draw viewers for only a few cents per pop. For a more detailed description of all the available video ad metrics for Google Ads, visit `https://support.google.com/google-ads/answer/2375431`.

REMEMBER

Watch how your campaign performs over time. When the view rate value drops and the CPV rises, it's time to optimize.

Getting earned metrics

The great part about YouTube advertising is that it can lead to increased viewer activity with your channel. These are *earned metrics*, measured in terms of the past seven days, and they include

» **Earned views:** The number of new video views that occur from viewers who've seen an ad from your channel

» **Earned subscribers:** The number of new subscriptions that occur from unsubscribed viewers who've seen an ad from your channel

» **Earned playlist additions:** The number of playlist additions that occur from viewers who've seen an ad from your channel

» **Earned likes:** The number of video likes that occur from viewers who've seen an ad from your channel

» **Earned shares:** The number of video shares that occur from viewers who've seen an ad from your channel

Earned metrics aren't displayed by default, so you have to select them from the Modify Columns menu. Here's how:

1. **From the Campaigns tab, click the Columns button on the Table toolbar and choose Modify Columns from the menu that appears.**

   You're presented with a Modify Columns configurator, like the one shown in Figure 13-13.

2. **Choose YouTube Earned Actions from the list of column options displayed.**

3. **From the options that appear, select each of the earned metrics you want to add by selecting the check box next to each earned metric.**

4. **Click the Apply button.**

   You now have full access to your earned campaign metrics on the reporting grid.

REMEMBER

This technique can be used for customizing all reporting, including adding and removing other paid metrics as well as competitive metrics around impressions.

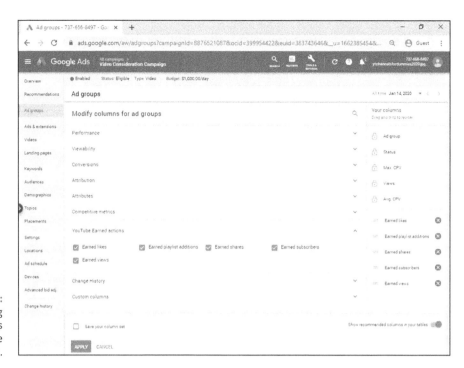

FIGURE 13-13:
Adding
earned metrics
data to the
reporting grid.

Optimizing Your Campaign

Because you pay for every click on your YouTube ads, you must choose highly effective targeting attributes for your campaign. When you initially create your campaign, you make certain assumptions about which targets will deliver results. Some assumptions may turn out to be wrong, and you may want to try other options over time.

Fortunately, YouTube offers a powerful way to manage targets for every video ad. Follow this step-by-step approach to learn how to optimize for CPV, as an example:

1. **From the Navigation menu on the left side of the screen, click on the campaign you want to optimize, and then click an ad group within that campaign.**

2. **Then, from the Page menu, select the appropriate targeting tab to review the ad group's targeting performance.**

   For example, if the ad group you select contains topics targeting, select the Topics tab from the Page menu. You then see the number of views you've received and the amount of money you've spent for each target.

3. **Review the list of targeting attributes to determine which ones are effective.**

   In this example, the important metric is the *cost per view,* or *CPV* — the amount you pay for every viewer who sees your video because of that particular targeting attribute. Really low CPVs are attractive, but sometimes you may want to spend more on targeted keywords or placements.

4. **To optimize a targeting group, identify the lowest-performing targeting attributes by sorting the grid from highest CPV to lowest CPV.**

   You can automatically sort any reporting column by clicking on its name within the grid. In this instance, you should click Avg. CPV on the reporting grid once, to sort the values from highest to lowest.

5. **Remove the underperforming targeting attributes by clicking the green button next to them and choosing Pause from the menu that appears.**

   By pausing underperforming targeting attributes, you free up more of your budget for better-performing targeting.

REMEMBER

Pause targeting attributes, instead of deleting them, because the performance information for paused targets is retained by the system.

6. **If you have ideas for additional targeting attributes after you have finished optimizing an ad group, click the big blue Plus Sign (+) button from the Table toolbar menu and follow the steps that are shown to add them.**

TIP

If you aren't drawing enough views, consider increasing the bids on your ad groups. This can be managed by selecting the Ad Group tab from the Page menu and editing the Max CPV field within the reporting grid. Simply click the Pencil icon next to a bid to open the bid window, edit the value, and then click Save.

YouTube SELECT

In 2014, YouTube announced the premium advertising platform Google Preferred, an in-stream advertising program that allows brands to target the top 5 percent of the most popular content on YouTube. In 2020, the program rebranded as YouTube Select. The lineup of YouTube Select changes regularly to stay up to date. To read about the latest lineup, visit https://www.youtube.com/ads/youtube-select/.

YouTube Select is targeted at big-brand spenders and has a premium price that Google will discuss with you privately. As an advertiser, don't despair if you can't buy 5 percent of YouTube. The other 95 percent of content on YouTube may actually be better suited for your channel objectives — and your budget.

IN THIS CHAPTER

» Joining the YouTube Partner Program

» Configuring your channel for monetization

» Creating an AdSense account for payment management and ad control

» Linking your YouTube channel with your AdSense account

» Understanding how ads work on your channel

» Making changes to increase ad revenue

» Adhering to FTC and COPPA regulations

Chapter **14**

YouTube Monetization: How to Earn Money on YouTube

f you have an active channel with fabulous content and you excel at social media and community interaction, you have a good shot at making some money from all your hard YouTube work. In YouTube and digital advertising lingo, this is known as *monetization*. If you've already read Chapter 13, you know all about how advertisers pay for YouTube advertising. You've probably figured out that the advertising money has to go somewhere. It does — into the hands of Google, your partners, and you: the channel manager/publisher/creator.

You can make money from your YouTube work in many ways:

- >> **Collect advertising revenue.** Charge users to view some or all of the content on your channel. Allow display, overlay, and video ads on your content.

- >> **Offer channel membership.** Allow members to pay a monthly fee for special perks you offer.

- >> **Provide Super Chats and Super Stickers.** Let your fans pay to highlight their messages on your channel's live chat streams.

- >> **Join a multichannel network (MCN).** Become part of an MCN. More on MCNs later in this chapter.

- >> **Benefit from YouTube Premium.** You can even get paid when a YouTube Premium subscriber watches your content (without ads).

- >> **Sell products.** Create a Merchandise shelf where your viewers can buy official branded "merch" directly from your watch pages.

- >> **Sign an endorsement deal.** Sponsorship deals work when they're made without too much over-the-top promotion.

You can read about monetization in this chapter, and you may already have, from earlier chapters, the basic info about MCNs and selling products. Completing the last item in the preceding list means that you've hit the big-time if you're getting six-figure deals to promote products.

REMEMBER

Nothing prevents you from combining some of these various monetization approaches. MCNs are the exception; you may have to speak with your MCN managers and lawyers about the rules around monetization.

Be patient on your monetization journey, though. If you focus on the basics of building your channel with content, discoverability, subscribers, and engagement, the ad revenue you receive will grow in kind. Your YouTube earnings will most likely come from multiple sources.

WARNING

Don't waste your time trying to conjure up a viral video that you hope to monetize. Instead, focus on steady channel-and-subscriber growth.

Your first step to generating income involves applying for the YouTube Partner Program (YPP), and your second step is connecting all of the AdSense and YouTube plumbing. You can find out more about these topics in the remainder of this chapter.

Partnering with YouTube

Every channel that meets the eligibility requirements can apply to be in the YouTube Partner Program (YPP). You probably want to make money off your YouTube channel, and this is the first step. To be a part of YPP, make sure that you play by the rules and follow all its policies and guidelines for your channel. It's not hard; just make good content that doesn't get flagged for bad behavior, profanity, X-rated material, and basically anything you wouldn't be proud to show your grandma. Just be sure to read the current channel guidelines provided by YouTube regularly, because they're constantly being updated.

You must also live in a country or region where YPP is available and have a lot of valid watch-hours on your content — 4,000 hours of watch-time on public videos in the past 12 months, to be precise. Perhaps even more difficult to obtain — 1,000 subscribers. Lastly, you need to sign up for an AdSense account. (More on that later in this chapter.)

REMEMBER

After you're a member of YPP, you need to follow all the policies regarding monetization, community guidelines, terms of service, and Google AdSense. Plus, you need to pay close attention to the kind of content you create if you want to maintain an advertiser-friendly environment on your channel. Not to mention, if your content is targeting children, pay extra close attention to Children's Online Privacy Protection Act laws — also known as COPPA laws. (For more on COPPA, check out the "Strikes" section, later in this chapter.)

REMEMBER

Don't expect your YPP application to be accepted immediately. After you agree to the terms of service and connect your AdSense account, your channel gets reviewed by both a machine and a human to ensure that your content follows all guidelines. You're given the ability to check your application status at any time, but it could take over a month after your channel is reviewed. If you're accepted, you can set up your personal preferences for the types of ads you want on your content and enable monetization on all your uploads. Don't give up if at first you get rejected from YPP; you can update your content and apply again in 30 days.

From Ads to AdSense

Google Ads is *the* way for advertisers to target YouTube and the Google Display network for ad placements. (For more on Google Ads, check out Chapter 13.) Publishers and creators can control what types of ads are shown against their content.

REMEMBER

Content owners often take a great deal of pride in the content they produce, so it only makes sense that the ads conform to their brands and ensure a good overall experience for their viewers.

Google AdSense is how web content creators and YouTube channel managers control ads and get paid from advertisements that run against their YouTube content and websites. Like Google Ads, AdSense is a huge topic — we don't have room to cover every nook and cranny in this chapter, but we can give you a sense of what's necessary to get you started with YouTube monetization. AdSense, like all Google products, evolves regularly. To stay current, check out `https://support.google.com/adsense`.

Setting up YouTube monetization

Before you can sign up your channel for AdSense, you need to be in YPP. Before you start seeing any money in your bank account, you need to set up your channel for monetization. Here's how it's done:

1. **Point your browser to** `www.google.com/adsense/start`.

2. **On the Google AdSense home page, click the Get Started button in the top right.**

3. **On the new page that appears, enter your YouTube channel URL in the Your Website text field.**

4. **Enter the email address associated with your YouTube channel in the Your Email Address field.**

5. **Choose the country you live in. (AdSense isn't available in all countries.)**

6. **Accept the Terms and Conditions (if you choose to accept after reading; that's your choice).**

7. **In the new page that appears, choose an individual or business account.**

   Choose Individual if you don't have a business bank account from the list of options.

8. **Enter your address and phone number and click Submit.**

   You need to verify your phone number, either by responding to a text or answering a phone call.

9. **After verification, start working on the Payments section.**

   After you earn your first $100, you have to manage your payment methods by adding a bank account and then verify your bank account and your billing address. This can take, in total, up to a couple weeks for the setup.

REMEMBER

All AdSense payments are delivered 21 days after the month being paid out has ended.

10. **(Optional) You can add multiple YouTube channels to a single AdSense account. Once logged into your AdSense account, select My Ads in the left-hand menu and choose URL Channels from the menu that appears.**

You can add your new channel URL in the new window that opens.

11. **To finish the process, you need to continue in YouTube.**

At this point, if you aren't in YPP, you can't go any further until you're officially accepted into the program.

REMEMBER

After you're accepted into YPP, you can complete these steps:

1. **On your YouTube page, click your channel's icon and then choose YouTube Studio from the menu that appears.**

Doing so brings up the YouTube Studio dashboard.

2. **Click the Channel item on the Navigation menu on the left side.**

REMEMBER

If your channel doesn't (yet) meet the minimum eligibility requirements for YPP, use the Monetization link in the Channel section to see a dashboard that shows you how many more subscribers and public watch-hours are needed to apply.

3a. **To monetize individual videos:**

i. *Using YouTube Studio's Videos tab, click to select a particular video and then choose Monetization from the menu that appears*

You can now choose the types of ads you want to run on that individual video.

ii. *Choose the type of ads you want to run and then click Save.*

You can choose the type of ads (display, overlay, skippable, non-skippable, and sponsored cards) as well as the location of the ad (before video, during video, and after video).

3b. **To enable multiple ads for monetization:**

i. *Using YouTube Studio's Videos tab, click on multiple videos to edit monetization settings in bulk.*

ii. *Choose the type of ads you want to run and then click Save.*

TIP

You can always monetize your entire channel from the YouTube Studio Channel tab. Just choose Status and Features and a new menu will open where you can click Enable under the Monetization section. In your Studio settings, you can then set your upload defaults for all future videos.

NOT EVERYTHING IS MONETIZABLE

If you're at all familiar with the ways of YouTube, you probably have already figured out that you can't just grab a copy of Harry Styles' "Lights Up" video, modify it slightly, and put it on your channel. Sure, everyone would love a few billion monetized views, but in the end, it all comes down to content ownership and copyright. To monetize anything, you need to own the rights to both the audio and visual components of the content. You also have to be careful about some of the visual elements, such as logos and other graphics, which may also be protected by the rights holders.

YouTube keeps tabs on copyrighted content with a feature it calls Content ID, a database of files that YouTube uses to compare copyrighted content against new content being uploaded to the site. Content ID can be used to make claims against your content, which may affect your ability to monetize. Note that with Content ID, the rights holder may choose to monetize *your* content.

Copyright is a tricky topic, and you can read more about it in Chapter 16. You can also check out https://support.google.com to find out more about the partner program, monetization, and copyright. When in doubt, consult with a lawyer or watch a YouTube video on the subject — assuming that it's not blocked by copyright, of course.

Analyzing ad performance with YouTube Analytics

You can view your revenue analytics in your AdSense account or from your YouTube channel. That way, you can get detailed information about your earnings that will help you make adjustments to your content and monetization strategy. The good part is that you can get lots of this information directly from YouTube Analytics, with helpful tips and premade reports. The ad performance data visualizations have been made easy to digest. Here's how to navigate to your Channel analytics:

1. **Log on to your YouTube account.**

2. **Click your channel's icon or your Google user icon in the top right, and then choose YouTube Studio from the dropdown menu that appears.**

    Doing so brings up the Channel dashboard.

3. **Choose the Analytics item from the Navigation menu on the left.**

    By default, you should go directly to the Overview submenu.

4. **On the Channel analytics navigation tab, the last tab is Revenue, where you can analyze your revenue.**

   See the next section for more on revenue issues.

REMEMBER

YouTube Analytics is your go-to resource when you want to find out how your channel is performing with your audience. Chapter 11 gives you the tools to understand your whole YouTube audience story; this chapter concentrates on how YouTube Analytics can help you figure out your ad-and-earnings performances.

Getting your YouTube revenue information

In YouTube Analytics, you'll find a section called Revenue, a vital resource for channel managers responsible for monetization. Within the Revenue section, you'll find many important metrics worth analyzing; the default topline metrics you can view by any duration of time requested include

>> **Your estimated revenue:** Estimated net revenue from Google-sold ads.

>> **Estimated monetized playbacks:** Counts the ad impressions served on your content, or impressions served that caused a viewer to abandon the video because of a nonskip ad.

>> **Playback-based CPM:** The gross revenue per 1,000 playbacks where ads were shown. This doesn't show you what the advertiser ended up paying for. CPM — technically cost per mille, where "*mille*" is the Latin word for "thousand" — is a common measurement used in the advertising industry.

REMEMBER

You can have multiple impressions (*impressions* are the number of times an ad is presented to a viewer) per playback. If a viewer is served a TrueView instream preroll ad, a display ad, and an in-video overlay, it counts as three impressions, not one.

Seeing which metrics are offered

YouTube Analytics is truly robust. Looking at only the Revenue tab, here are some of the other default reports you can use to monitor revenue:

>> **Monthly estimated revenue:** Covers the last six months of your channel's estimated revenue.

>> **Top-earning videos:** Highlights the videos that made the most money in the chosen timeframe.

>> **Revenue sources:** Covers how your channel actually made money in the chosen timeframe.

>> **Ad types:** Shows you which ad types were served on your content. This is especially helpful because you won't see all the ad types just by watching your own video content, due to targeting parameters set up by advertisers.

>> **Transaction revenue:** Shows estimated revenue from transactions like Super Chat and paid content for the chosen timeframe.

REMEMBER

You may experience a delay for certain metrics as Google confirms the validity of each ad impression and user. YouTube Analytics shows information — within reason — as it's occurring. Actual earnings are visible and available for download within 24 hours on YouTube or AdSense.

Figure 14-1 shows the standard Revenue tab.

FIGURE 14-1:
The Revenue tab.

REMEMBER

If you're not seeing performance data for a specific ad type, go back and make sure you have monetization turned on and all ad types enabled. You can find out more about configuring the monetization of existing videos a little later in this chapter.

TIP

Whenever you look at your analytics reports, keep an eye out for events that stand out in the charts — such as peaks or valleys in the data — to determine what's working well and what may need improvement.

Making changes to your video strategy based on the data

The Revenue reports can help you increase your revenue stream only if you're agile in your video strategy. Advertisers are more likely to want to advertise on your videos if the content is in line with their branding and company image. You should make authentic content and not worry about advertisers for the most part, but if you're making content about obscure or radical topics, you may be alienating your potential advertisers. YouTube has rolled out helpful guides to demystify the placements advertisers are looking for in running their ads. You can see all the advertiser-friendly guidelines at

https://support.google.com/youtube/answer/6162278

If you have hundreds of videos but only a handful of them are making any revenue, if might be time to make some changes to your video content strategy. To find out why the few videos are working, ask yourself these questions:

>> When monetizing the content, did you allow all ad types? Perhaps you need to update your monetization preferences across your channel.

>> Are the videos vastly different from the others? Are they funny, but the rest of your content isn't?

>> Did you have a guest speaker onscreen with you who might have a deal with sponsors or be vastly more popular?

>> Do the underperforming videos meet the advertiser-friendly guidelines that help you stay in good standing? (We tell you more about those guidelines later in this chapter.)

>> Are the title, tags, and descriptions for these successful videos more accurate?

>> Do successful videos have the best practice thumbnails, a face in the thumbnail, and/or larger text?

>> Are the best-performing videos directed at children or adults?

OTHER WAYS TO MAKE MONEY FROM YOUR CHANNEL

If you're just starting your YouTube channel and you're hoping to make some money so that you can create more content or do something fabulous, it might be hard to earn the revenue you need from your channel if you don't meet the YPP minimums yet, or even if you do and you're just getting off the ground. Consider trying out crowdfunding using sites like Kickstarter, GoFundMe, and Patreon. You can also try for brand sponsorships. If you're good at a sport, think about brands, like Red Bull, that sponsor athletes and sometimes even feature their video content. Name-dropping your favorite products in your videos can also help land you sponsorship deals. Some companies will even help match your content, with brands like Grapevine Logic and FameBit. You might even consider joining a multi-channel network (MCN). MCNs such as Kin Community are quite popular and offer even more ways to help you generate a following and additional revenue sources.

Strikes

There are community guideline strikes and copyright strikes. Both are handled differently by YouTube. A partner in good standing has no strikes or very few strikes. If you receive a community guideline strike, you're notified by email specifying the reason for the strike and the next steps you can take. As in baseball, draw three strikes and you're out. To avoid this situation, follow these community guidelines:

```
www.youtube.com/about/policies/#community-guidelines
```

If you get a copyright strike, it means that the legal owner of the content you posted has requested that YouTube take it down. Sometimes, this can be a mistake and YouTube corrects it, but if you did, in fact, illegally upload someone else's content, you will get a strike. The first strike requires you to complete YouTube's copyright school. Subsequent strikes will start to strip away your ability to monetize, livestream, and more.

WARNING

Avoid using copyrighted material or breaking the rules in the community guidelines in order to continue to monetize your content. If you do break the rules, you may have your channel disabled, and the ability to create new channels will be disallowed.

REMAINING IN GOOD STANDING

If you're a YouTube partner in good standing, try to stay that way. Follow the rules, and don't do what Paul Logan did. (You can Google him to find out how he lost millions of dollars in ad revenue from one bad video that he probably regrets posting.) Or learn what not to say from Pew Die Pie, whose insensitive language lost him many sponsorships and tons of money. The best way to think about your content is to focus on a video content strategy that you feel passionate about. Keep in mind that you need to appeal to advertisers along the way, to ensure your continued stream of ad revenue. The good news is that following the YouTube Partner Program advertiser-friendly content guidelines can help you do just that. Here are some of the contents types you should stay clear of: `https://support.google.com/youtube`

- Inappropriate language
- Violence
- Adult content
- Harmful or dangerous acts
- Hateful content
- Incendiary or demeaning content
- Recreational drugs or drug-related content
- Tobacco-related content
- Controversial issues and sensitive events
- Adult themes in family content

Brand safety and suitability

Brand safety and suitability have been issues since the beginning of radio and TV advertising. A brand advertiser doesn't want its brand to be associated with content that isn't in line with its vision and mission. For instance, you might be making content that's in accordance with the community guidelines about animal testing in the beauty industry, but even a beauty brand that doesn't test its products on animals won't want to run ads on your video. They're afraid that viewers will negatively associate their brand with the topic of animal testing. Some types of content are safe enough to run an ad on, but may not be suitable for the brand.

When creating your channel content strategy, research channels that are similar to yours to see what kinds of ads are appearing on their content. This is a good indication of what you might be able to expect.

Federal Trade Commission Guidelines and COPPA

In September 2019, the Federal Trade Commission (FTC) imposed a historic fine of $170 million on YouTube for alleged violations of child privacy laws. Many changes have now been rolled out for creators to comply with the ruling. As a creator, you need to either label your entire channel as content directed at children or identify the specific videos that are directed at children on your channel. Several gray areas exist here — like gaming, toy reviews, and family vlogging — that are difficult to manage, because they may target kids and adults. The FTC now requires that YouTube must treat anyone watching primarily child-directed content as children under 13 years old. Product features, such as comments, are disabled for content created for children. Content labeled for children also has different advertising opportunities and may in turn create different trends in your revenue stream.

WARNING

The FTC now holds *creators* liable for future violations, so be sure to carefully label your content designated for children or not. If they find that you have mislabeled your content, you could be fined.

To learn more about how the FCC is handling YouTube channels, check out this blog post:

```
www.ftc.gov/news-events/blogs/business-blog/2019/11/youtube-channel-
    owners-your-content-directed-children
```

Or visit the FTC's page regarding the Children's Online Privacy Protection Act (COPPA):

```
www.ftc.gov/tips-advice/business-center/privacy-and-security/children%27s-
    privacy
```

REMEMBER

When deciding whether your content might be seen as directed at children, ask yourself these nine qualifying questions:

>> Does the subject matter in the video appeal to children?

>> Is the thumbnail or video content something that would attract children?

- ❯❯ Does the video have animated characters or child-oriented activities?

- ❯❯ Is the music used in the video or other audio tracks something children might like?

- ❯❯ Are the actors or subjects of the video children?

- ❯❯ Does the video have any child celebrities or creators who appeal to children?

- ❯❯ Does the language used in the video or on your surrounding channel target children?

- ❯❯ Does the video feature any sponsorships that would appeal to children?

- ❯❯ Are the video's titles, tags, or descriptions appealing to children?

5

The Part of Tens

See how you can improve your YouTube search results.

Explore the intricacies of copyright law.

Chapter **15**

Ten Key Steps to Improving YouTube Search Results

YouTube is about one thing: getting people to watch your content. Before they watch it, though, they have to find it. Simple, right? In theory, yes, but your challenge is to help viewers find your channel and your content. That's what search results are all about: placing your content in front of the right viewers so that they can watch.

Unfortunately, YouTube doesn't share the secret sauce for getting found, but you can help improve the odds of your videos showing up in YouTube and Google Search as well as in the recommended videos on the Watch page. To get that search engine to work for you, you need to optimize both your channel and your videos. It may come as a surprise to you, but YouTube doesn't have a human watch all your videos to determine what topics they cover. To let YouTube understand what your videos are all about, then, you need to include metadata that describes the content for YouTube to index. (That's part of the optimization process.) In this chapter, we describe ten key steps for improving YouTube search results for your content.

Updating Video Metadata

Metadata are the words you use to describe your video — like the video title, keyword tags, and video description. When uploading new content to your channel, YouTube walks you through the steps to add metadata. If you want to go back and tweak that metadata later, as part of your optimization strategy, follow these steps:

1. **Log in to your YouTube account.**

2. **On your YouTube page, click the Channel icon and then choose YouTube Studio from the menu that appears.**

3. **Click the Videos tab in YouTube Studio.**

   By default, you should go directly to the Videos submenu.

4. **Find the video and click the Details button next to it.**

   The Details button is represented by a pencil.

5. **Modify the thumbnail, title, description, and tags to better reflect your optimization goals.**

6. **When you're done, click the blue Save button.**

The search results from the channel *Marty Music* in Figure 15-1 show good metadata — compelling thumbnail images, great titles, and punchy description data. Metadata helps visitors make viewing decisions, and good metadata helps visitors make better viewing decisions.

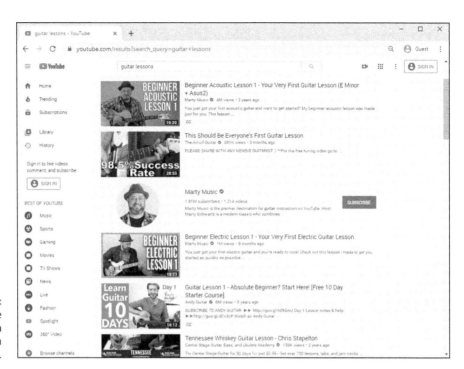

FIGURE 15-1:
How YouTube
video metadata
shows up in
search.

Managing Video Titles

Descriptive video titles are helpful not only for viewers to identify the content they may want to view but also for YouTube's search engine. The title is one key indicator used to index your videos. If you do nothing at all, at least be sure to use a keyword-rich title — a title full of descriptive words or adjectives, in other words. You always have the opportunity to rename your videos after you upload them to your channel. A good title tells the viewer what the content includes and who created the video, such as "Easy stretches for runners led by certified yoga instructor." You may also add a relevant hashtag in the title to help users more easily find your content. (We cover hashtags in more detail a little later in this chapter, in the section "Managing Video Descriptions.")

REMEMBER

Good titles are 70 characters or fewer. Any longer and the title gets cut off in search results. Mobile devices often show even fewer characters before the title is cut off. If you have a large mobile audience, put the most important keywords at the beginning of the title so that they're visible to all users.

Understanding Working Titles

Editors — whether they're of the Hollywood variety or the YouTube variety — often use a working title for a film being edited. That's all fine and dandy in the privacy of your studio, but we're here to tell you that you should never upload an asset using a working title. Always upload your videos with a descriptive title — say, `2020 Hawaii Vacation Highlights.mov`. Even if the descriptive title doesn't end up as the final title, it's important to have a descriptive title associated with the file. YouTube never loses this original upload title, so it always remains with your video file in YouTube's database. (This is simply another way to ensure that YouTube knows what your video is about, even if you forget to include any other metadata.)

Optimizing Thumbnails for Viewer Session Time

A *thumbnail* is a visual snapshot of your video, similar to a poster for a movie. It has a tremendous impact on a video's view rate, so choose a good one. By default, YouTube chooses thumbnails from three optional frames taken at the beginning, middle, and end of your video file. You can, however, create a custom thumbnail for each video. If you do so, choose a thumbnail that's illustrative of the content in the video. Thumbnails show up in the following areas:

>> Channel page

>> Watch page

>> Playlists

>> Suggested videos

>> Channel guide

>> Subscriber feed

>> YouTube search

>> Web search

>> Mobile display

>> Mobile search

Although it's vital that the title of your video accurately reflects its content, it's even more important for a viewer's mobile viewing experience that you add a compelling video thumbnail. Users often base the decision of whether to watch your video on the appeal of the video thumbnail. The thumbnail should not confuse viewers; it should prepare them for the entire viewing experience. Clear, striking images with easy to read descriptive text or branding work really well. You can even create custom thumbnails for your playlists.

REMEMBER

Playlists, which can show up in YouTube searches along with the video results, often lead to longer viewing sessions. The longer a viewer's session watch time, the better your video and channel ranking. Viewer session watch time is the primary ranking factor on YouTube's search engine.

Managing Video Descriptions

The video *description* is a 5,000-character field that YouTube provides for you to describe your video. It's a great place to add details about not only your video but also your channel, along with links for other videos, subscriptions, other channels, and merchandise. In other words, it's a goldmine for both metadata and user guidance. The viewers who care about your video will read the description, so make it worth their while.

The first two lines of the first paragraph of the description (approximately 100 characters) comprise the only element that shows up in YouTube search results; thus, it's the most important part of the description copy. Everything to follow is consumed by YouTube's algorithms and passionate followers who click the Show More link below the description copy. The first line should describe the content of the video and grab viewers' attention with alluring copy to lead them into the viewing experience. If you don't have a lot of time, focus your creative energy on the first paragraph.

The first line should also include a link to your website or other content you've uploaded. The best practice is to include a short link to save space — you can compress any link by using a link shortener like bit.ly, a free link-shortening website. The link might lead to a playlist with the video, a landing page on or off the YouTube site, a product page, or a blog. Figure 15-2 shows a good description.

You can also include hashtags in your video description. A *hashtag* is a word or phrase that is spelled out without any spaces and preceded by the pound sign (#). Hashtags are used on social media websites to label content, making it easier to search for a specific topic. If you don't use a hashtag in your video title, YouTube displays the first three hashtags you include in your description above your video on that video's Watch page. Using hashtags is a great way to help users find your content, especially if you're making videos that cover current trends. Be careful not to overdo it in adding hashtags to your videos, however, because YouTube penalizes you for including more than 15 in a video.

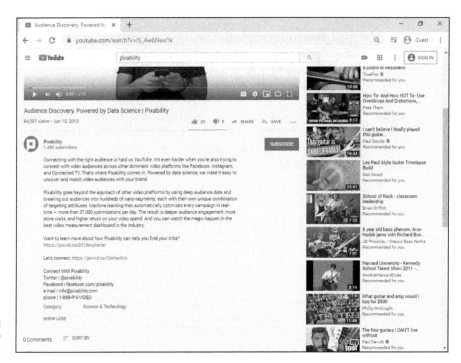

FIGURE 15-2:
YouTube video
description copy.

REMEMBER

You can set up default metadata for your new uploads. Always remember to customize the title, tags, and descriptions of every video. Your metadata should closely reflect each video's unique content.

Adding Closed Captioning

YouTube and certain other platforms let you upload text files that contain closed-captioning subtitles for your video. You can then reach people who have hearing impairments, and it pays off for your search engine ranking. The captions are used by YouTube Search to determine the topic of your video. (See Chapter 10 for information about adding captions.)

You don't have to write captions yourself. Several affordable services can create these caption files for you. Rev (www.rev.com/caption), for example, provides captions for only dollars per minute. Alternatively, you can use YouTube's automatic captioning feature, but keep in mind that because the captions are written by an algorithm, they're often imperfect.

Handling Tags

A *tag* is a keyword that identifies your video's content within YouTube for discovery. These unique, descriptive keywords are limited to 30 characters per keyword. Try to apply at least 15 tags per video, with a maximum of 500 characters per video. You can add tags when you upload a video or modify them later in YouTube Studio. Make the tags extremely relevant to your video content, and scatter them throughout the description copy. Start with the most specific tags first, to help viewers find your videos more easily when they're looking for a particular topic.

TIP

Start off with specific keyword tags, but if you have space, add some general ones as well to identify the category of your video, such as beauty or DIY or entertainment.

Refreshing Metadata

Recently published videos typically rank higher in YouTube Search because they have newer content — though we're not saying that all old videos disappear. Older videos that have been watched frequently and are contextual matches for specific searches will rank well. It's important to revisit your older video content regularly and add in any new or trending metadata terms that are relevant.

TIP

In addition to refreshing your metadata, be sure to refresh your end screens to link to newer, more relevant videos and playlists on your channel. (*End screens* are interactive cards that you can place in the last 5-20 seconds of your videos that allow you to promote additional channel content; see Chapter 5 for information about end screens.)

Understanding Channel SEO

Channels can show up in relevant YouTube searches along with video search results. If you search for one, you see the Channel icon and the first few lines of the channel description in the search results. To ensure that your channel appears in the search results, you have to let YouTube know what your channel is about. It has a description field that you can use to communicate precisely what content viewers can find here. (See Chapter 3 for instructions on how to update and edit your channel description.)

A channel also has a field for keywords that you can use just like you use the Tags field for videos. To update your channel keywords, follow these steps:

1. **Log on to your YouTube account.**

2. **On your YouTube page, click the Channel icon and then choose YouTube Studio from the menu that appears.**

   Doing so brings up the YouTube Studio dashboard.

3. **Click the Settings heading in the navigation menu on the left.**

4. **In the window that opens, choose Channel from the navigation menu on the left.**

5. **On the new screen that appears, click the Advanced settings option.**

6. **Scroll down and click on the link for Advanced Channel settings.**

   Doing so brings up a page dedicated to the Advanced channel settings, as shown in Figure 15-3.

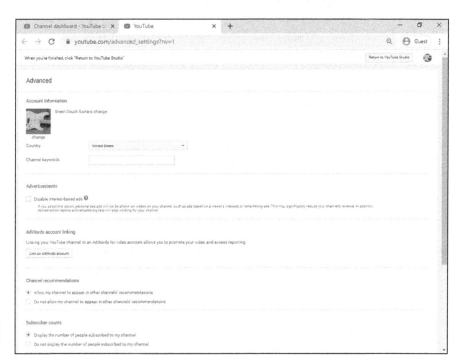

FIGURE 15-3:
YouTube channel metadata.

7. **Add relevant, descriptive keywords, separated by commas in the Channel Keywords field.**

   Use a maximum of five to seven keywords, to ensure that you're using the most relevant words.

8. **When you're done, click the Save button.**

TIP

Create a keyword-rich channel description. Craft an engaging first few lines of the channel description because those are the elements that are revealed across YouTube with your channel.

REMEMBER

Add specific keywords first and then finish off with broader terms, if space allows.

Avoiding Misleading Metadata

Using misleading or deceptive metadata is against YouTube policies. You cannot include metadata that isn't contextually relevant to your video content or that misrepresents the video's content. You cannot add a series of unrelated tags to your description copy to show up for additional search results. This is known as keyword stuffing. If Taylor Swift isn't in your video, don't add her name to the title, tags, or description. Adding repetitive words in the description copy and tags is interpreted as spam by YouTube and will hurt your discoverability.

REMEMBER

The most important thing is to not try to trick viewers into watching your content with misleading titles, thumbnails, tags, or description copy. These resources are at your disposal to add more contextual value to your video asset — not to fool viewers into clicking. Adding misleading metadata is a futile exercise. When viewers click on your video and fail to find what they're looking for, they click to go elsewhere quickly. This hurts your watch time statistics and definitely hurts your search rankings. YouTube excels at detecting spam and misleading metadata, so trying to game the system will never succeed in the long run.

Chapter **16**

Ten Things to Know About Copyright

ohn Locke said, "The end of law is not to abolish or restrain, but to preserve and enlarge freedom." In the same spirit, copyright law protects creators from having their material used, without permission, by people who didn't create it. The goal is to protect the creator's freedom to create without having to fear that others will profit unjustly. Create something, and the intellectual property belongs to you by way of copyright. If anyone palms off your intellectual property as their own, the law protects you and provides measures for legal action. And, if your copyrighted content should appear in video form on YouTube without your permission, YouTube acts as the law on your behalf.

That's great if someone is trying to take advantage of you, but sometimes it's you who gets put on the hot seat. Thanks to multimedia, people often create things that use other people's work — such as adding a piece of music you didn't write to a video you've made — and they don't realize that they're doing anything wrong. Collaboration is a good thing and is often encouraged on YouTube, but you need to have the proper permission to use any music, artwork, photograph, excerpt, or whatever else was created by an individual other than yourself before you put it in your YouTube videos.

When someone infringes on copyright — whether it's someone doing it to you or you doing it to someone else — there *are* consequences. YouTube takes the breach seriously and will take down the infringing video. It also penalizes the offender with a strike. And as in baseball, if you take three strikes, you're outta there! YouTube boots you and your channel if it gets to this point, ruining all your hard work.

To ensure that it doesn't happen to you, follow the advice in this chapter.

Remember Who Owns the Copyright

It's fairly simple: If you created the video, the copyright belongs to you; if you upload content created by someone else, the copyright belongs to that person, and you had better have permission to upload it.

As soon as the work is created, so is the copyright, and since 1992, there's no longer a renewal process. Copyright lives with the creator — and even lives on for a period after the death of the creator.

Basic stuff, right? But often it's the most basic rules that are not followed. People jaywalk all the time, and people violate copyright all the time on YouTube, too. That means YouTube is kept busy because, if another user uploads your content without your permission, or if you do the same, YouTube tracks down the offender, sends a take-down notification, blocks the infringing video, and sanctions the offender with a copyright strike. (All of this is managed with YouTube's Contend ID system, which we will cover in detail in this chapter.)

Attribution Does Not Absolve a Copyright Violation

Some people steal other people's work and claim it as their own, and that's blatant infringement. But it's no less of an offense when you use content and then add the line, "Created by so-and-so," "No copyright infringement intended," or "All rights belong to their respective owners." It's still a breach that can earn you a strike and a blocked video.

If you use someone else's work in your video without that person's permission, it doesn't make it less of an offense just because you give the person credit. You're still in violation because attributing the creator doesn't absolve you if you don't get permission. The only exception is fair use, which we tell you more about later in this chapter.

Here are some elements to watch out for in your videos:

>> **Music:** If you didn't write it, didn't play it, didn't record it, and didn't get permission to use it, you can't use it. If you're struggling to find royalty-free music for your YouTube video, check out YouTube's Audio Library to browse their massive collection of free-to-use tracks and sound effects at www.youtube.com/audiolibrary.

>> **Someone else's pictures or videos:** Pictures and videos found on the Internet are not yours for the taking. Instead, try a practical solution, like purchasing inexpensive rights to images or videos on various stock photo sites, such as www.istockphoto.com, www.shutterstock.com, and www.stock.adobe.com. If you're more budget conscious, look for websites that use the Creative Commons Zero (or CC0) license. Photos and videos released under the CC0 license are released without restriction and are free to use without attribution, even for commercial purposes.

>> **TV or movie clip:** Again, you can't simply use this type of content — unless it's already in the public domain — even if you provide attribution to the creator. Some exceptions are afforded under the principle of fair use, which we describe later in this chapter. And even though the studio may not track you down and ask you to remove it, YouTube eventually will, and it will throw you a fastball over the plate.

Know the Consequences

YouTube takes copyright issues seriously — and it blocks or takes down any video that infringes on copyright. Two things can happen on YouTube when there's a copyright violation, and though they sound similar, they're completely different:

>> **Takedown notice:** If someone spots content they've created being used without their permission, they can send YouTube a complaint. If it's a breach, YouTube takes down the video and issues the offender a copyright strike.

WARNING

If you feel compelled to lodge a complaint against someone else's video, just be extra sure that it's your content and that the breach is accurate, because you're initiating a legal process.

>> **Content ID match:** If YouTube's algorithms determine that someone improperly used material uploaded to their Content ID platform, YouTube files a copyright claim automatically on the copyright owner's behalf. YouTube doesn't immediately take down the video, however. Instead, it allows the copyright owner to take a few different measures of recourse.

Content ID is a system YouTube uses to automatically match content that violates copyright against the millions of videos uploaded every month to the site. For Content ID to work properly, copyright owners have to upload *reference* files — original versions of their work that prove they own the rights. Normally, record labels, movie studios, and TV stations complete this process for all the work they publish, so individual artists don't have to worry about it. Every new video uploaded to YouTube is checked against this huge library of reference files, and if it finds a match, YouTube automatically files a copyright claim for the owner of the work.

Unlike a takedown notice, a Content ID claim doesn't result in a copyright strike on your channel. Content ID claims are most commonly leveraged by copyright owners to profit from the use of their content in your videos by monetizing them with ads. Any ad revenue generated from the infringing video is then given to the copyright owner directly. Content ID claims can also be used to block your video from specific countries or even the entire world if the copyright owner really doesn't want you to use their content. Though these outcomes may sound frustrating, it's important to remember that if you remove the claimed content from your video, you regain full ownership of your creation. This could involve something as simple as swapping out the music in your video for a royalty-free soundtrack.

It's possible to have permission to use music, pictures, or video yet still have a Content ID claim filed against you. Content ID is an automated process, and the idea is that claims are triggered when YouTube's algorithms detect that the musical, photo, or video content belongs to a copyright owner other than yourself. But don't worry: If you had permission to use that content, you can file a dispute challenging the accuracy of the claim. To find more information about Content ID and the processes behind it, go to www.youtube.com/yt/copyright.

No matter how a copyright violation may have been discovered, if you breach another content creator's copyright, that creator is in a position to have YouTube take down or block your content. In the event of a mistake, you can dispute the infraction, but you had better be darn sure that there was a mistake. If the claim ends up being proven correct, or if you were untruthful in any way, you may find yourself in much bigger trouble, including facing legal action.

The Profit Motive Is Irrelevant

Some folks will say, "Hey, it's all right if I use someone else's content, because I'm not looking to make any money." Tell that to the judge and the verdict is still "Guilty of copyright infringement!"

Whether you intend to make money from the video or you simply want to share your masterpiece with the world, it still doesn't mean that you can violate copyright law. You need to get permission from the copyright owner. Having no intention to profit doesn't absolve you if you use someone else's content without permission.

Rather than take any chances, reach out to the copyright owner, explain your intended use of the content — profit or otherwise — and see what the person says. Sometimes, the copyright owner gives you written permission with no stipulations, whereas at other times the owner may attach restrictions on the type of use, length of time of use, or content.

Get Permission for Using Copyrighted Material

Getting permission to use someone else's copyrighted material is often well within the realm of the possible. A nicely written note explaining how you would use the content usually is enough for a rights owner to grant permission. Just remember that it can get dicey because sometimes permission comes with the caveat that you cannot monetize the overall video. That restriction can hurt big-time if your intention is to quit your day job, but it could be a bittersweet solution if you're merely looking to add flavor to your video.

If you're having difficulty reaching a copyright owner to ask for their permission or you don't want to wait for a response, consider using content made available under a Creative Commons license. Any content released under a Creative Commons Attribution license (sometimes called a "CC BY" license) is free to repurpose on YouTube, as long as you give credit to the original creator. You can find many other types of Creative Commons license designations (such as CC0, which we mentioned earlier), so be sure to determine whether a piece of content has any specific use limitations before adding it to your own video. For more information on Creative Commons licenses, visit `https://creativecommons.org`.

Fair Use Is Complicated

Fair use is a legal doctrine that permits limited use of copyrighted materials in your YouTube videos without requiring permission from the copyright owner. Many misconceptions exist surrounding fair use, and among them is the notion that you can use anything you want in your video as long as you don't go beyond some arbitrary time constraint. But it's much more complicated than that. In some editorial situations, you can use copyrighted material without permission, but you must fully understand those situations to avoid future trouble.

If you feel the need to exercise fair use, here are a few acceptable uses to consider:

>> **Criticism:** Reviewing a movie or some form of music makes it perfectly acceptable to use copyrighted material without permission — short clips on the work you critique, for example.

>> **Parody:** If you're poking fun at something, it's acceptable to use content without first gaining permission.

>> **Commentary:** This one depends on how you use the material. If you use just enough to illustrate your point, it's acceptable. For instance, gamers on YouTube often record themselves playing a new video game and offer funny observations. This is, within limits, fair use.

>> **Academic:** If you're creating educational content, it's considered fair use to reference other works in certain situations.

In all these cases, consider whether your contribution to the original copyrighted work is "transformative." If you're adding substantially new meaning or expression to the original work, you're likely within the bounds of fair use.

And now, for some misconceptions:

>> **You can use 40 seconds of anything:** It's completely untrue. You can't use even *4 seconds* if it doesn't comply with the circumstances in the preceding list. As a best practice, use the least amount of copyrighted material to get your point across and always credit the original copyright owner.

>> **You can decide fair use for yourself:** Fair use is complicated for many situations, so you may not be sure exactly what you're allowed to do. The thing is, if you stretch the limits of fair use too far and harm the original copyright owner's ability to profit from their work, you can be sanctioned by YouTube. That's why a copyright attorney should decide any serious question over fair use.

Don't Let Copyright Issues on YouTube Lead to a Strikeout

"Three strikes and you're out" is a common understanding when playing baseball. But in baseball, you get another chance after another eight batters have had their try. YouTube doesn't share this benevolence, so if it gives you strikes — especially for copyright issues — that means a lifetime ban from its partnership program. That's something you don't want on your record; worse yet, once that happens to you, you can't recover any of your videos. So, avoid getting strikes at all costs.

You can draw two types of YouTube strikes:

>> **Community guideline:** This type can result from a variety of causes, ranging from uploading objectionable content to having a misleading thumbnail or caption. To read more about YouTube's community guidelines, please visit `www.youtube.com/about/policies/ - community-guidelines`.

>> **Copyright:** If some part of your video includes content from another creator and that creator did not grant you permission, you can get a copyright strike. You can appeal it or take down the video to avoid a possible strike.

Other things you should know:

>> **Mandatory copyright school must be completed:** After your first strike, YouTube requires that you complete an online course and take a quiz to be sure you're up to speed on copyright regulations.

>> **Strikes come down, eventually:** As long as you haven't struck out, community guideline strikes and copyright strikes disappear after 90 days from the time they're issued, at which point YouTube restores any channel privileges you lost while you waited out the strike. If you draw three community guideline strikes or three copyright strikes over a 90-day period, your YouTube channel will be terminated.

>> **Your fate usually lies with the copyright owner:** As we mentioned a little earlier, the copyright owner can decide whether the video you uploaded should be removed, flagged in certain regions, or even monetized. Yes, that's right: Even though the video may contain only a small portion of the person's material, that person is entitled to all monetization proceeds — and can even put ads on your video, if you haven't added monetization.

We cover how to check your YouTube account status for copyright strikes in Chapter 9 under "Preparing Your Channel for Uploads."

Wipe the Slate Clean

When it comes to removing strikes from your account, these two contradictory idioms come to mind:

» The squeaky wheel gets the grease.

» Don't open a can of worms.

If you draw a copyright strike from YouTube and you're positive that you're in the right, go ahead and appeal the strike with a copyright counternotification. By not staying quiet, you can fulfill the prophecy of the first idiom by having that strike removed.

Yet let's examine that second idiom. If you're not sure you can win, maybe it's better to wait it out until the strike expires. You see, after you appeal the strike, your personal information goes to the copyright owner, and that person can possibly sue you for copyright infringement. If the situation reaches this level, you still can work out an agreement directly with the copyright owner and see whether that person will file an appeal with YouTube on your behalf, if you both agree that you were within your rights to use the copyrighted material. It's worth a shot. An alternative you may want to consider before filing a copyright counternotification is to kindly ask the copyright owner to retract the claim of copyright infringement if you believe that an error has been made. If it was a case of mistaken identity, you might get lucky and get the strike removed immediately. Or, if your video has truly violated copyright, you can work out a deal to remove the offending content. This is likely the least complicated way to dispute a copyright strike. As for strikes related to the community guidelines, feel free to appeal those, because they're only between you and YouTube.

YouTube's Algorithms Are Good at Finding Copyright Infringements

Whether intentional or inadvertent, sometimes the content of other creators gets used in a YouTube video. Sometimes the breach is noticed, and at other times it goes undetected by the original creator. But as YouTube continues to refine its copyright detection system, it finds the breach more quickly than ever. With over $100 million dollars invested in the development of Content ID, and billions more paid out to copyright owners from ads on infringing videos each year, it's clear that Google has made copyright detection a major priority on YouTube.

Part of these refinements to YouTube's copyright detection system include sophisticated algorithms that scan every uploaded video and compare it to similar uploaded content, looking for matches with music, video, or pictures. It seems music gets detected the most. Even if it's background music, you may get sanctioned. Usually, YouTube blocks the video, and you must submit a dispute form to keep your video public.

Copyright Is (Almost) Forever

Copyright lasts for 70 years past the death of the author; after that point, the copyrighted content enters the public domain. When that happens, the content is no longer protected by intellectual property laws, and anyone can use it without permission. Of course, for many people on YouTube, that content isn't available to use without permission until we near the next century. And don't forget, if the creator (or the creator's heir) files a copyright extension, they can hold on to the rights even longer — that way, the video of your dog dressed as a spider can stay in the family for as long as possible.

Index

About the Authors

Rob Ciampa is a sales, marketing, product, and media strategist, speaker, and author. He works with brands, agencies, tech firms, media companies, and creators on their go-to-market and competitive strategies. Previously, Rob was CMO and VP of Sales for Pixability, helping turn it into one of the world's top YouTube marketing and media platforms. While there, he launched brands and artists on YouTube and led Pixability's famed YouTube brand studies across fashion, beauty, consumer electronics, and automotive. Rob holds a BS and MS in computer science and engineering from the University of Massachusetts and an MBA from Boston University, all with honors. He and his team have previously received two Cannes Lions nominations for the use of YouTube video and data. Rob can be found at www.ciampa.com.

Theresa Go is VP of Platform Partnership at Pixability, a YouTube Verified Partner for brand suitability, contextual targeting, and content insights. She manages Pixability's partnerships with leading social platforms and premium video inventory sources. Theresa is a leading YouTube strategist for many premiere brands and agencies and received one of the first YouTube certifications available. She has spent more than ten years expanding Pixability's customer base and provides strategic consulting for customers in New York, Chicago, San Francisco, Boston, and the UK. She is also obsessed with immersive video formats and enjoys capturing 360° underwater video while freediving.

Theresa holds a BA in cinematic arts and technology from California State University - Monterey Bay.

Matt Ciampa has been a video creator and producer for more than a decade. Matt currently produces long-form YouTube content for BuzzFeed's Tasty, producing more than 60 videos and generating over 60 million views. Previously, he worked at several other award-winning agencies and studios around Los Angeles. Many years ago, as a teenager, Matt and his brother co-created a wildly popular LEGO YouTube channel, which served as a lot of the inspiration behind the first edition of this book. Matt has a BA in Writing for Film and Television from Emerson College, magna cum laude.

Rich Murphy is a Product Manager at Pixability, a YouTube Verified Partner for brand suitability, contextual targeting, and content insights. Before joining the Product team, Rich was a member of Pixability's Ad Ops team, responsible for executing millions of dollars in gross video advertising spent for some of the biggest brands in the world across YouTube, Facebook, and other video platforms. Previously, he was an Assistant Editor and Coordinator at 43Films, where he helped manage the production of original programming on AHC, part of the Discovery network. Rich graduated summa cum laude from Syracuse University with a BS in Television, Radio, & Film, and Marketing Management.

Dedication

Rob Ciampa: I wish to dedicate this book to my wife, Laura, who tastefully balances being both an admiring fan and an impartial critic. I also dedicate this book to my sons Matt and Zach, who turned our attic into a YouTube studio, built a popular channel, and complained about cutting the grass because they were too occupied making videos instead.

Theresa Go: This book is dedicated to my mother, Hope, for always pushing me to be the most creative version of myself and for showing me that hard work and dedication to one's passions is the only way to move forward in life. I also dedicate this to my supportive husband, John, and my wonderful daughter, Charlie. All are my inspirations.

Matt Ciampa: I dedicate this book to my parents. Thank you for giving me the world. And Zach.

Rich Murphy: I am dedicating this book to my nieces, Grace, Lily, Evelyn, and Lucy Mae, whose enthusiasm elevates everyone around them. I hope this shows them that they can make great things happen in the world.

Author's Acknowledgments

Rob Ciampa, Theresa Go, Matt Ciampa, and Rich Murphy: Keeping up with the YouTube world is not so different from minding a two-year-old in a toy store; it's fast-moving and often feels as if everything is out of control. Fortunately, we had many helping hands to keep us up to date and help deliver the book you're now holding in your hands (or viewing on your tablet). We would like to thank the team at Wiley who came to us with a great idea and a system to make it so, including Steven Hayes, Paul Levesque, and Becky Whitney. A big thank you also goes out to collaborators Adam Wescott of Select Management Group and Heather Peterson of Pixability. Heather provided excellent technical reviews to ensure the accuracy of our content.

Sincere thanks to both the alumni of and team at Pixability, the most groundbreaking team of YouTube professionals ever assembled. A special shout-out to Bettina Hein, its founder, and Andreas Goeldi, its first data scientist, for bringing us all together. We'd also like to thank our many friends and supporters at YouTube, along with our brand and agency partners over the years. Most importantly, we're grateful for all the feedback from the YouTube community and readers of the first edition of the book. We hope this second edition exceeds your demanding expectations.

Publisher's Acknowledgments

Acquisitions Editor: Steve Hayes

Senior Project Editor: Paul Levesque

Copy Editor: Becky Whitney

Tech Reviewer: Heather Peterson

Production Editor: Umar Saleem

Cover Image: © warrengoldswain/Getty Images

Leverage the power

Dummies is the global leader in the reference category and one of the most trusted and highly regarded brands in the world. No longer just focused on books, customers now have access to the dummies content they need in the format they want. Together we'll craft a solution that engages your customers, stands out from the competition, and helps you meet your goals.

Advertising & Sponsorships

Connect with an engaged audience on a powerful multimedia site, and position your message alongside expert how-to content. Dummies.com is a one-stop shop for free, online information and know-how curated by a team of experts.

- Targeted ads
- Video
- Email Marketing
- Microsites
- Sweepstakes sponsorship

20 MILLION PAGE VIEWS EVERY SINGLE MONTH

15 MILLION UNIQUE VISITORS PER MONTH

43% OF ALL VISITORS ACCESS THE SITE VIA THEIR MOBILE DEVICES

700,000 NEWSLETTE SUBSCRIPTION

TO THE INBOXES OF

300,000 UNIQUE INDIVIDUALS EVERY WEEK

# of dummies

Custom Publishing

Reach a global audience in any language by creating a solution that will differentiate you from competitors, amplify your message, and encourage customers to make a buying decision.

- Apps
- Books
- eBooks
- Video
- Audio
- Webinars

Brand Licensing & Content

Leverage the strength of the world's most popular reference brand to reach new audiences and channels of distribution.

For more information, visit **dummies.com/biz**

PERSONAL ENRICHMENT

Staying Sharp

9781119187790
USA $26.00
CAN $31.99
UK £19.99

Facebook

9781119179030
USA $21.99
CAN $25.99
UK £16.99

Guitar

9781119293354
USA $24.99
CAN $29.99
UK £17.99

Investing

9781119293347
USA $22.99
CAN $27.99
UK £16.99

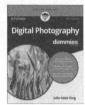

Beekeeping

9781119310068
USA $22.99
CAN $27.99
UK £16.99

Digital Photography

9781119235606
USA $24.99
CAN $29.99
UK £17.99

Meditation

9781119251163
USA $24.99
CAN $29.99
UK £17.99

Pregnancy

9781119235491
USA $26.99
CAN $31.99
UK £19.99

Samsung Galaxy S7

9781119279952
USA $24.99
CAN $29.99
UK £17.99

iPhone

9781119283133
USA $24.99
CAN $29.99
UK £17.99

Crocheting

9781119287117
USA $24.99
CAN $29.99
UK £16.99

Nutrition

9781119130246
USA $22.99
CAN $27.99
UK £16.99

PROFESSIONAL DEVELOPMENT

Windows 10

9781119311041
USA $24.99
CAN $29.99
UK £17.99

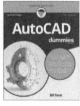

AutoCAD

9781119255796
USA $39.99
CAN $47.99
UK £27.99

Excel 2016

9781119293439
USA $26.99
CAN $31.99
UK £19.99

QuickBooks 2017

9781119281467
USA $26.99
CAN $31.99
UK £19.99

macOS Sierra

9781119280651
USA $29.99
CAN $35.99
UK £21.99

LinkedIn

9781119251132
USA $24.99
CAN $29.99
UK £17.99

Windows 10

9781119310563
USA $34.00
CAN $41.99
UK £24.99

SharePoint 2016

9781119181705
USA $29.99
CAN $35.99
UK £21.99

Fundamental Analysis

9781119263593
USA $26.99
CAN $31.99
UK £19.99

Networking

9781119257769
USA $29.99
CAN $35.99
UK £21.99

Office 2016

9781119293477
USA $26.99
CAN $31.99
UK £19.99

Office 365

9781119265313
USA $24.99
CAN $29.99
UK £17.99

Salesforce.com

9781119239314
USA $29.99
CAN $35.99
UK £21.99

Coding

9781119293323
USA $29.99
CAN $35.99
UK £21.99

dummies®
A Wiley Brand

Learning Made Easy

ACADEMIC

9781119293576
USA $19.99
CAN $23.99
UK £15.99

9781119293637
USA $19.99
CAN $23.99
UK £15.99

9781119293491
USA $19.99
CAN $23.99
UK £15.99

9781119293460
USA $19.99
CAN $23.99
UK £15.99

9781119293590
USA $19.99
CAN $23.99
UK £15.99

9781119215844
USA $26.99
CAN $31.99
UK £19.99

9781119293378
USA $22.99
CAN $27.99
UK £16.99

9781119293521
USA $19.99
CAN $23.99
UK £15.99

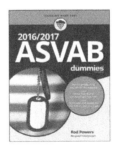

9781119239178
USA $18.99
CAN $22.99
UK £14.99

9781119263883
USA $26.99
CAN $31.99
UK £19.99

Available Everywhere Books Are Sold

dummies.com

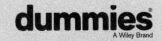

Small books for big imaginations

9781119177173
USA $9.99
CAN $9.99
UK £8.99

9781119177272
USA $9.99
CAN $9.99
UK £8.99

9781119177241
USA $9.99
CAN $9.99
UK £8.99

9781119177210
USA $9.99
CAN $9.99
UK £8.99

9781119262657
USA $9.99
CAN $9.99
UK £6.99

9781119291336
USA $9.99
CAN $9.99
UK £6.99

9781119233527
USA $9.99
CAN $9.99
UK £6.99

9781119291220
USA $9.99
CAN $9.99
UK £6.99

9781119177302
USA $9.99
CAN $9.99
UK £8.99

Unleash Their Creativity

dummies.com

dummies
A Wiley Brand